# Middle Country

# Middle Country

An American Student Visits
China's Uyghur Prison-State

## Grayson Slover

YBK Publishers
New York

Middle Country
Copyright © 2021 by Grayson Slover

All rights reserved including
the right of reproduction
in whole or in part in any form.

YBK Publishers, Inc.
39 Crosby Street
New York, NY 10013

ISBN: 978-1-936411-69-6

**Library of Congress Cataloging-in-Publication Data**

Names: Slover, Grayson, author.
Title: Middle country / Grayson Slover.
Description: New York : YBK Publishers, [2021] | Includes bibliographical
   references.
Identifiers: LCCN 2021009137 | ISBN 9781936411696 (paperback)
Subjects: LCSH: Xinjiang Uygur Zizhiqu (China)--Description and travel. |
   Slover, Grayson--Travel--China--Xinjiang Uygur Zizhiqu. | Uighur (Turkic
   people)--China--Xinjiang Uygur Zizhiqu--History--21st century. |
   Xinjiang Uygur Zizhiqu (China)--Ethnic relations. | Muslims--Violence
   against--China--Xinjiang Uygur Zizhiqu. | Xinjiang Uygur Zizhiqu
   (China)--Politics and government--21st century.
Classification: LCC DS793.S62 S56 2021 | DDC 951/.60612--dc23
LC record available at https://lccn.loc.gov/2021009137

Manufactured in the United States of America
for distribution in North and South America
or in the United Kingdom or Australia
when distributed elsewhere.
For more information, visit
www.ybkpublishers.com

*To Aynur, and the countless others like her*

# Contents

| | | |
|---|---|---|
| Introduction | | ix |
| Chapter 1 | Leaving Beijing | 1 |
| Chapter 2 | Plane to Kashgar | 5 |
| Chapter 3 | Arrival in Kashgar | 12 |
| Chapter 4 | Kashgar, Day One—Afaq Khoja | 24 |
| Chapter 5 | Kashgar, Day One—The New Old City | 34 |
| Chapter 6 | Kashgar, Day One—Sue's Shop, the Dancers | 39 |
| Chapter 7 | Kashgar, Day One—Afternoon and Evening at the New Old City | 44 |
| Chapter 8 | Kashgar, Day Two—Breakfast and Getting to Id Kah | 50 |
| Chapter 9 | Kashgar, Day Two—Id Kah Mosque | 56 |
| Chapter 10 | Kashgar, Day Two—The Old Old City and the Night Market | 62 |
| Chapter 11 | Kashgar, Day Three—The Livestock Market | 72 |
| Chapter 12 | Kashgar, Day Three—A Uyghur Neighborhood and the Bazaar | 77 |
| Chapter 13 | Train to Ürümqi | 90 |
| Chapter 14 | Train to Ürümqi—New Friends | 98 |
| Chapter 15 | Overnight and Arrival in Ürümqi | 112 |
| Chapter 16 | Ürümqi, Day One—Settling In, Hongshan Park | 118 |
| Chapter 17 | Ürümqi, Day One—Erdaoqiao Bazaar and M-Plex | 128 |
| Chapter 18 | Ürümqi, Day One—The Mosque | 142 |
| Chapter 19 | Ürümqi, Day Two—Encounter on the Road | 146 |
| Chapter 20 | Ürümqi, Day Two—More Questions | 153 |
| Chapter 21 | Ürümqi, Day Three—Heavenly Lake | 163 |
| Epilogue | | 180 |
| What We Can Do | | 184 |
| Notes | | 187 |
| Acknowledgements | | 194 |

# Introduction

For most of us, the struggles faced by people in other countries tend to occupy less of our attention than the problems we face closer to home. Understandably, our mental energy is primarily directed toward addressing domestic issues because these issues are tangible in our own everyday lives.

In recent years, the domestic problems in the United States have only become more pronounced. Acute political polarization, and its inflammation during the years of the Trump Presidency; long-standing societal ills coming to the fore, and a concerning rise in violent extremism; the burgeoning power of unaccountable tech giants, and declining public confidence in government; growing income inequality and widespread economic anxiety; climate change and its increasingly observable effects; and on top of all that, a global pandemic that has killed more than half a million Americans (as of the time of this writing), kneecapped the economy, and dramatically rewired all of our daily lives.

With no shortage of challenges confronting us at home, the first reaction most people will have when confronted with something taking place in another, less familiar part of the world is, to put it bluntly: How can we worry about that when our own house is on fire?

While this America-centered focus is generally reasonable, and actually prudent at times, it can blind us to crises outside our usual sphere of attention. And among these distant concerns are some injustices that are so odious, so utterly contrary to what we would all agree constitute basic human rights, that they deserve our immediate and unflinching attention.

One of these generational evils is occurring right now, in China's far-western Xinjiang Uyghur Autonomous Region (XUAR), also known as East Turkistan.

In 2017, the Chinese Communist Party (CCP) government began to introduce in Xinjiang thousands of what it calls "re-education camps" and "vocational training centers." At these facilities, instead of the practical professional training that their official names suggest, detainees spend their days being forced to learn the Mandarin language, to recite Communist Party propaganda songs, and to renounce Islam. Along with these "training" activities, many are routinely subjected to atrocities that include rape, torture, and forced organ harvesting.

The United Nations estimates that these camps hold more than one million people—other estimates are even higher—but there is no certainty as to the precise number, due to the CCP's pervasive penchant for secrecy. What we can be certain of is that the majority of the camps' occupants are Uyghur—an ethnically Turkic, predominantly Muslim group who have called the region their home for more than 1,000 years; far longer than it has been part of China.

Outside of the camps, the government has established in Xinjiang what has been characterized as an "open-air prison," where benign displays of faith are fastidiously monitored and often lead to actual imprisonment. Even activities that have nothing to do with religion, such as using too much electricity, contacting people outside of China— for any reason—or having too many children, are deemed suspicious, and cause for detention. Mosques and other religious sites, including ancestral graves, are being destroyed indiscriminately in great numbers. Some of the most sacred and well-known of these sites have been spared destruction, only to be repurposed by the CCP for the amusement of Han (the predominant ethnic group in China) tourists. Uyghur women are being forcibly and systematically sterilized at a genocidal rate, and some are coerced into marriages with Han Chinese bachelors. Uyghur children are being taken from their parents to be put in government-run orphanages, where they are "re-educated" in many of the same ways as their parents.

I had the opportunity to visit East Turkistan, for about a week in the summer of 2019—after a college semester of study abroad in Seoul, South Korea—to see what I could of what is taking place, and to report what I saw.

For the past several years, the CCP has practically banned foreign journalists from traveling to the region—and any journalists who are granted access are tightly controlled by government minders. I wasn't officially a journalist (although I had published some political opinion pieces), so I was able to truthfully identify myself as a tourist on my visa, which allowed me a much greater degree of freedom of movement.

What I saw during my short visit aligned with everything I had read about the CCP's brutal policies in the region. Of course, being purposely hidden from view, most of the worst aspects of these policies were impossible for me to observe directly. But I've been able to contextualize what I experienced during my brief time there by digging into as much in-depth reporting, expert analysis, and relevant history as I could consume since then. The contextual asides that I've included throughout the book, taken together, constitute what I believe, based on my research, to be the most pertinent information on the current situation in East Turkistan. Because this book is structured around my own narrative account, it wasn't practical for me to include every piece of relevant information. I hope that this book will motivate readers to continue to educate themselves on this humanitarian crisis.

The very name Xinjiang, the name bestowed on the region by China, meaning "New Frontier" in Mandarin, is considered to be inaccurate and offensive by many people whose families have lived there for centuries. In this book, I try to use the term Xinjiang when I am referring to the actual political state that exists there today, as well as in direct quotes and in dialogue. When I speak about the region historically, and in my own descriptions when I can, I refer to it as East Turkistan.

In the interest of their security, I have withheld the real names of most of the people I met, as well as the specific dates when I was in East Turkistan.

What follows is an account of the week I spent in East Turkistan. It is based on my vivid memories, refreshed by notes I took while I was there, and bolstered by additional context contributed by my subsequent research. I hope that anyone who reads this will be able not only to learn about what I experienced in East Turkistan myself, but also, much more importantly, to be informed about the experiences of the Turkic peoples of East Turkistan, and the unspeakable crimes being committted against them by the Chinese Communist Party.

Chapter 1

# Leaving Beijing

"Today China's economic power makes U.S. lectures about human rights imprudent. Within a decade it will make them irrelevant. Within two decades it will make them laughable."

—Former U.S. President Richard Nixon
(1969–1974), writing in 1994

"Why are you traveling to Xinjiang?"

I was at the customs clearance desk at the Beijing Capital International Airport, having just arrived from Ulaanbaatar, Mongolia. The uniformed customs officer behind the desk was asking me this question for the first time in my life, but I'd hear it again countless times over the next week.

"I'm going there for tourism. I'm a student and I was studying in South Korea. I'm on summer break now." I was unsure of how this response would go over, since I had only ever practiced it to myself. *Was I saying too much? Perhaps too little?*

He looked down again at my passport and registration card.

"How long will you be there?" He asked. He already knew the answer—this information was listed on the registration card still occupying his gaze.

"Seven days," I replied.

After another minute of investigation, he quickly stamped my passport, stapled my registration card to the stamped page, and handed it back to me.

"Thank you," he said, without looking up. I moved swiftly along, down the concourse toward the main terminal.

I wasn't even in Xinjiang yet. I would have been two time zones away, in fact, if not for the uniquely Chinese practice of putting the entire country on the same Beijing Standard Time. Yet I was already being questioned about my personal travel plans and my motivations for going there. At the very least, it seemed like an unpersuasive method to encourage international tourism—a goal for Xinjiang that the CCP has been quite transparent about.[1]

1

After a surprisingly long walk through bland airport hallways, I reached the escalator that took me down into the center of the main terminal. The complimentary bag of chips from my last flight was the only thing I'd eaten for around twenty-four hours, so I began scanning all of my dinner options immediately as I started my descent.

A bountiful number of choices lay in front of me. Generic Western-style burgers and pizza to my left, South Asian to my right, and, of course, a wide variety of East Asian cuisines farther down on either side. It was nearly overwhelming, but in the best of ways.

---

Some of us in the West still think of China as an undeveloped, poverty-stricken nation, whose economy is best characterized by its deep reservoir of eager and reliable cheap labor that Western companies are always seeking to tap into. But this could only be believed by someone who isn't aware of what it's like there today—the cornucopia of food options at this airport being only one tiny example. In 1978, following the death of the People's Republic of China's infamous first leader, Mao Zedong, his successor Deng Xiaoping decided to "open up" China's markets to the outside world, and to institute some liberalizing reforms to China's domestic economy. Since then, China has managed to pull more than 850 million of its people out of poverty—more than any other country in history.[2]

Indeed, by certain metrics, such as purchasing power parity and foreign direct investment, China is already the preeminent economic power in the world; but that hasn't assuaged the CCP's growing ambitions. When he took office, current Chinese President Xi Jinping announced that the central goal of his rule was to achieve "the great rejuvenation of the Chinese nation." To do this, he laid out a set of specific goals: By the year 2025, China would be the world leader in ten different crucial technologies, including quantum computing and artificial intelligence. By 2035, China would be the innovation leader across all advanced technologies. And by 2049, the hundredth anniversary of the founding of the People's Republic of China (PRC), Xi aims for China to be unambiguously number one. If present trends continue, they are well on their way to hitting all of these targets.[3]

The idea of China surpassing the United States may seem far-fetched to many of us. But from the Chinese perspective, this is the way that the world is supposed to work. As the China expert and author Michael Schuman observes:

> Today in the West, China is described as an "emerging" economy, catching up to the richer, more advanced United States and Europe. But that situ-

ation is an aberration. China was either the largest or second-largest economy in the world continuously from 1 AD to the nineteenth century . . .. In the Chinese history of the world, its economy never had to "rise" to the world stage. China was comfortable on top, watching everyone else scrambling to catch up. For most of recorded history, China was an economic superpower.[4]

---

By the time I got to the bottom of the escalator, I'd homed in on a Korean restaurant nestled in the corner of the main food court, and to my pleasant surprise, there was no line. I made a beeline straight for it. It still felt strange to think of Korean food as "familiar"—having only lived there for six months.

I walked up to the counter through the steam billowing from the kitchen and, without even glancing at the menu, told the cashier I wanted a pork cutlet and two beers—my Korean meal of choice. Having ordered this same thing in excess of a hundred times, often at restaurants where there were no English-speakers on the staff, I was relatively adept at pronouncing it in smooth Korean. This elicited a gasp from the cashier, who was either Korean herself or spoke the language fluently, as was made clear to me in her wordy reply. I could make out a couple of words in what she said—"wow" and "American" stood out in particular—but the substance of her full response was lost on me.

"Sorry," I said with a shrug and a smile, as she handed me my change.

I found a large booth in the corner of the restaurant that looked perfect—one side for me, the other for my colossal, sweaty Osprey backpack. I knew that I still had some time before my flight began boarding, so I took out the book that I'd bought in Mongolia: *Genghis Khan and the Quest for God: How the World's Greatest Conqueror Gave Us Religious Freedom.*[5]

I'd purchased this book for two reasons. The first was the same as why anyone goes into a bookstore and spends money—the book looked interesting to me. I've always been fascinated by the interaction between religion and politics, and when I read the end of the title—that the bloodthirsty Mongol legend Genghis Khan is who actually "gave us religious freedom," not Thomas Jefferson, I just had to see it for myself.

My other reason for getting this book was much less ordinary. As part of the extensive planning for my trip to Xinjiang, I knew that it would be necessary to develop an alibi of sorts for being there as a tourist if I were pressed to be more specific. After all, college students more often go to places like Cabo San Lucas or Daytona Beach for their vacations. Some of my study-abroad friends chose to spend a couple of weeks at Bali's picturesque beaches. Xinjiang, on the other hand—which is arguably the most remote inhabited region on Earth[6]—isn't the best destination for those seeking peaceful white sand beaches or shore-side keggers.

To address this concern, I decided to say that I wanted to travel to Xinjiang because I was interested in the history of the ancient Silk Road trading network. The Silk Road, which at its peak stretched all the way from Constantinople to Beijing, would not have been possible if it weren't for the central hub cities located in Xinjiang (although it wasn't known to anyone as "Xinjiang" until much later). This alibi, I reasoned, would be plausible to the Chinese authorities I encountered. It would also convey to them that my purpose for being there had nothing to do with seeking my own first-hand look at the effects of their culturally destructive policies.

When I came across the book (which, believe it or not, was *after* I had decided on my Silk Road story), I knew it would be an effective grist to explain myself; something I could easily pull out of my bag and show to a curious police officer to cut through the verbal miscommunications that were likely to occur. I expected that most of the Chinese officers I'd be stopped by wouldn't be able to read English, and if they could, the name Genghis Khan is the part that would stand out the most, and they'd instinctively associate him with the Silk Road.

Sure, it wasn't perfect—the title didn't have "Silk Road" in it, and it did, inconveniently, contain the term "religious freedom." But they unfortunately appeared to be out of Silk Road foam fingers at that particular bookstore, so I decided this was my most practical option.

As I was breezing through the pages, my order was called. Thankfully, access to beer was never in question at any point during my travels, but I knew this could be the last pork cutlet I'd have in Asia for the foreseeable future. I made sure to savor every bite.

# Chapter 2
# Plane to Kashgar

"The greatest force is common blood."
—Sun Yat-Sen, Chinese political philosopher
and provisional President of the
Republic of China (1912)

One of the cultural differences that stood out most to me in East Asia was the normalcy of staring at strangers—foreign-looking ones, such as myself, at least. It wasn't only in China; I noticed it in South Korea, too. When I was in the less-international parts of Seoul, I could expect at least a handful of passersby on the street to gawk at me. Sometimes they'd point directly at my face, and occasionally they'd even ask me to take a picture with them. I was flattered by it at times, unsettled at others, depending mostly on the mood I happened to be in. In general, though, I could tell that most of it came from a place of good-natured curiosity—a desire to understand a foreign culture. At the root, it wasn't so different from some of my own reasons for being there.

As I lined up to board my flight to Kashgar, about half a dozen of my fellow passengers were giving me this treatment that I was getting used to—they were staring at me, unabashedly. I noticed one girl near the front of the line not-so-subtly snap a picture of me with her phone. The man and woman standing with her, probably her parents, looked at the picture and chuckled.

I suddenly felt an aggressive buzzing in my pocket. It was my Chinese burner phone, notifying me that I had received a text from my Airbnb host, who I will call Sue.

Sue was the only Airbnb host in Kashgar who was willing to have me as a guest. The majority of the lodgings listed for the city explicitly prohibited foreign guests—these I never even attempted to reserve—and the dozen or so I found that didn't mention an anti-foreigner policy all ended up denying me for presumably the same reason after they'd received my booking request. Sue, on the other hand, put "FOREIGN-ERS WELCOME!" in her description, and she responded to my booking by mentioning how excited she was to meet me, and asking whether I would need to know where to find American-style cuisine. The disparity between her hospitable attitude and the lack thereof from seemingly every other Airbnb host in the city was enough to even be a bit suspicious, but I didn't have an alternative, so I went ahead with the booking.

I should also briefly explain why I was taking the precaution to have a Chinese burner phone. Knowing of the Chinese government's propensity for surveillance, even of foreign visitors,[7] it seemed like an undue risk for me to use my American iPhone during my trip; so I chose to keep it turned off completely (with a couple of exceptions) while I was in China. I would instead buy a cheap Chinese phone and cellular plan that I could use for that week.

During an earlier part of my journey, in Beijing, I spent the better part of one of my days inside a China Mobile store, navigating the convoluted process of getting a week-long phone plan. I left with the closest thing I could get to a phone plan that made sense for my circumstances, along with a device called a *Guangphone*.

The Guangphone was easily the lowest-quality cell phone I'd ever owned. Text messages sometimes never came through, and when they did, there was often a delay. Sending texts on it was tedious, there being no keyboard or touch screen. I'd have to type out texts the old-fashioned way, by locating the number button with the corresponding letter and cycling through until I finally reached the correct letter. It reminded me of texting with my basic-level Tracfone in the fifth grade—but with spottier service and fewer recognizable ringtones. The industrial-grade flashlight and impressive battery life (I only had to charge it once) were its only positive attributes.

"At what time will you be making your arrival at my condominium?" Sue's text read.

I had no idea when I'd be arriving at her home. Our flight was scheduled to land in Kashgar around midnight, but I didn't know how long it would take to get from the airport to her house, or even how I would get there.

"I will text you when I land, probably around midnight. Thanks!" I replied. By the time I managed to type the whole thing out and hit "send," I was next in the boarding line to flash my ticket and visa to the flight attendant.

I made my way onto the plane and down the aisle. My seat was almost at the very back, and since I was among the last passengers in the boarding line, I was again the recipient of many stares while en route. I kept my head down as I went.

Upon my arrival, a Han Chinese man sitting in the aisle seat looked up from his chest—where his attention was occupied either by his phone or the adjacent pack of cookies. When he saw me, his face took on an odd expression, a sort of mix between confusion and elation.

"Can I squeeze in there?" I asked with a smile.

As he got up to let me in, an avalanche of crumbs plummeted from the top of his expensive-looking button-down shirt. The pack of cookies itself soon followed, all of it ending up on the floor. His phone, luckily, was spared by the soft cushion of his seat.

Sitting next to the window was a man who looked to be about my age, staring at his phone with headphones in—ostensibly unaware of the peculiar traveler who had just sat down next to him. Notably, he was the only person I had seen on this flight who was obviously not Han. He looked more Central than South Asian, his slightly darker skin pigmentation and difference in facial structure suggesting to me that he was probably an ethnic Kazakh.

Kazakhs are the second largest predominantly-Muslim ethnic group in East Turkistan,[8] and, along with the other Turkic ethnic groups in the region, including Kyrgyz, Uzbeks, and Tajiks, have been systematically oppressed by the CCP in the same ways as the Uyghurs have been. The Chinese government technically draws distinctions between all fifty-five of the nation's officially recognized ethnic groups (which they call *minzu*),[9] but when it comes to the Turkic Muslims in East Turkistan, these distinctions lose their significance.

An hour after I took my seat and re-immersed myself in my book, the pilot made an announcement over the intercom in Mandarin—without a subsequent English translation. My Kazakh-looking co-passenger and I briefly glanced at each other, silently acknowledging our shared confusion. I began to wonder if there might be a problem, since we were still sitting idly at the gate.

I knew that my lack of candor in disclosing the true reasons behind my journey could, if discovered, lead to the Chinese authorities pulling me off this flight (if not worse). The mere possibility, unlikely as it was, gave me a pang of anxiety.

The flight attendants began walking down the aisles, taking early drink orders from the disgruntled passengers. In the nervous state I was in, just being able to order a cuppa without complication provided me some reassurance. *If I was going to be escorted off the plane, there's no way this flight attendant would have taken my order without saying something, right? And she certainly wouldn't have done it in such a cheerful manner.* I rationalized this to myself, self-servingly, as if the attendant's warm demeanor provided even a shred of evidence about the Chinese travel authority's attitudes toward me one way or another.

As I waited for my tea, TV screens throughout the plane dropped down from overhead. I'd been reading for over an hour by that time, so I thought I might as well give my brain a rest with some visual entertainment. I searched for a button on my armrest to browse the channels, but to no avail. When I looked up again, there was a movie playing—the same one on every monitor throughout the plane. I assumed this meant there wouldn't be much of a selection to choose from.

I plugged my earphones into the outlet on the armrest. As expected, the dialogue was entirely in Mandarin, but I was relieved when I saw English subtitles.

A Chinese shipping vessel has been hijacked by a band of armed pirates in the Gulf of Aden. The exact patch of ocean they're in (the subtitles tell us) bears the menacing nickname "pirate alley." The pirates have the ship's crewmembers set up as human shields, creating a perimeter around the main cabin windows to guard the pirates on the inside.

It looks as though all hope is lost. The cargo will never reach its destination, and the crewmen will almost certainly be killed . . .

But wait! Here comes the Chinese navy to save the day!

The camera pans to several teams of Chinese special forces officers, all draped from head to toe in high-tech military gear. Each squad is strategically positioned throughout the hijacked vessel, in preparation for what we can already predict will be a surgically coordinated attack.

The captain of the Chinese navy ship warns the extraction squad's leader that they must complete the mission before the commandeered ship reaches territorial waters, which will happen in ten minutes. (That this would be a deterrent for them was particularly amusing, since the Chinese navy routinely intrudes on the territorial waters of other countries.[10]) The squad leader agrees, then confirms with the team's sniper, who we see perched in a helicopter flying toward the ship.

The squad leader gives the go-ahead as the helicopter swings around the main cabin. The scene shifts to slow motion as the camera zooms in on a small gap between the heads of two hostages, revealing one of the pirates behind them, who has a gun pointed at the head of yet another hostage. An impossible shot for the sniper to make? If he wasn't a Chinese soldier, perhaps. The sniper pulls the trigger, and in a *Matrix*-like ultra-slow-motion shot, we see the bullet explode out of the barrel of his rifle, inching progressively closer to the target. There's a ticking clock in the background to add another timely touch. The camera pans to the team in the hull of the ship, who detonate the charge they had planted at a door to gain access into another room to dispatch a different crowd of pirates; then quickly pans back to the bullet, as it breaks through the glass, flies through the gap between the two hostages, and makes contact with the first pirate's head.

The movie was the blockbuster Chinese action film *Operation Red Sea*. Its plot is essentially a Chinese version of the well-known American film *Black Hawk Down;* but instead of being based on the real story of American troops extracted from war-torn Mogadishu in 1993, it is based on the real story of Chinese troops extracting Chinese nationals from Yemen as it descended into civil war in 2015. It's an above-average action movie, and I'd recommend it if you don't mind near-parody numbers of explosions and improbable killing moves—it is the second-highest grossing Chinese film of all time.[11] But it stood out to me for a different reason.

It made sense for Air China to show this particular movie during a flight from Beijing to Kashgar, because it effectively reinforces the CCP narrative that the Han Chinese are in an existential war with brown-skinned Muslim extremists. If it weren't for the brave Han Chinese soldiers who work to keep the peace in Xinjiang, they would have you believe, the region would descend into theocratic Sharia hell.

---

The CCP has gone to great lengths to convince the world that "the two pans"—pan-Islamism and pan-Turkism—are so deeply ingrained among the region's Turkic Muslims that they pose a critical threat to regional and even national stability. To its own citizens, the CCP preaches not just that East Turkistan is a hotbed of Islamic extremist and separatist violence, but also that the only pacifying force strong enough to civilize the Turkic peoples living there is the paternal guidance of the ethnically superior Han Chinese. According to China scholars John M. Friend and Bradley A. Thayer, this racist infantilization of Xinjiang's Muslims is a symptom of an overarching ideology they call "Han-centrism," premised on the idea that the Han Chinese are "considered to be racially pure and the true descendants of the 'ancestral nation.' " Friend and Thayer trace Han-centrism back to the ideas of Sun Yat-Sen, who declared explicitly that "the government of China should be in the hands of the [Han] Chinese."[12] He is widely revered in China today, and CCP leaders regularly invoke his name to energize Chinese nationalism.

Indeed, the CCP actively nurtures the ideology of Han-centrism in China's population. Friend and Thayer note how Xi Jinping "has effectively tapped into the sense of vulnerability, humiliation, and revenge at the core of Han-centrism" through his appeal to racialized historical grievances in his promotion of "national rejuvenation." They go on to say that the CCP is especially eager to stoke Han-centrist attitudes "when pressured by foreign forces or by non-Han minority groups that are viewed as an obstacle to the country's development."[13]

Evidently, the CCP believes that the most benighted of these "non-Han minority groups," and the group that is currently most guilty of holding China back from reclaiming its rightful position atop the global hierarchy of nations, are the Turkic peoples of East Turkistan.

---

"Excuse me, sir," I heard in crisp English coming from outside my headphones.

I looked up to see the flight attendant standing there with my tea. Exactly what I needed for a touch of relaxation after all that terrorist-busting epic carnage I had just witnessed.

She handed me the cup of hot water and the tea bag, still with her same cheerful smile from earlier. But as I reached for the tea bag on my tray, I accidentally nudged the cup of water with my elbow, spilling it on the Kazakh-looking man in the seat to my right.

He jumped up and let out a sharp yelp—an understandable reaction to hot water being splashed across his lap without warning. I called the attendant back, painfully aware that the most she could do would be to bring the poor man something with which to dry himself.

"I'm so sorry!" I exclaimed.

He looked over and gave me a slight hand-wave paired with an equally slight smile.

"Eto oka," he replied. I later learned that this means "it's okay" in Russian, the predominant language spoken in post-Soviet Kazakhstan. But I got the basic message well enough in the moment.

I offered the man his pick from my assortment of travel snacks as penance, but he graciously refused.

I felt horrible. Because of my clumsiness, this man would soak in his damp clothes for the entire four-hour flight. And I had no satisfactory way of giving him a proper apology.

The flight attendant came running back with a fistful of napkins, her radiant smile from earlier now a scowl. She handed them to the man, frantically questioning him on his state of well-being as he calmly wiped up the affected surfaces around his seat. She hovered over us until the man had finished, and then marched back up the aisle, seemingly no less vexed than she had been when she arrived.

But minutes later, she appeared at the front of the plane, having reverted to her formerly cheerful facial expression, as the pilot came on the intercom. She began to demonstrate proper seat belt-fastening and oxygen mask-wearing, smiling throughout, as all good flight attendants do. It seemed we were finally about to take off.

And then, just as I felt the plane slowly begin to move, I felt a warm sensation running from my nostril, rapidly approaching my upper lip. I sent my index finger to investigate. It came back with a blotch of red. I instinctively tilted my head back to pinch the bridge of my nose, waiting for the flight attendant to complete her presentation before I called her back to attend to me yet again.

If I were the superstitious type, I might have taken all of this as an omen that my trip wasn't going to go as planned—that maybe I should get off the plane while I still had the chance.

# Chapter 3

# Arrival in Kashgar

"China is a sleeping lion. Let her sleep, for when she wakes she will shake the world."

—Napoleon Bonaparte

I was abruptly wakened by the feeling of large hands on my left shoulder. It was the man sitting to my left, shaking me with a sense of urgency. I opened my eyes, and looked around to find that all of the lights were on throughout the plane. The passengers in front were unloading their luggage from the overhead bins, and those farthest ahead were walking down the aisle toward the exit.

We had made it to Kashgar.

I quickly turned on my Guangphone. There was only one notification, a text from Sue.

"Please answer. I would like to go to bed soon," it read. My phone clock said it was 2:30 a.m. *Shit.*

Worse still, there were no other texts in my inbox, which meant my Guangphone had, for some reason, failed to receive any of the other texts her message implied she had also sent. The last thing I wanted to do was make a lackluster first impression on Sue—the only host in Kashgar willing to take me in. I was already off to a poor start.

"Sorry! My flight just landed," I replied, while jogging to the baggage claim area. "I'm picking up my luggage now, and I'll get a taxi to your home right after that. I hope you're still awake."

There were windows surrounding the walkway, but it was too dark to see anything outside except for a few scattered lights. The airport was tiny compared to Beijing's, and everything was closed for the night. Some of my co-passengers were speaking loudly in Mandarin on their phones, irritable after their taxing flight across the country. I sympathized with them.

I arrived at the baggage claim to see just a single carousel. Even at a small regional airport like Kashgar's, I'd expected at least a couple.

But we were the only flight listed on the recent arrivals board, so many of our bags were already available.

As I approached the carousel, I saw a figure coming toward me from the right.

"Hello," he said in slightly-accented English. I turned to see a uniformed Chinese police officer at my side. "Passport, please."

I looked around to see if anyone else was being asked the same. No one. Not even my Kazakh co-passenger, who was standing at the carousel, unbothered.

My instinct was to protest, to ask why I alone was being subjected to a delay while everyone else was free to get their bags and go home. But I knew that doing so could only make things worse for me.

"Why are you in Kashur?" He asked. (Kashur is the Mandarin pronunciation of "Kashi"—the Chinese name given to the city when the CCP first colonized it.)

The officer's impressive English, along with the fact that I was the only passenger being questioned, made me wonder whether this police officer might have been sent here specifically because I was on the flight manifest.

"I'm a student tourist, on summer break," I told him. The brevity of this response compared to the full one that I had given at the Beijing airport was due to my exhaustion from the flight. But judging by this officer's reaction, it seemed to be effective enough.

He continued scanning my passport, then handed it back to me.

"Thank you. Have a good time in Kashur," he said.

He turned around and headed through a side door a dozen feet to my right. Hanging above it was a small headshot picture of President Xi, angled in a way that made it look as if he was staring right at me.

I briskly made my way over to the baggage claim carousel, and spotted my green Osprey bag almost immediately, stretched out of shape from my cramming it far past what it was designed to hold. I grabbed it and headed toward the exit.

I felt another buzz in my pocket. "Yes, I am awake," read Sue's text. "How will you get here?"

*Great, I have a place to sleep tonight . . . But how **would** I get there?* I'd anticipated there would be a generous number of taxis waiting outside; it was an airport, after all. I was disappointed when I stepped through the exit doors into the front parking lot.

There were a few cars, as well as a couple of white vans—both of which looked to be private shuttles—but not a taxi in sight. I scanned for airport personnel, hoping that I was just in the wrong pickup lot.

I spotted a couple of uniformed men talking with some of my Han Chinese co-passengers, and made my way over after their conversation had ended.

The outside air was incredibly dry, as you'd expect in a desert, but also quite clean. It was a welcome change from the permanent haze of polluted air in Beijing, and it illustrated Kashgar's geographic separation from the Chinese capital.

"Hello, taxi?" I asked them, mindful to keep my question to the basics.

Still, the only initial response I received was a pair of blank stares.

"Taxi, to hotel?" I clarified.

This seemed to hit on something. One of them got out his phone and opened up what I recognized as WeChat—essentially the Chinese version of Facebook—which I knew had a translation function. He typed up a message and handed it to me.

"Do you need a ride to your hotel?" It read.

"Shi, xie xie"—Chinese for "Yes, thank you"—I verbally replied as I returned his phone to him, satisfied with myself for using two words out of my paltry Mandarin vocabulary.

"Enjoy Kashur," he said with a subtle grin. His co-worker gestured at me to follow him.

On our way to what I hoped would be a ride to the Airbnb, we weaved through a few small clusters of my co-passengers, as they were being greeted by family members and friends who had come to pick them up.

At the edge of one of those clusters was an older Han couple, sharing a warm embrace. From the angle at which we passed them, I was able to get a look at the woman's face. It emanated a deep reassurance, as if the earth had only just begun spinning again the moment she came in touch with her husband. I wondered where he might be returning from, and what he might have been doing there, to warrant her strong, visceral display. Or perhaps she was just happy that he had arrived safely after flying all the way from Beijing. They were certainly old enough to have been alive when a 4,000-kilometer journey across China was a significant and potentially hazardous undertaking, rather than just an inconvenient day trip.

---

For one group of men in particular, a fateful flight from East Turkistan to Beijing was of pivotal historical significance. In 1949, the plane carrying the leadership of the semi-autonomous East Turkistan Republic (ETR), one of two independent nations that existed in parts of present-day Xinjiang under this name, at different times in the early/ mid 1900s, crashed en route to a meeting in Beijing. The leaders were supposedly headed there to express their solidarity with Chairman Mao and the newly formed PRC. It is unclear whether this original delegation would have pushed for formal independence at this meeting—some official statements made by them around this time suggest they wouldn't have. But these statements were likely influenced by the Soviet Union, who had been instrumental in helping the ETR originally come to power, but who now supported Mao.

In fact, according to a 1953 CIA report,[14] declassified in 2011, it was the Soviets who engineered the plane crash. They knew that Mao intended to occupy East Turkistan that same year, and they were also expecting that the leaders of the ETR would resist Mao's occupation. So, in order to prevent a conflict with their newly-minted Communist ally in Beijing, the Soviets chose to eliminate the ETR leaders who would stand in the way. A new delegation was quickly appointed in their stead, which unanimously (and conveniently) declared that they would abandon any claims for autonomy.[15] Xinjiang has—officially— been a part of China ever since.

---

After turning a corner into another parking lot, we arrived at a van of the kind I'd seen as I came out. Beside it was a circle of people, gathered around a woman in a white polo shirt and khaki pants in the middle of doing a roll call.

My escort approached the woman and said something in Mandarin. She looked at me and smiled before she replied to him.

He turned to me and proceeded to explain the situation . . . in Mandarin, as if he had forgotten already why I needed him to bring me to a ride in the first place.

"He says you can ride to your hotel with us," the woman translated. I was a bit surprised by her heavy British accent.

"Oh, that's great. Thank you so much," I replied, nodding to the man who had escorted me over before he walked away.

"Where are you going?" the woman asked.

"To the city center, close to the Mao statue," I said.

"Ahh, that is fine. We will have to drop the others off first, because they have reservations, but we can certainly take you after that. Is that okay?"

"Yes, of course."

"Okay, good. You can get in the van now. Just take the seat behind me."

I was a bit confused by what she meant at first, since she hadn't yet entered the van herself. But I looked inside to see that there was only one seat unoccupied, directly behind shotgun.

"Hello!" I heard yelled from the back as I ducked my head in to enter.

I turned to see a younger Han boy grinning up at me from the next row.

"Hello! How are you?" I replied, trying to match the boy's enthusiasm.

He looked at me and laughed, clearly unable to provide an answer. I joined in, along with the rest of the passengers. Now that I knew my Airbnb host was awaiting me, and I had secured a ride—and one with a positive atmosphere—I was feeling much more at ease.

Seconds later, the woman entered the van along with the driver. She told him something in Mandarin, and he started the engine and began driving away, past the few remaining people in the arrivals lot, toward the airport exit.

"So what is your name?" I heard the woman ask.

I continued looking out the window for a moment, ignoring her question, assuming she must have been talking to one of the other passengers. But I quickly reminded myself that I was probably the only person in the van who could understand her.

"Grayson," I answered. "What is yours?"

"Liqui, but my English name is Cindy. You can call me that."

"Nice to meet you, Cindy. Did you live in England?"

"Yes! I studied at university there. How did you know?" she asked. Her British accent sounded even more pronounced, maybe because of her generic use of the word "university."

"Just a lucky guess," I replied jestingly. She smiled softly and turned back around, seeming not to catch my drift.

Out the window there still wasn't much to look at. We had been driving along the same highway since we'd left the airport. It was well lit by columns of tall street lights, all designed with an oriental flavor, lining either side of the road and stretching interminably ahead of us. Beyond the roadway, the lighting was so sparse as to conceal almost everything.

It also struck me that there didn't appear to be any other vehicles on the road with us. Three a.m. certainly wasn't rush hour, to be sure, but the level of development of the highway suggested that it was a major route—one that you'd expect to see at least a few cars on at any time of day.

"Where are you from?" Cindy turned back again to ask.
"I'm from the United States." I heard a couple of *ohhhhh*'s from behind me.
"Oh wow, very interesting. What part?"
"From around Washington, D.C.," I replied.
I waited a few seconds for her to say something before I looked up. For some reason this fact seemed to surprise her; it almost looked like it frightened her.
"Really?" she asked, wide-eyed.
"Yes I am. Do you not see many people from D.C. here?"
"No, you are the first one."
There was a brief, uncomfortable silence.
"I'm really excited to see Kashgar," I said, to change the subject.
"Yes, it is a beautiful city. One of the best tourism spots in China, now that it is so secure," she declared.
"I have heard that. I'm sure I'll feel very safe."
As I said this, I looked past her, through the front windshield, to see a luminous array of buildings several hundred yards in front of us—my first real glimpse of the city.
Out my side window, I tried again to get a look at Kashgar's "outskirts." But instead of mud brick homes or poplar trees, I got my first good look at a Xinjiang police station.
The building straddled the side of the highway opposite us, and by the look of it, was actually built right into the side of the road. It had red and blue lights flashing from the top of the building—something I had never seen on a police station before. I noticed a couple of vehicle entrances as well. One of them appeared to lead to a small parking lot on the side, where two police vans were parked. The other went into an enclosed area within the station—probably a checkpoint for inspecting suspicious vehicles.
As we entered the city, the Han Chinese passengers behind me got out their phones and began filming and snapping pictures of our surroundings. I couldn't tell what they were so excited about. All I saw outside were modern-looking office and apartment buildings—nothing particularly noteworthy from my perspective. On second thought, though, I reasoned it could have been because these were tourists from eastern China—which has been highly developed for decades—and they were impressed by the modernization of what they likely considered to be a peripheral city.
Indeed, the section of the city we were driving through looked indistinguishable from Beijing. High-rise buildings, coffee shops, depart-

ment stores—we even passed by a Kentucky Fried Chicken. I hoped this wasn't representative of the current state of the ancient Silk Road city as a whole. I hadn't traveled all this way just to buy discounted Polo shirts or eat American fast food.

The van soon pulled into a luxurious hotel, coming to a stop at the front entrance between two sleek marble dragon statues. Cindy said something to the passengers behind me in Mandarin, and they all began exiting.

"We are going to get out now, but the driver will take you to your destination," she said.

"Great. Thank you so much for taking me, Cindy. How much should I pay you?" I asked.

"Fifteen yuan [around two dollars] please. And no problem." I handed her the money through the still-opened van door.

"Have a great time in Kashur, Grayson!"

"Thank you. I'm sure I will," I said to her, as the last passengers were exiting from the back.

"Goodbye!" I heard from outside, recognizing the voice of the boy who had greeted me earlier. Looking back at him, I got a kick out of the smile he showed me again, seemingly from how proud he was of having instigated our very brief—yet technically, successful—conversation in English. I waved at him as the driver sped off.

We continued down the main road that we'd been on before. I figured we couldn't be too far away. Meanwhile, I was satisfied with getting a little bit more time to look at the city in its state of repose.

As I gazed out the window, we pulled up to a red light. To our left, I saw something else of significance.

Sitting between two apartment buildings was a long wall, partitioned in the middle by a tall metal gate. With the addition of some barbed wire, or perhaps some armed guards, it would have looked like a prison or a police facility—although it would probably have been the first prison in history to have colorful cartoons painted on its outer wall. There was one of a girl jumping rope, one of a couple of anthropomorphized birds playing on a swing set, another with some monkeys playing basketball; things you'd expect to see on the walls of a kindergarten classroom.

I knew immediately what this place likely was: a "boarding school" for Uyghur children whose parents had been sent away to "re-education."

---

When Uyghur parents are forcibly interned, the most typical next step taken by the Chinese government is to send their children to a state-run boarding school, instead of allowing them to live with a relative. In these schools, the children are indoctrinated in many of the same ways that their parents are being indoctrinated in the camps. They learn Mandarin, and are immersed in and made to adopt Han Chinese cultural practices, as well as to condemn their former cultural and religious practices and values that are deemed insufficiently Chinese. The children are also interrogated by officials at these schools in an attempt to extract more information about their parents. They are asked questions like "Do your parents read the Quran?" and "Did you celebrate Ramadan with your parents?" If they provide the "wrong" answer, their parents are presumably given a more severe sentence.[16]

Adrian Zenz, a Senior Fellow at the Victims of Communism Memorial Foundation, who is widely considered the world's foremost expert on Xinjiang's re-education camps, has released a number of papers on the camps (as well as on other aspects of the CCP's genocidal policies in Xinjiang), largely based on the PRC's own documents and publicly available government information.

Tragically, as Zenz explains, "The number of students in Xinjiang who live in boarding facilities grew by over 380,000 between 2017 and 2019, from about 500,000 to just below 900,000."[17] Today, an estimated 40% of Uyghur children in Xinjiang reside in these boarding schools.[18]

Scholars have noted how integral this boarding school policy is to the broader success of the CCP's genocide in East Turkistan. Not only is it criminalizing non-Han culture and religious expression among adults, which is reprehensible enough in its own right. By also extending it to children, who are just beginning to discover the nature of the world and to form their own views about it, the CCP is creating an army of indoctrinated youth who will rapidly suffuse Xinjiang's Turkic population once they grow into adulthood. It turns what would otherwise be a slow death of Uyghur culture from the stultifying effects of adult re-education into a more abrupt demise, one that could come to fruition within a single generation.

---

Minutes later, the driver pulled over to the side of the road.

I looked outside, scanning the dark sidewalks and buildings around us, but I couldn't spot my host, or even any buildings that appeared residential.

The driver turned toward me and grumbled something in Mandarin, somehow expecting me to understand.

"Are we at this address?" I asked as I handed him the piece of paper I'd written it on.

He looked at it and pointed to the building directly to the van's right. All I saw was an enormous metal door with two cars parked in front of it. Certainly not what the pictures online had looked like; but then again, those pictures had not been taken at three in the morning.

"Are you sure?" I pressed. "I don't see my host."

He just pointed again to the same building, this time impatiently. I followed his finger toward the giant gate. This time when I looked, there was a figure standing in front of a smaller door next to it, and now coming our way.

"Mister Grayson?" the shrouded figure inquired, with a trace of fatigue.

"Hello! Sue?!" I shouted out the window. The driver shook abruptly, and I adjusted my loud volume. "Yes, it's Grayson."

"Yes, it is me. Come out and we will go inside," she replied, in a far more considerate decibel level for the late hour than the one I had just used.

I nodded at the driver, thanking him for the ride as I got out.

It was at that very moment, as I stepped out of the van, when I first felt the full weight of where I was. I wasn't in America. I wasn't in Seoul. I wasn't even in Beijing. I was in Kashgar, the epicenter of the worst human rights crisis on Earth. And I was about to meet my conspicuously gracious host for the first time, with whom I'd be staying for the next two nights.

"Hello Sue, I'm so sorry for making you stay up this late," I apologized as I approached her.

She came into the light a bit more, but it still wasn't optimal for my getting a good look at her. My tired state, along with the bad lighting, made it impossible to tell for sure whether the young woman in front of me was the same one as in the picture on Airbnb.

"It's okay. It's nice to meet you. Are you ready to go inside?" she asked.

"Yes, definitely. I'm exhausted."

She entered a code into a keypad to the side of the large gate. It opened mechanically, upward, just like a typical electric garage door, but at least five times the size. The now-open gate revealed a large, well-lit parking lot in the center of an apartment complex.

With the improved lighting, I could see Sue clearly. Her face had a weary look to it, due to lack of sleep, I presumed, but I could see that aside from being a bit unkempt, she was quite pretty. It also clearly matched the face in the picture I'd seen on Sue's Airbnb profile. She was wearing full-body pajamas, decorated with Hello Kitty faces, that ended with a pair of oversized red flip-flops that loudly slapped the ground on her every step.

"How was your flight?" Sue asked. Her voice was monotone, in a way that suggested she thought asking this question was a cordial formality.

"It was alright . . . long, though. Very ready to sleep," I said with an unnatural chuckle.

I had thought that this gate was an entrance to a single apartment building, but I counted five separate buildings on just this first walk-through. I had never seen this sort of layout in America: a behemoth of a gate, not guarding luxury condos or McMansions, but a community of decidedly modest apartment buildings. It seemed misplaced, but I considered that it might have some official "security" justification behind it.

We eventually came to the door to what looked like the last apartment building in the complex, all the way at the back.

"This is your key," Sue told me, holding out a circular fob at the end of a purple keychain. "You press it against this thing on the side of the door to open."

She demonstrated for me, then handed me the keychain as we entered the building. I followed her up a cramped, poorly lit staircase. On the second flight, I almost lost my footing after catching my foot on a stray stair tile. I looked down to see dozens of loose tiles scattered haphazardly around, as if whoever last renovated the place had just emptied a bag of them onto the stairs on his way out.

Sue stopped at the third floor, in front of a door that was noticably better kept than the rest of the stairwell. A small wooden sign hanging on it read "What a wonderful life," in English, reminding me of the similarly titled black-and-white Frank Capra movie I'd watch with my family every Christmas.

It was a cozy apartment, with enough room for a kitchen, a couple of tables, and what looked like a new leather couch facing a flat-screen TV in the first room; but not much more. It smelled of a pleasant, earthy incense, and was decorated with many items that were iconically native to southern Xinjiang—a region historically called "Kashgaria" or "Altishahr" ("Six Cities") by the Uyghurs. A beautiful gold and white Kashgari rug took up most of the living room, and two smaller rugs had been repurposed into what looked like makeshift doors to other rooms. A large yak-skin painting was hung on the wall behind the couch, depicting a camel caravan making its way through the Taklamakan desert, which surrounds Kashgar on all sides.

"Do you need anything before you go to sleep?" Sue asked, hinting unsubtly that this question was meant to be taken as a final "good night."

"No, thank you. I'd just like to get to bed. Where is my room?"

"Right in there," she said, pointing to one of the rug doors. "There are already sheets, blankets, and pillows on the bed for you. If you have to use the bathroom, it's right over here," she said, pointing to a door—this one, thankfully, not made from a rug. "Just be careful when you go in. It can be loud, and my mother's room is right next to it."

*Mother's room?*

"Oh, uh, is she staying here, too?" I asked reflexively.

"Yes, we both are. And there will be another guest arriving tomorrow as well, to stay in the other guest room. Is that okay with you?"

I was surprised to learn I'd be sharing this small apartment with three other people. But, since I wasn't planning on spending much time inside, I really didn't mind. In fact, I thought it could end up being a positive part of the trip.

"Yes, that's perfectly alright," I said. "Before I go to bed, though, I wanted to ask you, do you know where I might be able to buy an English map of Kashgar?"

"Um, I have some maps here, but none of them are in English. That might be hard to find. You could use the map on your phone?" Sue said with a perplexed look.

"My phone actually doesn't have a map function," I told her as I took out my Guangphone. "It only sends texts."

She burst out laughing at the sight of it.

"Where did you buy that thing?" She asked, barely able to get the words out.

"In Beijing, at a China Mobile store. I prefer navigating the old-fashioned way. It makes me feel like a real explorer," I said, tongue-in-cheek.

"Ah, okay. Well maybe I can put some English directions on one of my maps tomorrow." Clearly, she took my explorer quip seriously.

"That would be fantastic, Sue."

"Okay, my mother and I have to go to work tomorrow at eight. Will you be awake by then?"

"Yes, I can be," I replied, hiding my disappointment with not being able to sleep in longer.

"Okay, great. Goodnight, Mr. Grayson!" she said.

"Thank you, Sue. And please, just call me Grayson."

"Okay, Grayson. See you tomorrow." She disappeared into a room past the kitchen.

I headed straight to my room and onto my bed, without even bothering to turn the lights on to see what the place looked like. I had barely four hours before I needed to start my day, and I intended for those four hours to be as rejuvenating as I could make them.

Tomorrow, I would explore the ancient city of Kashgar.

Chapter 4

# Kashgar, Day One
—Afaq Khoja

The winter of 2012 was an especially consequential time in Chinese politics. The outgoing President, Hu Jintao, had overseen a series of reforms during his tenure that seemed to vindicate the optimists in the international community: China, just as they had predicted, was moving toward liberalization.

Based on the reforms that had taken place, it wasn't an entirely unreasonable extrapolation. Under Hu Jintao, Chinese journalists were given a greater degree of freedom than they ever had in the past; religious groups were permitted to worship with relatively minimal interference; there were even human rights organizations, cautiously-but-openly critical of the CCP's policies, that were allowed to operate in Beijing. Hu's successor, however, had other plans for China.

The incoming president, who also happened to be Hu Jintao's former vice president, was an austere Party veteran and pomade enthusiast named Xi Jinping. During the interregnum, in December of 2012, the soon-to-be president gave one of his first speeches in that capacity. The only publicly available version of the speech is from a leak, and it does not provide the location where the speech was given or who was in attendance. But we can assume that many of the Party members who were present for it expected to hear a panegyric to his predecessors' work in strengthening the economy and ingratiating China into the international community.

Instead, Xi used this speech to apprise his comrades of the dangers of the very sorts of liberal reforms Hu Jintao had instituted.

"Why did the Soviet Union disintegrate?" Xi asked. "An important reason was that their ideals and beliefs had been shaken." He continued: "To dismiss the history of the Soviet Union and the Soviet Communist Party, to dismiss Lenin and Stalin, and to dismiss everything else is to engage in historic nihilism, and it confuses our thoughts and undermines the Party's organizations on all levels."[19]

Less than a year later, the Party's General Office circulated "Document Number 9" throughout the bureaucracy. It laid out a list of "false" Western values, including freedom of the press, civil society, and general elections, and it attributed any advocacy for these values within China to the surreptitious meddling of Western governments. It also reaffirmed the centrality of strict adherence to Socialism with Chinese Characteristics, as well as the importance for all Party leaders to "preemptively resolve all problems in the ideological sphere."[20]

From the moment he took office, President Xi has been obsessively focused on preventing the Chinese Communist Party from disintegrating in the same way as he believes their Soviet comrades did a few decades ago. His commitment to the preservation of the CCP's founding ideals, and his hubristic confidence in himself to oversee this preservation, led him in the spring of 2018 to orchestrate the passage of a constitutional amendment that effectively abolished presidential term limits.[21] It has reflected Xi's admiration for the old, unreformed Soviet Union—the Soviet Union of Joseph Stalin and his paranoid totalitarian police state—as well as Xi's aversion to the reformist inclinations of his predecessor, Hu Jintao.

And what could be a more quintessential expression of Xi's dewy-eyed reverence for the Soviet Union's peak gulag era than his putting millions of Xinjiang's Turkic Muslims in concentration camps?

---

Xi's face was distorted on Sue's grainy kitchen television. The wisps of smoke from her mother making breakfast obscured the image further, but I could still tell he was giving a vigorously-toned speech at some sort of military parade. Not what I would have picked for my morning television, but it wasn't my house.

"Do you want to buy souvenirs?" Sue asked.

"Uh, maybe. What kinds of souvenirs?" I replied.

Sue's mother placed a couple of poached eggs atop the mountain of steamed rice already on my plate. She didn't seem to speak any English, judging by her silence during my dialogue with Sue. She had on an extra-large T-shirt of the American TV show "Friends," which I approved of wholeheartedly.

"Like special Kashgar souvenirs. There are Kashgar rugs, teas, sculptures, and other things," Sue explained. "My mother and I own a shop in the New Old Town. You can come meet us there once we are set up."

It seemed what she really meant to ask was, "Do you want to buy souvenirs *from me?*" I had to respect her hustle, and considering how hospitable she and her mother had been to me thus far, I felt it would only be right to see if I could find a couple of things at her shop to take home for my family.

"That would be great. Can you mark where it is on the map?"

She made a small X near the center.

"This is our shop," she said, pointing to the X. "I also marked some other places you should go to. My English writing isn't good, so if you cannot read it, send me a text and I will translate."

She handed me the map, which had at least a dozen other marks scattered across it. Most of them were near the center city, in or around the New Old Town. But it was the one mark that was not centrally located, barely within the eastern limit of the map, that caught my eye.

"Is this Abakh Hoja?" I asked.

"Yes!" Sue exclaimed. "How did you know that?"

"I'd read some stuff about it before I came. I remember that it's near the city limits."

As with many other tourist destinations in Xinjiang, the English translation of its name found on most tourist resources, such as the one I had used, left much to be desired. The proper translation for the place I was talking about is actually "Afaq Khoja." It is named after Khoja Afaq, the most famous of the Kashgari Khojas, or "masters"—the name for the leaders of a sect of Sufi Islam he founded, known as Afaqiyya, which became incredibly influential in Kashgaria in the late seventeenth century. Among the things Afaq is famous for is enlisting the Tibetan Dalai Lama to help him regain control of Kashgar in 1678, after he had been chased out by a rival Sufi sect, the Ishaqiyyas. According to one legend, the Dalai Lama agreed to assist him only after he had been able to defeat the Dalai Lama in a "contest of miracles"; but more likely, His Holiness thought it was simply a prudent foreign policy move.[22]

The place called "Abakh Hoja" that Sue and I were talking about is the tomb where Khoja Afaq and the rest of his family members are buried.

I continued, "I think I'd like to go there first this morning, then maybe I can meet you at your shop."

"Are you sure? We are much closer to the New Old Town. Only a short walk away," she replied.

"Yeah, I'm sure. I want to see everything I can while I'm here, and from what I've heard about the New Old Town, I worry I'll have trouble leaving once I see it for myself."

Sue let out a quick laugh. "Oh yes, you might!" she said, "it is even better after being remodeled. It is much safer now."

*Safer?* I was unsure whether she was referring to the government's bulldozing of the *real* Old Town, to be replaced with sturdier new structures, or to the draconian anti-terrorism policies. In reality, however, these two seemingly disparate issues are closely intertwined.

I had read about how the original Old Town Kashgar, the one that had been there for more than 1,000 years, has all but disappeared in the last decade. Beginning around 2009, the ancient buildings of Old Town have mostly been demolished and replaced by an assortment of new structures that, according to Kashgar's vice mayor, would be designed with the utmost consideration to "preserve the Uyghur culture." This collection of replacement buildings is what is now known as the "New" Old Town.[23] What was left of the original Old Town had been relegated to just a few blocks of buildings.

The justification provided by the CCP for the project was that the new structures will be better at withstanding damage from earthquakes, which are somewhat common in southern East Turkistan. But this excuse is dubious when viewed in context. The Chinese government hasn't only demolished the Old Town, they've also razed countless Muslim religious sites, like mosques and cemeteries, as well as non-religious sites that are culturally or historically significant to the Uyghurs. If these renovations were purely to do with safety, it would be quite the coincidence that all of the most hazardous buildings happen to be the ones that are most important to the non-Han ethnic groups.

"Great, I'm excited to see it!" I replied, finishing off my last poached egg. I tried to get up to clean my empty plate myself, but I was intercepted by Sue's mother, who smiled at me while snatching it out of my hands.

"How do you plan to get to Abakh Hoja?" Sue asked.

"I was thinking I would take a taxi, would you recommend that?"

"Yes, the buses are confusing sometimes," she said. "How about you come by our shop at one in the afternoon?"

I checked my Guangphone. Only 8:45—plenty of time to go see Afaq Khoja and get back before one.

"That sounds perfect. I'll text you if I need anything before then. Thank you so much for breakfast," I said, adding a "xie xie" to the end upon remembering it was Sue's mother who had crafted the hearty meal.

"No problem. See you then!"

I walked back to my room, grabbed my black daypack—filled with my notebook, a couple of water bottles, and a hat and a pair of sunglasses for the unrelenting Kashgar sun—and headed out the door.

On my way down, one of the unfastened stair tiles almost got me again, leading me to slip over a couple of steps.

When I stepped outside, I got my first real taste of Kashgar's punishing heat. The sun's intense rays reflected off the black asphalt with an incandescent glow, as if they were about to melt it all into the ground. I could feel the skin on my face stiffen, attempting to adapt to the brutal desert climate.

I thought I was familiar with intense summer heat, but this was beyond anything I had been exposed to before. *Welcome to Kashgar*, I thought as I moved along.

I made it to the enormous front gate, and reached into my pocket for the fob Sue had given me upon my arrival. I had been excited—laughably so, in retrospect—by the thought of opening this monster myself, but once I pressed the fob to the receptor, prompting the door to swing up, I was a bit underwhelmed. The process had looked much more impressive in the blackness and quiet of Kashgar at four a.m.—although what it now revealed on the other side was far more exhilarating.

Old brick sidewalks were packed with throngs of people; most of them looked like commuters, making their way to work, but others were dressed more like tourists. The streets beyond them were filled just as tightly, underscored by the chorus of car horns, cursing out into the ether. At the edge of the sidewalk nearest to me, there was a lone street vendor, selling *doppas*—the iconic skull cap traditionally worn by Uyghur males.

I stepped past the gate's perimeter to join the commotion, and made my way along the crowded sidewalk, in search of an auspicious corner to hail a taxi. I could feel the gaggle of eyeballs fixed on me as I went—many more than I had ever attracted before. I hadn't even made it down a single block before being intercepted for the first of what became three separate pictures with star-struck pedestrians.

And, yes, I do mean star-struck—the first one, a young Han Chinese woman around my age, screamed "Keanu Reeves!" prior to politely requesting a photograph.

Like Keanu Reeves, I too have a pasty skin pigmentation. My hair was also on the longer side. These two qualities, let me emphasize, were the full extent of our similarities.

It's a strange feeling, having foreigners confuse you for an action-movie heartthrob with whom you bear only passing, if any, resemblance. A part of you, naturally, is flattered. And amused, of course. But it's also a bit disheartening, in a way, because it suggests that the person making the comparison has had such a dearth of personal encounters with Westerners during their lifetime that we remind them of movie stars.

Before others got the chance to buttonhole me further, I was able to get away.

Not long after, I arrived at a busy intersection—both streets packed with near-standstill traffic in each of their four lanes. I could see a Uniqlo department store, a two-story Luckin Coffee (the Chinese equivalent of Starbucks), and between them, most notable, a massive electronic billboard of President Xi Jinping.

It depicted him at what looked like a construction site, pointing confidently at a blueprint spread across a table. He was surrounded by a group of laborers—most of whom were clearly Uyghur or some other Turkic ethnicity. President Xi had on the same neatly tailored suit he can be observed sporting at virtually any Party event. He looked like he had just stopped by after a meeting with the Politburo. (Though he was wearing a hardhat.)

The laborers surrounding Xi were dressed their part, with splotches of dirt unevenly distributed across their uniforms. You could even see sweat glistening on the face of one of the Turkic men closest to the president.

The scene came off to me as specious—a fraudulent display to make the Chinese president look like a man of the people and the CCP a party of diversity and equal opportunity. Apparently, the observer was intended to believe that President Xi had taken the time to go to a construction site, fill in for the foreman, and while putting his expertise in construction management to use, he just *happened* to be photographed prominently with Turkic workers on the crew.

When the billboard shifted to a different, less farcical advertisement, I refocused on the task at hand. I couldn't spot any taxis close by, so I decided I'd try my luck near the larger buildings farther down the street.

After what couldn't have been more than a minute, I heard a shout from up ahead.

"Taxi!?"

I looked to see an older Han Chinese man, smoking a cigarette while leaned up against a black sedan, about twenty feet in front of me.

"Yes! To Abakh Hoja," I answered as I approached him.

"Aaa-baka Hoja?" he asked.

"Uhhhh, here." I took the map from my bag and pointed to it.

"Ahhh," he exhaled, then asked me something in Mandarin to which I simply shrugged my shoulders.

For payment, he requested an egregious forty yuan—more than double what I had paid for my red-eye airport shuttle. On top of that, the lack of any markings on the sedan made clear this wasn't a registered taxi.

"Too high!" I exclaimed, aiming to be just loud enough to get the message across in spite of the language barrier.

I countered by miming the number fifteen with my hands, but realized that this would probably mean nothing to the man either, since China has its own complicated system for signing numbers. I dug into the money pouch strapped to my waist and took out fifteen yuan, holding it up for him to see.

After a brief silence, which I anticipated would be followed by a cavil retort, the man nodded his head in agreement, gesturing to the door of his sedan. I hopped in the back, and once my driver was able to light his next cigarette, we were off.

The first blocks took a while to clear, but once we got outside the city center, things moved much more efficiently. I was grateful that the driver had agreed to my non-verbal request that he put all the windows down. I don't mind cigarette smoke in most circumstances. But when I sense there are more noxious fumes in an enclosed environment than there is oxygen, that's where I draw the line.

As we continued on, we passed over the Tumen River. I could see water flowing down it, but only enough to fill a very small fraction of the riverbed. I wondered whether this was the product of a purposeful irrigation decision by the government, or if the river had simply dried up, and fixing it was deemed a lower priority than other infrastructure projects in the city. I knew that climate change has made its mark in East Turkistan—particularly in the form of severe droughts in the southern half of the region—so this could have been an unavoidable result.

After we crossed the river bridge, things began to look more how I had envisioned Kashgar. The side streets we passed were lined by poplar trees, creating canopies against the onslaught of the desert sun. A young Turkic man in a roadside stall was selling pomegranate juice to some women around his age. He was doing an admirable job, holding up a conversation with them while holding off a couple of Turkic boys from stealing some of the inventory stored behind him.

Punctuated by these side streets, there were rows of less-modernized buildings with storefronts at the ground level. Most were still the familiar Han Chinese storefronts, with Chinese inscriptions, but for the first time, I saw signs written in the modern Uyghur script.

---

The original Uyghur script, or "Old Uyghur script," was a vertically written, Syriac-based system developed in the ancient Uyghur Empire, which existed in what is today northern Xinjiang and Mongolia for a large part of the eighth and ninth centuries. Several hundred years after that ancient empire had disintegrated, a successful Mongol Khan by the name of Chinggis (also commonly spelled "Genghis") was seeking a system of writing for his new and growing empire, and was convinced—with the help of some of his knowledgeable captives-turned-advisors—to adopt the same one that the Uyghurs had used. This wasn't the only thing Genghis Khan adopted from the ancient Uyghur civilization. He also appropriated their philosophy of religious pluralism, and used it as a foundation for constructing the largest and most diverse empire in all of human history.[24]

Because of some of the twists and turns that make the history of this part of the world so complex, the modern (or "new") Uyghur script—the one that the Uyghurs use today—is a derivation of traditional *Arabic* script. And the modern spoken Uyghur language is derived from the *Turkic* Karluk language.

---

It was about five more minutes into the cab ride when I saw the top of a striking turquoise dome above the roadside poplar trees and scattered buildings. The driver whipped a hard U-turn, veering across all three lanes of (thankfully) sparse traffic, and stopped at the front gates. He didn't seem like the type to waste time with goodbyes, so I exited the car quickly, giving him a wave and a "xie xie."

I approached the ticket desk, where a Han Chinese woman was seated. The rear wall of the ticket window displayed a large PRC flag.

"Hi," I said, putting up one finger.

The sign on the outside of the ticket booth showed an English translation of the prices. I handed her the thirty-five yuan for the cost of admission.

She smiled, clearly satisfied that we'd managed to avoid a more challenging attempt to communicate, and handed me a ticket. I took it and entered through the gate.

About thirty feet in front of me was a large white stone fountain with elaborate decorative carvings around its outside. The fountain was set in the middle of a large circular depression on the white stone path I was on, equidistant between me and the main mausoleum building. Hugging the perimeter of the path were a variety of plots of earth containing flowers in various colors; to my eye, slightly more of the bright red ones.

I had come at a perfect time. In the entire garden area, I couldn't see anyone else. It seemed strange for an iconic place like Afaq Khoja

Mausoleum, a place of such cultural significance, to be completely empty at ten in the morning on a summer weekend. I didn't even see any Han Chinese tourists.

I noticed a sign that read "Fragrant Princess," with an arrow pointing in the direction of the main building. I made my way through the garden and the opened gate on the opposite side.

There it lay before me, completely unobstructed: Afaq Khoja Mausoleum. The same turquoise tiles on the dome that I had seen on approach also graced the edges of the main mausoleum building—along the outward-facing side of the roof as well as the floor beneath it, along the enormous archway to the main entrance, all the way to the corners, and up to the minarets atop each of them. I also noticed, now that I was closer, that the turquoise color that dominated its appearance was made up of smaller tiles of a variety of similar, but slightly distinct hues. Other sections were made up of various grey tiles, in the same style as those in turquoise.

I could imagine what it would be like to have been a weary Silk Road traveler, traversing hundreds of miles of treacherous terrain, on the verge of succumbing to the unrelenting desert, and miraculously coming upon this divine refuge.

As I got closer to the front doors, I heard a man speaking Mandarin into a microphone. When I entered, I saw a tour group of a dozen or so Han Chinese, and their tour guide in front of them, pointing to a line of dusty caskets behind him. I understand next to no Mandarin. But there was something about the combination of the tone of his voice, and the few scattered laughs I heard from the tour group, that told me I had walked in just in time to witness one of those forced, uncomfortable puns that all tour guides are required to make.

After the tour group had moved on to the opposite corner, I was able to take my time looking at the caskets.

It was exactly as I expected an old tomb would look: rows of ancient, mud-brick caskets, with the most important ones—those with signs in front indicating the names of the deceased—elevated slightly higher than the others. I don't recall the names I saw on the signs in front of the caskets, except for two: Khoja Afaq and, next to him, Xiang Fei, or "Fragrant Princess" in English, as the sign noted.

---

I have since learned that Khoja Afaq's place in history is complicated. While he is revered by some Uyghurs today, others view him—and the Khojas in general—in a negative light. The brand of Sufism brought to Kashgaria in the seventeenth century by the Khojas was distinct from other types of Sufism, most importantly in its strict Islamist interpretation of the Quran.[25] Although the Khojas did not always govern in practice purely according to the Shari'ah, their interpretation of Islam had enough of an influence on the people in Kashgaria that some Uyghurs today blame the Khojas for the traces of Islamism that can still be found within their community. Additionally, after power over Kashgaria had shifted hands multiple times, eventually ending up with the Qing Dynasty in 1759, the Qianlong Emperor reinstalled the Khojas as titular rulers of many of the various city-states, serving at the pleasure of the Qing. Predictably, this has not helped the Khojas' image in the eyes of many Uyghurs.

In regard to Afaq Khoja Mausoleum, there is a strong case to be made that the CCP is preserving and operating it to help bolster claims that they are showing reverence for Uyghur history.[26] They point to Afaq Khoja to show that they respect Uyghur culture; but they have simultaneously been undertaking massive destruction of the gravesites of less-famous Uyghurs throughout East Turkistan. Satellite data have shown that in just two years—since 2018—the Chinese government has destroyed more than one hundred Uyghur cemeteries across Xinjiang.[27] A separate report from the Australian Strategic Policy Institute found that "30% of important Islamic sacred sites (shrines, cemeteries and pilgrimage routes, including many protected under Chinese law) have been demolished across Xinjiang, mostly since 2017, and an additional 28% have been damaged or altered in some way."[28]

---

I went back outside and found a small garden shaded by poplar trees. I sat down on a bench beneath their protection, and got my notebook and pen from my daypack to write down some of my observations. I tried to do this regularly, at least once at the end of every day, but often more frequently if I was someplace where I could do so without drawing attention.

Soon I was ready to move to my next destination: the New Old Town.

I made my way back to the entrance, and out, turning to take one last look at the mausoleum exterior before hailing a ride with one of the cabs conveniently stationed along the curb.

Chapter 5

# Kashgar, Day One
## —The New Old City

"You can't uproot all the weeds hidden among the crops in the field one by one—you need to spray chemicals to kill them all. . . . re-educating these people is like spraying chemicals on the crops. That is why it is a general re-education, not limited to a few people."

—Chinese Official in Kashgar
at a public meeting in 2017, reportedly[29]

My taxi driver took the same route as the one earlier that morning. We continued along it for a short while, and then, to my right, the gargantuan statue of Mao Zedong emerged. I hastily told the driver to let me off in front of it, and refused his offer to refund a portion of my fare for the shorter-than-expected ride.

As I stepped out of the car, a flock of pigeons that had congregated on the sidewalk took flight, setting me aback for a moment. My eyes followed them up to Mao's stone statue head, where dozens of their friends were already perched. (I didn't learn until later that the locals have fittingly nicknamed the statue "The Pigeon Keeper."[30])

The statue depicted Mao in his distinctive Communist coat—the one also worn by Joseph Stalin and other Soviet leaders, having two parallel columns of buttons down the front, and an oversized collar at the top. The Chairman was also wearing a hat, the red star in the center of it the only coloration on the entire statue. He had his hand outstretched in an awkward posture—evoking something between a handshake and a Nazi *Sieg Heil* salute—pointing toward the People's Park across the street.

---

For many of us in the West today, the name Mao Zedong doesn't elicit the same visceral reaction as do those of some other twentieth-century totalitarians. It surprises most people to learn how exceptionally ruthless he was.

## The New Old City 35

We'll never know precisely how many died under Mao's rule. But based on the data available (which includes some of the CCP's own records), in just four years, between 1958 and 1962, Mao's Great Leap Forward policy killed *at least* forty-five million people. Most of these deaths were due to the famine caused by Mao's messianic decision to corral China's farmers into poorly structured agricultural communes. But according to historian Frank Dikötter, somewhere between two and three million people were either tortured to death or summarily executed.[31] (This isn't even to mention the 1.5 to 2 million killed during Mao's Cultural Revolution, from 1966–1976, and the many lives "ruined through endless denunciations, false confessions, struggle meetings, and persecution campaigns."[32])

The disaster of the Great Leap Forward brought hundreds of thousands of Han Chinese to East Turkistan for the first time. This included the government-directed resettlement of Han Chinese—both willing and unwilling—from the east to help with the economic development of the region, in addition to the flood of millions of Han refugees from eastern Chinese provinces, where Mao's collectivization policies were being implemented more comprehensively. This period of mass migration, as well as several subsequent periods that followed it, dramatically altered the ethnic composition of East Turkistan.

East Turkistan did not escape from this period untouched. In the far northwest corner, Ili Kazakh Autonomous Prefecture, the famines became so crippling that they led to a mass exodus of ethnic Turks and ethnic Russians into the Soviet Union. But the most destructive policies of the Great Leap Forward—such as farm collectivization—happened at a much slower rate in Xinjiang relative to other parts of China, largely because of the CCP's effort to avoid inflaming tensions with the Turkic people there.[33]

In fact, one of the key events in the deterioration of relations between the Soviet Union and the People's Republic of China beginning in the mid-1950s (known as the Sino-Soviet split) was when Nikita Khrushchev, Joseph Stalin's successor, supported some high-ranking CCP apparatchiks who opposed Mao's Great Leap Forward and its resulting widespread devastation and dislocation.[34]

---

After taking a few more minutes to reflect on the exalted image of the most murderous man in modern history, I felt it was time to move on to check out the New Old City. My map indicated that an entrance was only a couple of blocks away.

I quickly covered the two blocks. Turning down a side street, I saw a gate about fifty yards in front of me, guarded by four Chinese police officers. Even from a distance, I could see that at least two of them were armed with military-grade assault rifles.

There was nobody else on the street at the time, aside from some shopkeepers on either side opening their stores. Two of the officers were leaning side by side against the booth that operated the gate, one of them cackling at something the other had just said. Then, one of them noticed me, his countenance instantly shifting to high alert.

"Ni-hao!" I blurted out.

I was too far away to comfortably address them, so this came out more as a shout than the friendly greeting I'd intended. It was loud enough to get the attention of the two officers on the other side of the booth, who hustled around to join their colleagues.

"Passport please," one of the officers requested coolly. I extracted it from my bag and presented it to him.

"Why are you in Xinjiang?" he asked as he flipped through.

"I am a student on vacation," I told him. He looked up from my passport and gave me a blank stare.

"Tourist." I clarified with a chuckle.

The officer's face slowly morphed into a disarming smile. It seemed my alibi had convinced him that I wasn't there for any illegal activity.

"Kashur Ancient City!" he declared while giving me a thumbs up. I replied with a "xie xie" and headed on my way.

That was my first interaction with the infamous Xinjiang police (aside from the airport cop), and it left me feeling ambivalent. They were members of the same police force who round up Uyghurs to be sent to concentration camps; who uphold Xinjiang's all-encompassing surveillance state; who brutalize Muslim citizens for even the most routine and innocent displays of faith. But these men I'd just encountered seemed like perfectly friendly guys. I understood how even normal and ethical people can be convinced into committing atrocities under a powerful authoritarian political system. Wrestling with this contradiction as I experienced it in person, though, was more difficult.

At the end of the block I found a wooden bench, where I sat down to plan out my route.

I could tell I was in the New Old City. The modern architecture of Sue's neighborhood had been replaced by an unending line of gaudy buildings with smooth sand-colored stone walls, and folksy curl-pattern carvings imprinted around and above the building entrances. Many of the windows and doors were painted in a lurid burnt orange, like they were constructed out of plastic and fashioned to vaguely resemble some exotic type of wood. White golf carts buzzed down the road in front of me, shuttling groups of gleeful Han Chinese tourists to their next destination.

It was uncanny how much it looked exactly as the name "New Old City" suggests. The architecture was clearly designed to imitate the feel of an ancient Silk Road city, with a rich 2,000-year history and culture, but in a cartoon version.

The mark that Sue had made on my map indicated that her store was just down the street. It wasn't even noon yet, and we were meeting at one, but I decided I'd walk by the place, just to make sure I knew where it was.

On my way, shops lined either side of the street, selling a wide variety of Kashgari items. Some were filled with meticulously designed Kashgari rugs; others sold various kinds of Uyghur pottery; one offered an array of aromatic spices; and there were many selling clothing and miscellaneous souvenir items. Several shops flew bright red PRC flags, prominently hung above their entrances for every passerby to see.

I stopped for a moment to admire an instrument I spotted hanging from the ceiling of a music shop. I mis-identified it as a sitar, but later discovered that it was a *dutar*—the two-stringed lute that is iconic in East Turkistan, as well as some other parts of Central Asia and Iran. The shopkeeper, an old Uyghur man wearing a white doppa and white shirt with a black and red embroidered collar, noticed me almost immediately. He emerged from the shop with an excited smile.

"Very good!" He exclaimed, while pointing to the instrument.

"Yes!" I agreed.

This must have given him the false impression that I was a prospective buyer, as I realized when he began taking the instrument down.

"Oh! No. Thank you!" I attempted to clarify.

He was undeterred. Once he'd managed to get it off its post, he handed the delicate thing to me. I felt it would be rude to refuse even to hold it, so I accepted, despite my fear of accidentally dislodging some crucial piece, rendering it beyond repair and myself liable. After pretending to give it an expert pre-purchase inspection, I handed it back to him.

"Very good! Thank you!" I reiterated.

I began to step back, planning to move on to find Sue's shop, but the man suddenly started plucking the strings. At first, I assumed he was just trying to prove to me that the dutar was fully functional, but he continued with what quickly became a discernible melody. Then, he began to sing.

I had never heard the Uyghur language spoken before in person, and here I was, for my first experience, being serenaded by it. To my unlettered Western ear, it sounded a lot like Arabic, but less tonal, and with a harsher emphasis on the sounds at the ends of words. I looked around to see if others were gathering to enjoy the man's performance, but it appeared that there was nobody else on the street aside from other shopkeepers, who I was sure had heard this countless times before.

I gestured at a plastic chair I saw next to the shop, seeking permission to sit. He nodded in approval, without a break in the lyrics.

My Guangphone showed that it was 12:15—forty-five minutes to explore more of the New Old City and come back to find Sue's shop. It would have been impolite to leave in the middle of this wonderful surprise performance, so I decided to stick around for as long as Uyghur Sinatra would have me.

As it turned out, he had plenty left in the tank—almost thirty minutes more. I'm sure I exhibited the epitome of an ignorant tourist when, after he'd finished, all I did was applaud, and regale him in a flurry of "xie xies." He laughed, and gave his best effort at an English "thank you."

I felt it was only right to repay him somehow. There was no musical instrument in his shop that, played in my hands, wouldn't offend the ears of every musician in Kashgar, let alone anything that I'd be able to fit on a plane. So I thought to give him a crisp American five-dollar bill.

His reaction was close to what I expected, knowing how valuable American currency is in this part of the world. His eyes lit up for a moment, but he refused to take it—surely out of a sense of politeness. I wouldn't have it. After several rounds of my insisting and his refusing, he acquiesced. When he finally took the bill in his hands, he seemed to be at a loss for words. I spared him the difficulty of thanking me by giving him one last "xie xie" before walking off.

I knew I would have to hurry to make it to Sue's on time. I did not want to be late.

Chapter 6

# Kashgar, Day One
## —Sue's Shop, the Dancers

"Ethnic unity is the lifeline of all ethnic groups in China and the foundation of economic progress in Xinjiang."

—Shohrat Zhakir, Xinjiang Regional Governor

I saw Sue immediately on rounding the first corner. She was standing in front of the store, looking at her phone, while her mother was sweeping around some clothing racks just outside. They were stocked with a variety of traditional clothing commonly worn by Uyghur women. As I got close enough for Sue to sense me, prompting her to turn in my direction, I saw that she was wearing one of those items—a black shirt made of what looked like silk, with an embroidered rose pattern circling the collar.

"Hello Grayson!" she said. "Would you like some water? You look hot."

"Hi Sue! Water would be great. Thank you," I replied, wiping a film of sweat from my forehead, as she invited me inside the store.

The place felt quite cramped, although I couldn't tell whether it was truly small or if the large stockpiles of inventory just made it feel that way. Every shirt hanger on the walls was full, and there were towers of items stacked on the clothing racks below them, each of the racks stuffed with items as well.

We arrived at a table in a back corner that held a pitcher of water. Sue poured a small paper cup and handed it to me. As I went for a sip, I was disappointed by its slightly-hot temperature.

One thing I did not love about China was that water was almost always served either lukewarm or hot. You would have to request that your water be iced (*bing* in Mandarin) if you wanted it colder than room temperature, and even this was sometimes ignored. The exception was bottled water, which was usually at least mildly chilled. I'm ashamed to say that the number of plastic bottles I went through in Asia would make Al Gore's environmentalist head spin.

"How do you like my shop?" Sue inquired.

"I love it. The clothes here look so nice. Are they made of silk?" I asked while thumbing one of the Uyghur dresses hanging on the wall in front of me.

"Some of them. Those aren't though," she said, pointing to the dress I was examining.

"Really? What is this one made of? It feels just like silk."

"I don't know, sorry," she said, in a tone that seemed to convey amusement at my misperception. "How did you like the Fragrant Princess?"

I thought it interesting that she seemed to be referring to the whole of the mausoleum by this name.

"I got to see where she was buried. The building and the grounds was one of the most beautiful places I've seen in China so far," I added, truthfully. "Do a lot of people call that place the Fragrant Princess?"

"Yes, most Chinese call it that," she said, using the designation "Chinese" rather curiously. "Did they tell you her story while you were there?"

"No," I replied.

---

Sue recounted the Han Chinese version of the story, which goes something like this: The Fragrant Princess, or Iparhan, was one of the many wives of the Qianlong Emperor between 1760 and 1788. The emperor, on discovering her in Kashgar, was taken in by her beauty, and even more so by her recherché natural scent. Some versions of the story claim that she even washed herself every day in camel's milk during her journey to Beijing, so that her fragrance would be preserved. When she got to Beijing, she was too homesick to come to bed with the emperor, so he tried everything in his power to recreate the things that she missed about Kashgar. After many of his attempts, she finally fell in love with him when he brought her a jujube tree from Kashgar that bore golden fruit. Her legend endures as a symbol of ethnic unity.

I learned later that the Uyghurs tell a very different Fragrant Princess story. According to them, her name was Nur Ela Nurhan, and she was kidnapped by the Qianlong emperor to be part of his vast harem in Beijing. While in captivity, she was able to obtain some daggers, which she used to protect herself against the lascivious emperor's constant advances. She continued fending him off until the emperor finally gave up, and had her poisoned. For the Uyghurs, her legend symbolizes the bravery of Uyghur resistance to Chinese imperialism.

Naturally, these two versions of the story are irreconcilable with one another, each serving to support the respective side's overarching narrative in regard to the historical relationship between the Uyghurs and the Chinese.

(It's important to note here that the Qing Dynasty, and the Qianlong emperor, were actually Manchu, which is an ethnicity distinct from the Han. Manchus have even been singled out by Han ethno-nationalists at various times in the past for being particularly to blame for China's problems. Today, however, the Manchu are not subjected to the same oppressive policies as are other ethnic groups—such as the Tibetans, and the Turkics in Xinjiang—because they are perceived as being more fully assimilated into the dominant Han culture.[35] And for their part, the Turkic peoples of East Turkistan draw little distinction between the Manchu and the Han, viewing them both as "Chinese" colonizers.[36])

The Uyghur side of the story wasn't even hinted at, as far as I can remember, at the Mausoleum. There was no plaque that told the story, or described the difficulties of interpreting controversial historical topics for contemporary visitors, or acknowledged that this woman, whoever she was, was most surely brought to Beijing against her will. This complete expurgation of disagreeable narratives is a microcosmic example of what the CCP does with many of the unflattering parts of Chinese history.

---

"Wow, I had no idea she was such an important figure," I said.

Even without knowing yet that there was a far different Uyghur version of the story, I suspected that there was more to it than Sue had told me. But even so, it's perfectly plausible that Sue herself did not know the Uyghur version

"Have you tried Kashgar food yet?" Sue asked, as her mother shooed us both out of the shop to clear some space for her to continue to sweep.

"Not yet. I'm really hungry, though. Are there any places nearby that you'd recommend?"

"There are a few. You should go toward the entrance archway. They have really good Uyghur street foods there."

"That sounds great. Is it close by?"

"Yes. Just keep walking down this street for maybe ten minutes and you will arrive," she said, pointing down the road in the opposite direction from where I'd come.

"Awesome. Do you want to come with me?" I asked. "I might need a translator."

"I can't, I have to stay until the shop closes. But maybe we could have dinner after that. There is a lamb restaurant near my apartment where we can go."

"I'd love to. What time do you close?"

"At eight. If you meet me here it will be easier."

"Sure, I'll come back here at eight. See you then!" I said, as I walked off down the street.

Sue's mentioning the lamb restaurant was a strong reminder of how famished I was. It took every ounce of my willpower not to stop off at one of the restaurants I encountered on the road.

Sure enough, after maybe ten minutes of walking—through the same synthetic Uyghur neighborhood that I'd seen everywhere thus far—I saw in front of me the inward-facing side of the giant beige sandstone archway. It was built over an offshoot of the same paved road I was on, which led off downhill for about forty yards before intersecting with a highway, and what looked like some more authentic parts of Kashgar city across it.

Between me and the archway there were perhaps thirty different street vendors, most of them selling delicious-looking street foods—such as pizza-sized circles of Uyghur naan, and sizzling kabobs—and others selling the kinds of clothing items and trinkets I had seen in the area I'd just walked through.

To the side of the archway was a small park, shaded by some trees, where a group of Uyghur women were dancing together, a crowd of fans gathered around them. They were all wearing matching red traditional Uyghur dresses with jeweled sleeves, and had red flowers pinned to their braided black hair that ran the length of their backs. The pop music they were dancing to emanated from a speaker that a Uyghur boy of about twelve crouched next to; he looked proud to have been accorded the role of DJ.

It was a pleasant scene, except for the fact that every last one of the observers was Han Chinese. In fact, surveying the rest of my surroundings, the only Uyghurs I could find were either street vendors or performers.

Kashgar was supposed to be the "Cradle of Uyghur Culture," and the Old City was supposed to be a cradle within that cradle. In terms of how Uyghurs view Kashgar, it is comparable to how the world's Jews, Christians, and Muslims view Jerusalem.[37] But what I saw was far from that. This was no longer a place for Uyghurs to live; this was a place for Han tourists to be entertained.

These Han tourists had most likely come to Kashgar from relatively comfortable lives in eastern China, doing so on the recommendation of some CCP-concocted advertisement that marveled at how "safe" the "New" Kashgar was. They could observe and experience an alien culture while being in the protection of even more of that vigilant state security they had grown accustomed to in Beijing or Shanghai. They could take videos of their strange compatriots practicing their curious cultural rituals and celebrations, and show all their friends back east how they got to see it all up close, without even having to leave the country.

The Uyghur dancers, on the other hand, wore practiced fake smiles, with no real joy behind them. Admittedly, this deduction was based only on my own observations in the moment. I had no hard evidence that these women weren't as happy as they appeared. But how could they be, having to showcase one of the treasures of their culture to a group of people who, in all likelihood, only felt safe enough to travel to Kashgar because of the very "counter-extremism" policies that were immiserating their community?

I couldn't even know for sure that these women were here performing of their own free will. It was possible that they were doing it out of an ordinary desire to make a living. But more likely, they were pressured by the CCP to be there—made to play a useful role in bolstering the CCP's narrative that the changes they have made in Kashgar are to benefit all of Kashgar's citizens.

As the Xinjiang expert Adrian Zenz has described it, "the level of coerciveness of one's occupation may vary, but being outside a government-approved work category, or failing to comply with the state's opinion of what you in particular should be doing, is no longer an option."[38]

I stayed until the end of the performance, to take part in the thunderous applause that followed it. After taking a bow with the rest of the troupe, one of the women had to run over to the speaker to turn it off, upon realizing that the DJ had abdicated his position several songs earlier, and was now playing soccer with some other adolescent Uyghur boys in the small field behind them.

# Chapter 7

# Kashgar, Day One
## —Afternoon and Evening at the New Old City

" . . . all of Xinjiang has become an open-air prison, with the difference of internment and non-internment being a matter of degree."

—Adrian Zenz, Senior Fellow, Victims of Communism Memorial Foundation

The rogue DJ was in a tough spot. Having just assisted one of his soccer mates on an impressively struck goal, it appeared his team had the momentum on their side. The two gave each other a fleeting embrace and exchanged a few words of friendly trash-talk with their opponents before going to defend against the coming counter-attack. But the young soccer star's mother, rapidly approaching the pitch, posed an existential risk to their chances. When he turned and saw her, his face quickly shifted from a confident smirk to a rueful sulk—he knew exactly what was to come. Having seen this stark reversal in her son's emotions, the Uyghur dancer felt no need to walk all the way over to him. She stopped, and he promptly ran to her. Without either of them saying a word, they turned and headed off down the road.

Among the most important rules all boys come to learn—in any part of the world—is that it is always ill-advised to embarrass your mother in public. I hoped he would be allowed near a soccer ball again sometime soon.

My immediate concern, however, was what to eat. My nose took over as I noticed the inviting smells coming from the nearby food stalls—cumin and grilling meat being the strongest among them. Right in front of me was a string of three kabob stands, each selling a different type of meat. One of them I knew to be chicken, and one smelled like lamb. The third was a mystery, and I lacked the vocabulary to ask the grill master about this one. They all smelled equally enticing, so I decided to try one of each.

I found a shady seat near the soccer field to enjoy my meal, eager to see how the team would fare without its star player. The kabobs tasted every bit as delicious as I had expected; the smokiness of the tender meat interacted with the cumin seasoning to create a richly flavorful taste. I was hooked from the first bite.

I was able to relax long enough to watch multiple full games before three police officers, armed with assault rifles, marched over to me. They asked for my passport. One of them got out his phone, making use of the translation app to ask me the usual questions. I gave him the usual answers. After two or three minutes, they moved on.

I watched as they marched down the street, in the direction of Sue's shop. Before they had even turned the corner, another three-man patrol emerged from that direction, coming toward the central square where I was.

Above their heads, attached to the sides of a second-story window, I spotted three white surveillance cameras arranged to cover 180 degrees. Directly across that street, in an identical position, were three more cameras.

I adjusted my eyes to scan my surroundings for more of them. The result was overwhelming: On just about every building, there were at least six surveillance cameras. On most of the light posts that lined the street on the park side of the central square, there were at least three. Without moving from my seat, looking around the entire square, and down past the archway to the other side of the highway, I counted sixty-two cameras. A subsequent counting of police officers within view turned up fifteen, not including the three who had approached me minutes earlier.

I felt the true inescapability of being in Kashgar's surveillance state.

But I was a fortunate man with a golden ticket out—a U.S. passport. If a police officer thought I looked suspicious (which they frequently seemed to), all I needed to do was show proof of my American citizenship, and after the same few questions, I'd be free to go. I would have to do something pretty reckless for the police to detain me. What Chinese cop would want to be responsible for further inflaming the already-strained tensions between China and the United States—for goading the global superpower that the CCP wishes to furtively surpass?

I knew how much worse it would be were I to trade places with a Uyghur—where everything that made me uncomfortable as an American tourist would instead have me fearing for my life and the lives of my loved ones each time I took a step outside.

---

The full extent of the CCP's surveillance apparatus in Xinjiang is almost unfathomably worse than what I knew about at that time. In an incisive report published in June 2020 by the Uyghur Human Rights Project, William Drexel notes that spatial surveillance (cameras) in Kashgar "cannot be fully understood without a prior basic understanding of the biometric, communicative, and behavioral modes of digital surveillance that accompanied it."[39] The following paragraphs summarize the key points of his report.

To collect biometric information, the government in Xinjiang required Turkic people to submit to physical examinations in which they provided DNA samples, iris scans, fingerprints, voice signatures, and facial signatures. Just one of a number of programs that conducted these examinations reported having thirty-six million participants between 2016 and 2017—more than the official population of Xinjiang.

As to communications surveillance, officials monitor everything a Uyghur does online. Uyghurs are forced to download an app called Clean Net Guard, which "monitors everything said, read, or written on smartphones." Online activity on computers is subject to similar surveillance. The activities that can lead a Uyghur to run afoul of the government and be sent to a camp are shockingly numerous, vague, and arbitrary. For example, being discovered to have communication with people outside of China is deemed suspicious. Or failing to use a properly surveilled device. Or possessing "religious imagery," engaging in "non-compliant speech," or having "suspicious sentiments." It does not matter if a Uyghur committed these transgressions only prior to the enactment of the stricter policies. Drexel notes that, "Even content that was posted and deleted on the internet before 2017, when much of these systems reached full fruition, can be retroactively recovered and used as grounds for suspicion."[40]

Surveillance of behavior overlaps with surveillance of communications in certain ways. The "suspicious activity" that the government looks for in a Uyghur's online activity is similar to what it looks for offline. Public displays of religious adherence are considered the most dangerous—this includes men who grow long beards or women who wear any form of headscarf. There are other behaviors, entirely unrelated to religious observance, that are treated as suspicious as well. Traveling outside of the country, for instance, regardless of the reason, is considered suspicious, and particularly so if the travel is to a predominantly Muslim country. Listed in the Drexel report as cause for suspicion are a Uyghur household's electricity usage; vehicle usage; exiting their home through the back door too often; and not socializing enough with neighbors.

All categories of surveillance—biometric, communicative, and behavioral—are systematized by the AI (artificial intelligence) technology built into every camera in Kashgar. Put simply, a Uyghur walking down a street in Kashgar will be tracked by cameras at every step. The cameras employ facial and voice analytics to identify that person; these are then cross-referenced to their associated profiles that contain their biometric, communicative, and behavioral surveillance histories.

There is also the massive and ever-present non-digital surveillance apparatus that exists side by side with the digital surveillance in Kashgar. There are "convenience police stations," each assigned a given "square" of 500 people, and tasked with overseeing their activities. There is the "Becoming Family" program, instituted in 2017, in which Han Chinese Party members come to live in Uyghur homes as "relatives" and monitor the intimate activities of these families to see whether they exhibit any signs of "extremism." Uyghur women whose husbands have been sent to the camps are often forced to share beds with male Han observers, in what has been called "state-sanctioned mass rape."[41] And finally, the CCP has also gone to great lengths to instill the more traditional Mao-era community-based surveillance system in which Uyghurs who report other Uyghurs for suspicious behavior accrue rewards from the government.

Taken together, these combine to make today's Kashgar what Mr. Drexel pointedly calls an "upside-down smart city." The full arsenal of China's available surveillance technology has been built into Kashgar's foundations, turning the heart of Uyghur culture into a dystopian nightmare.

---

To take my mind off the ever-present eyes watching me, I returned my focus to the soccer game.

It wasn't long before one of the younger soccer players, who had noticed me observing them, walked over to me sheepishly. He stopped about ten feet in front of me, with a rapt look, unable or unwilling to speak.

"Hi!" I said to break the silence, with a smile and a wave.

He seemed to think that some part of this greeting was hilarious, because he burst into laughter the second I'd finished delivering it. He ran back a few steps, calling to his mates, who quickly came over to join him.

There were now five of them in front of me, each grinning from ear to ear. The boy in the middle, who looked slightly older than the others, maybe fifteen, was holding the dilapidated soccer ball. Here, I saw an opportunity.

I got up and pointed to the ball, gesturing at the kid to kick it to me. He obliged, still laughing. I took a couple of touches to get used to the feel of it on my feet, and to lull the kids into letting their guard down. As I looked up at the boy who had passed the ball to me initially, I kicked it—hard—past the group's right flank, and ran quickly to retrieve it. I looked back to see that I had successfully baited them into a game of keep-away.

I managed to retain possession for all of thirty seconds before their relentless swarming overwhelmed me. But I was happy when they invited me to join their match.

I had a great time playing with them, but in my head, I was wondering how to interpret this situation. There was no way to be certain in this environment what was genuine and what wasn't. The boys were laughing and screaming ebulliently; but it was unclear how much of their friendliness might be born of an understanding that they were expected to make nice with all the tourists who ventured through there.

There was something else I perceived in their eyes: what appeared to be a deep tiredness of the spirit. Its emergence was ephemeral, and I had only seen it twice thus far—earlier on the face of the shopkeeper musician, and now on the faces of at least a couple of the kids I was playing soccer with. It was as if they were so used to the artificial, choreographed nature of their lives in the new Kashgar, that they were unprepared for a foreigner treating them like human beings worthy of respect. And so they seemed to unconsciously let down their emotional guard for a moment, revealing a glimpse at the depths of their true feelings for the tragic state of their homeland.

As I continued to play with the boys, we gradually accumulated a small group of spectators, all of whom, predictably, were Han Chinese. They were gawking and pointing, their phones documenting our game. Being watched in this way felt stranger than the stares I had already gotten used to. It almost felt like we were animals in a zoo, entertaining onlooking visitors as we played among ourselves. I just focused on the game as much as I could, and the crowd became less of a distraction. I wondered if that might be how the boys had learned to cope with it, too.

We played for several hours, until dark. I gave high-fives to my teammates, gathered my things, and headed back to the central square.

Almost as soon as I left, I remembered my eight o'clock dinner meet-up with Sue, and realized that I had almost certainly missed it. Sure enough, my Guangphone read 9:30.

I felt awful. After making Sue stay up into the early hours of that morning because of my late flight, I had now inadvertently blown off her very considerate offer to join me for my first dinner in Kashgar, at a restaurant she thought I'd really enjoy.

I decided to see if she might still be hanging around her shop; but I knew there was hardly any chance she'd be there. Part of me hoped she wouldn't be. I was not looking forward to having to explain myself. "I lost track of time playing soccer with the local Muslim children" didn't strike me as an excuse that would resonate with her.

Just as I had expected, when I arrived back at Sue's shop, she was gone and the store was closed. I grabbed a late dinner at a lone chicken kabob stand nearby, and then returned to the apartment.

When I arrived, it was clear that no one else was home—presumably they were having a lively Saturday night out without me. Just as well. It would have been difficult for me even to pretend to have a good time that night, given my realization that so much of Kashgar had essentially become an imperialist theme park.

# Chapter 8

# Kashgar, Day Two
## —Breakfast and Getting to Id Kah

"To destroy a people, you must first destroy its history."

—Xi Jinping, quoting the Chinese intellectual
Gong Zichen (1792–1841)

I briefly rehearsed the apology I would give Sue, before gently brushing the rug door to the side and exiting my room. In the kitchen, I found Sue's mother making breakfast, and Sue sitting at the kitchen table, talking to a young Han Chinese man I hadn't seen before. He was wearing a plain white T-shirt and baggy athletic shorts, and had a strikingly bad case of bedhead, all of which reassured me that he wasn't there in any official capacity.

"Good morning!" Sue greeted me as I entered. "How was your night?"

"It was very good. I got so caught up in everything in the city that I forgot about the time," I explained, having decided to leave out the specifics. "I'm really sorry about missing our dinner. I feel horrible. I hope you didn't wait for me for too long."

"That's okay. I'm very happy that you enjoyed the city. It's so much fun at night, isn't it?"

"Definitely. I had a great time."

"So what do you plan to do today?" she asked.

"Well, the two things I want to see most are the bazaar and Id Kah Mosque," I told her, "but other than that, I thought I would just explore the city some more."

Out of the corner of my eye, I saw the seated Han man staring at me intently. I must have turned my attention away from Sue for a moment, because she seemed to pick up on it immediately.

"Oh, this is Li," she said. "He is the other guest who will be staying with us."

"Hello, you are Grayson, right?" he inquired as I turned toward him.

"Yes, I am. Nice to meet you, Li," I replied.

Li told me that he had been born in Chengdu (which Sue helpfully clarified is the "Panda City"), but that he now lived in Tokyo as a graduate student in biology. He was visiting Kashgar because his parents had come there recently and had raved about its significant improvement as a vacation spot. He was also a big fan of spiced lamb—which gave me high hopes for a congenial relationship between us.

"Do you want to see the animal market?" Sue asked.

I had read some about the livestock market in Kashgar, and that it was one of the few bastions of authentic Uyghur culture left in the city. It used to be far more central—quite literally, as well as figuratively—in that it was based right outside of Id Kah Mosque, near the center of the city. However, as part of the government's sweeping reconstruction plans, it was forced to move to the far outskirts in 2001.[42]

"Yeah, I would love to. Are you going there today?"

"No, Li and I are going tomorrow morning, I think. Would you like to come with us?"

"Absolutely. Thanks for inviting me."

Sue's mother placed a couple of plates of rice and poached eggs in front of each of them, and headed back to the pot to fix a plate for me.

"Oh, I think I'm going to eat breakfast in the city somewhere today," I told Sue. "Please tell your mother thank you, though."

She turned to inform her mother, who looked at me and smiled, indicating that she took no offense.

"I should get going now, I have a lot I want to see. I'll see you both tonight," I said.

"Okay, I'll see you then. Please text me or come by the shop if you need anything," Sue offered.

"It was nice to meet you, Grayson," Li added.

"Nice to meet you too, Li. What do you plan on doing for your first day?" I asked.

"I don't know yet. Sue is giving me recommendations."

"I'm sure they'll be great. She helped me out a lot yesterday," I told him sincerely. "See you guys later."

I had two additional destinations on my itinerary for the day that I thought best to withhold from Sue and Li. The first was to see if there was any part of the *real* Old City that I could access. I hadn't yet seen it for myself, but I'd learned from my reading that there was still a several-square-mile section that had not yet been demolished. Time permitting,

I also hoped, more ambitiously, to visit a randomly chosen part of the outskirts of the city, where there might be some remnants of the real Kashgar still there to see.

But first, I needed breakfast—something more filling than roadside kabobs. I wanted to go to a real restaurant. I recalled some places that I had passed on my walk through the New Old City the day before, so I decided to make my way over there.

I took a different entrance to the New Old City this time, one that looked on my map to be quicker. When I arrived at it, though, I immediately regretted this choice. On the right side of the road, there was a line of maybe a dozen Uyghurs waiting to go through a checkpoint of metal detectors beside a police desk. The rest of the road was open, with crowds of Han Chinese strolling through.

As I was waiting my turn at the detectors, one of the officers at the police desk noticed me. He yelled something in Mandarin to get my attention, and when I looked up at him, he aggressively directed me to get out of the line. I hesitated for a moment after I had passed the police desk, anticipating a passport-check and the usual questions; but no one even looked in my direction. It seemed that a wizened Uyghur man, inching through the detector with the aid of his cane, required the undivided attention of all four of the officers—two of whom, interestingly, were Uyghur themselves.

Soon after, I arrived at the central square in front of the archway. I hadn't yet explored farther along the main road I was on, which divided the square and seemed to lead into other parts of the New Old City. Surely I'd find some good restaurants down that way.

To stay on schedule, I committed to eat at the first decent-looking sit-down restaurant I came to. It took only minutes for me to arrive at a quaint dumpling establishment, tucked between two shops selling Uyghur clothing. I was still intent on finding an authentic Uyghur restaurant, but my gut feeling suggested there was little chance that any restaurant I'd find in the New Old City would be owned and operated by Uyghurs, which I considered an essential part of a genuine experience.

I took a prime people-watching seat on the outer edge of the empty restaurant. A middle-aged Han woman near the back noticed me and brought over a tea kettle and a steel cup. She hovered over me as I perused the menu, all written in Chinese. The tricky thing about relying entirely on pictures at a dumpling restaurant is that most dumplings look the same on the outside. I pointed to the largest dumpling picture on the menu, thinking that its size might be correlated with its popularity. The woman smiled before shuffling back to the kitchen.

When I poured myself a cup of tea from the ornate kettle she'd brought over, I was surprised by its blackish color—and even more so by its earthy, bitter taste. After a few sips, it began to grow on me. I had gotten used to the smoother green teas in Korea and Beijing, but as someone who insists on always having my coffee black, this turned out to be quite to my liking.

It took about ten minutes for a plateful of dumplings to arrive. The first bite released the unmistakable taste of spiced pork mixed with cabbage.

---

Eating pork is considered unethical—haram—by most practicing Muslims. This, one might expect, would make pork difficult to find in Kashgar, but that is not the case. A component of China's cultural edification in East Turkistan is to force Muslims to consume haram products, such as alcohol and pork, to demonstrate that they have successfully acculturated into Han society by rejecting "extremist" ideas. A Muslim's refusal to eagerly participate can lead to internment.

There are some particularly sardonic examples of this policy being carried out, such as the regular "beer-drinking contests" put on by the government in Xinjiang, often scheduled around Ramadan. Supposedly, these events are justified because, as one Chinese academic disingenuously put it, "many Uyghurs like to drink."[43] Another example occurred on the first day of Ramadan in 2020, when Konasheher County in Kashgar signed an agreement to raise 40,000 pigs annually to "secure Kashgar's pig supply." It was designated a "poverty alleviation project"—as are many of the CCP's cynical schemes to obliterate Uyghur culture.[44]

---

I scarfed down every dumpling on my plate, and after agreeing to pose for a picture with the waitress, I went on my way.

My first destination, a short walk away, was the historic Id Kah Mosque. Id Kah is the largest mosque in all of China, and considered by most Uyghur Muslims to be the holiest site in East Turkistan.

This passage from *The Silk Road: From Xi'an to Kashgar*, published in 1993, paints a picture of the atmosphere around the mosque during a time when the CCP's policies toward religious practice were relatively tolerant. It depicts Id Kah on the Muslim holiday of Eid al-Adha:

> This mosque, the largest in China, can see as many as 10,000 worshippers at prayers on Friday afternoon. Muslims come by the truckload from towns as far away as Yengisar, many dressed in traditional chapans (three-

quarter-length coats of striped cotton), embroidered dopas and knee-length leather boots. Veiled women and young children stand at the exits of the mosque, holding small teapots of water or pieces of nan in cloth. As men stream out from prayers they bestow on these their holy breath or spit, blessing them; they will then be taken to feed a sick relative. [45]

I did not anticipate a high-spirited scene of this kind. Considering the parts of the New Old City I had already seen, reconfigured into a plastic Uyghur display, it seemed likely that Id Kah would neatly fit that same theme. Its centrality to Uyghur culture, I feared, would only have made its unchanged existence a greater target for the CCP's malicious goals for Kashgar's reconstruction.

Soon I arrived at another police checkpoint. Behind it, and across a full-width city street, in the middle of a vast clearing, stood Id Kah Mosque. Even from that distance, I noticed the natural desert-yellow tinge of its walls—a welcome sight compared to the grandiloquent New Old City neighborhood I'd just come through. Apparently the CCP had left some of this beautiful structure alone.

I passed through the police checkpoint, undergoing the now-tedious routine of ID check and questioning, and undergoing the same process again a few yards on, at the entrance to an underpass.

I emerged from the underpass on the opposite side of the road, deliberately turning away from the kabob stand strategically placed next to the exit.

In front of Id Kah Mosque was Id Kah Square, a massive grey-stone semi-circle of open space where Kashgar's central market used to be. The square was largely empty, aside from some scattered pedestrians and a "camel ride," where you pay a Uyghur man to parade you around the square on a camel's back. I decided to skip that.

The only Uyghur in sight was the camel handler. Everyone else was Han, and most looked like tourists. It seemed an unhealthy inversion of the place's natural state—the closer I got to what should have been the center of the Uyghurs' homeland, the fewer of them I saw.

I wasn't the least bit surprised to find a ticket desk at the entrance to the mosque. *Welcome to Id Kah Mosque: The Heart of Old Kashgar,* read an English sign, written also in Chinese and Uyghur.

"One ticket?" the Han man behind the counter asked in perfect English.

"Yes, please," I answered.

"Fifty yuan."

I handed him the fifty, and he handed me what looked like an oversized postcard.

"Good for three days," he chirped.

The left half of the front side of the ticket was a professional photograph of the New Old City architecture—taken either in early morning or late afternoon, so the sun illuminated only the top half of the buildings. The right half of the ticket was filled with writing that I scanned for English. All I could find, in the bottom right corner, was a section headed *Tourist Guide* that included what the ticket paid for (maintenance), the opening time, and an admonition for visitors to "respect customs, protect cultural heritage."

I looked back into Id Kah Square to see a young Han Chinese girl riding on the camel. She was screaming with laughter as five or six of her relatives stood off to the side, cheering her on while taking video. It was an adorable scene, causing the misanthropic look on the Uyghur camel-handler's face to be all the more noticeable. He was staring bitterly down to the ground as he paraded the girl around the square, clearly hating every moment of it. Strangely, the first thing I felt was not pity for the man, but concern for his well-being: he wasn't playing his part convincingly, and maintaining the spectacle was the highest priority for the CCP. I entered the mosque wondering how much longer he would last in the job.

I still remember that man's face.

Chapter 9

# Kashgar, Day Two
## —Id Kah Mosque

> "Only in the late nineteenth century did the Chinese realize that civilization had a plural."
>
> —S.C.M Paine, Professor of Strategy and Policy, U.S. Naval War College

The entrance to the mosque gave way to a spacious courtyard, perfectly shaded by poplar trees lining the edges of the stone path. They were all marked with curious identical red lines at about chest level, reminding me of the trail markers you would see while hiking in national parks in the U.S.

In the center of the courtyard was an open space with benches for visitors to sit. A group of five or six Han Chinese were gathered around one of them, speaking at a much higher volume than I thought was considerate for the austere religious setting. There was another similar-sized group at a bench farther down, silently and respectfully taking in the beauty of their surroundings. One of them had his head bowed and eyes closed—appearing, perhaps, to be subtly praying.

Near the end of the path was a dark green wooden gate, with yellow brick pillars on either side. The doors of the gate were open, and there was a loudspeaker mounted at the top. I doubted it was used for the call to prayer.

Through the gate, and up a short flight of stone stairs, I found the prayer hall. It was just far enough away to render insignificant the noise coming from the tourists in the center courtyard.

The hall was enclosed on its other three sides by white walls that contained a few worn lines of Uyghur script, and was held up by green pillars, roughly ten feet apart. Directly to my right, at the top of the stairs, was an empty rack for shoes. There were no worshippers.

However, had there been anyone desiring prayer, they would have been deterred from entering the prayer space by a line of white rope that was tied around the perimeter pillars. The white string was draped with triangular flags of different garish colors—an addition that struck me as carelessly insensitive. It was as if a design specialist had been assigned the task of fabricating a feel of authenticity for Id Kah, while rendering useless its authentic Islamic features. The designer's creative solution upon arriving at the question—what will Muslim tourists do when they have come to visit the mosque, and find that the prayer room is inaccessible?—was to decorate the rope barrier with some rainbow-colored pennants.

---

Islam as it is practiced in East Turkistan is particularly diverse. Most Uyghurs today are part of the Hanafi school of Sunni Islam, which is distinct from other schools in that it allows Muslims to pray in non-Arabic languages. Sufism also remains a prominent presence in East Turkistan. But that surface-level description fails to account for the complexities within Uyghur Islam.

Remnants of the various religions that first entered East Turkistan along the ancient Silk Road remain salient in the region. Buddhist influences left over from the Khotan Kingdom in the late ninth/ early tenth century, as well as Zoroastrian, Manichean, and various forms of Shamanism that date back even further, appear in the religious rituals performed by many Uyghur Muslims.[46]

The general normalization of these hybrid forms of Islam in East Turkistan would suggest that the Uyghur terrorist attacks in the region during the past few decades were not instances of Islamist terrorism, as the CCP claims. A key characteristic of Islamism is the prioritization of punishing Muslims who stray from a doctrinaire interpretation of Islam; thus a society rife with Islamists would be unlikely to accommodate the many Muslims in East Turkistan who hold a more liberal interpretation. Instead, the evidence suggests that these Uyghur terrorist attacks were more likely secular in nature.

This is a significant distinction. If the attacks were driven by religious belief, this might offer at least a veneer of plausibility to claims made by the CCP that Islamist extremism is dangerously prevalent among Xinjiang's Muslims. But if one looks at the reported terrorist attacks in Xinjiang over the last several decades, hardly any of them bear the hallmarks of Islamist terrorism. Indeed, as Georgetown University historian James Millward noted in his 2004 report on violent extremism in Xinjiang: "While individual Uyghurs may be involved in Islamist organizations in Central Asia, by all indications the groups that are accused of militancy against the PRC espouse primarily nationalistic, as opposed to religious, motives and goals."[47] Even Uyghurs who have traveled outside of China to join jihadist organizations, such as the Turkistan Islamic Party (TIP) in Syria, seem largely disinterested in the ideology of global jihad, and to be focused instead on training for a singular commitment to freeing East Turkistan from Chinese occupation.[48]

China has a damning track record of dishonesty in its portrayal of the terrorism situation in East Turkistan to the rest of the world; it even successfully convinced the United States to unwisely lend credence to its spurious claims. In 2002, in the aftermath of the 9/11 attacks, China induced the Bush administration into labeling a group called the East Turkistan Islamic Movement (ETIM) as an officially designated terrorist organization. There was never much information available on the group—the first time it was ever publicly mentioned was in a PRC document released in November 2001. Experts who did look into ETIM, such as Sean Roberts of George Washington University, concluded that there was very little chance that the group ever even existed.[49] Secretary of State Mike Pompeo revoked the misguided designation of ETIM in late October 2020;[50] but this mistake had already caused irreparable damage.

As it stands, the CCP's habitual misrepresentation and exaggeration of the terrorism environment in East Turkistan, and the evidently secular nature of the vast majority of terrorist attacks that have been carried out in the region, points not to rampant Islamist sentiment among East Turkistan's Muslims, but instead to a violent outgrowth fed by widespread and deeply-rooted frustration with China's long-standing failure in addressing Uyghur grievances.

---

After circling the prayer room's flagged defense barrier a couple of times to see what I could, I retreated back down the stairs and toward the central courtyard. The loud group of visitors from earlier had now been replaced by an even louder, and larger, group—this one entirely composed of middle-aged Han men.

I sat down on the farthest bench from the group, retrieving my water bottle and notebook from my daypack, trying my best to ignore their chatter from across the courtyard. But just minutes later, a barrel-chested Han man came strutting through the entrance toward the group, raucously chanting in Mandarin. He carried an enormous PRC flag, swinging it around triumphantly, like he intended to plant it in the center of the courtyard as a symbol of conquest. As he approached his comrades, they eagerly joined him in chanting. They formed a circle, while two of them in the middle hoisted the flag as high as they could, the top of it disturbing the leaves on the lower branches of the poplar trees.

At least there appeared to be no Uyghurs present to witness this chauvinistic flag-waving spectacle; but this was little consolation. By all reason, Id Kah was a Uyghur mosque, but Uyghurs were now unable to safely go there. Instead of being the heart of Uyghur Islam, it had become a stage for old Han Chinese men to act out fantasies of being brave conquerors. I lingered there only a few minutes longer before heading for the exit.

As I walked out, I passed another group of Han tourists entering the mosque. They were laughing and taking pictures of the older Han men's disrespectful flag performance. It was the family I had noticed earlier—the one with the girl riding on the camel.

When I got outside, I saw the camel-handler sitting on some steps, taking a cigarette break between customers. He looked a bit happier than when I had seen him earlier, now that he had some time to himself.

---

Chinese nationalism, the kind I saw inside the mosque courtyard, is difficult for many people outside China to understand. It can be roughly broken down into three principal components. One of them—Han-centrism—is rapidly becoming the defining feature of Chinese nationalism under Xi Jinping. But the other two components, which are often intertwined with Han-centrism, also play a critical role in how Chinese nationalism is conceived of today.

The second component is the idea of China's territorial integrity. Chinese historians have long emphasized the importance of having China in control of the land (and in some cases, bodies of water) that they consider to be part of China. The problem that arises with this oft-uncompromising view is that what the Chinese consider to be "part of China" frequently isn't aligned with the views of its neighbors.

Of course, China isn't totally unique in this regard. Many nations construct exaggerated or fictitious stories to legitimize their territorial integrity. To an extent, it makes some practical sense to create these stories, in the interest of social cohesion; but China's claims to East Turkistan are especially self-interested and dishonest.

Today, the CCP insistently promotes the idea that Xinjiang has always been a part of China. It is a crucial piece of their narrative, as it seeks to delegitimize any claims to the independence of East Turkistan.

The CCP cites the beginning of Chinese rule over Xinjiang as during the Han Dynasty (202 BCE–220 AD). But, as James Millward points out, this claim is a "distortion" of history. During the majority of the time when the Han Dynasty existed, southern Xinjiang can more accurately be characterized as being engaged in a "tug-of-war, the waxing and waning of one power or another."[51] The northern half of Xinjiang (Zungharia, on the other side of the Tian Shan range), was never under Han Dynasty control.

Millward goes on to describe how the Tang Dynasty consolidated rule over roughly all of contemporary Xinjiang at around 730 AD—but only for about thirty years, until the An Lushan rebellion. After this, he notes, "there would not be direct rule over Xinjiang by a China-based state for almost exactly one thousand years."[52]

The third principal component of Chinese nationalism is the idea that Chinese leaders, traditionally called "Sons of Heaven," are divinely ordained as the rulers of "all under heaven." For the majority of Chinese history, Chinese emperors refused to engage with any foreign leaders as peers. In order to have any economic or political relations with China, foreign rulers and their emissaries would first have to acknowledge their subordination to the Son of Heaven. It would be inconceivable for a Chinese emperor to conduct bilateral diplomacy in the way we think of it today, or even how Western nations thought of it in the nineteenth century, because to do so would imply that the Son of Heaven had worldly equals.

Officially, this system of relations no longer exists. Xi Jinping is technically a Chinese President (and a host of other titles he's given himself), not the emperor of a dynasty. But as Michael Schuman has observed, the Chinese state that exists today is "not all that removed from the dynasties of earlier chapters."[53]

A useful way to grasp how this sort of thinking is still foundational in China is to consider what the Chinese word for "China" is: "Zhongguo," which translates to "Middle Country."

The name dates back to what was (probably) the first unification of China, in the Qin Dynasty in 221 BCE, and it illustrates well China's expectations for itself in a global context. For much of history—before the discovery that the earth is not flat—claiming the title "Middle Country" would be quite reasonable. That this remains the name for China in *today's* Chinese vernacular says more about their deeply rooted sense of superiority than it does their understanding of geography. It reflects the idea that China believes that its rightful place in the global community—from the origins of Zhongguo until the end of the world—is at its center. That Chinese civilization, presided over by the Son of Heaven, is the point from which other civilizations get their light as it radiates outward.

What I saw in Id Kah was a declaration of this thinking: that the Uyghurs should be grateful to be a part of China, because China is, by definition, the most important place in the world. What that version of history neglects, however, is that China could have never become the power it is today but for its relations with what was actually the geographic "middle" of Eurasia, and its commercial crossroads—East Turkistan—and with the people who have lived there for thousands of years.

Chapter 10

# Kashgar, Day Two
## —The Old Old City and the Night Market

"The most crucial thing is to raise the standard of administration, not to exploit the Hui and the Turban-Wearing Muslims."

—Yang Zengxin, Xinjiang's First Governor under the Republic of China (1911–1928)

The neighborhood behind Id Kah looked even more plastic than the rest of the New Old City. When he visited in 2013, the journalist Nick Holdstock aptly described this area as "a kitsch fantasy of a southern-European street."[54] It did have the feel of how Disney might choose to depict Rome or Naples in its next animated movie. Everything seemed twice as gaudy, and the colors twice as bright.

(Coincidentally, Disney enjoys a friendly relationship with the Xinjiang government. Disney even thanked Xinjiang's publicity department for allowing it to use the region to film part of its 2020 remake of Mulan.[55])

It became more bearable once I had reached the edge of the New Old City, as the street emptied out onto a busy city highway. The area was similar to Sue's neighborhood—just a more modest version. Instead of posh coffee shops and Western-style restaurants, there were working-class noodle and tea houses, with rows of motorbikes and electric scooters parked in front. It reminded me of the dualism I had seen that distinguished some of the upper- and working-class districts in Beijing.

I found a bench to sit and get my bearings—I wanted to try to find remnants of the Old Old City. Predictably, the map that Sue had given me had no indication of where this might be. I assumed it would probably be somewhere in the vicinity of the New Old City, since the New Old City used to be simply the Old City. So I decided to walk around the New Old City's perimeter, hoping to come across it.

No more than ten minutes after I began walking down the sidewalk next to the highway, I had already noted two convenience police stations, eight armored police trucks, and seventeen police officers. Just like the police officers I had seen in the New Old City—with the exception of the ones running the checkpoints—they didn't seem to be doing anything. They were just standing around, chatting among themselves. It was as if their only purpose was to remind Uyghurs that Kashgar was a police state, and to reassure Han Chinese that the city's new security apparatus was every bit as airtight as state television had informed them.

Eventually, the restaurants and apartment buildings on one side of the road gave way to the Tumen River, and on the other side to an unobstructed view of the massive sandstone archway that marked the main entrance to the New Old City.

Once I'd made it to the arch, I stopped for a moment to have a better look at the front-facing side of it, which until then I hadn't seen. "Ancient City of Kashgar" was spelled out on it in big, gold letters—in Uyghur, Chinese, and English—in a refreshingly simple style that complemented the structure's ecru-toned base.

A troupe of Uyghur dancers were performing under the arch, with a crowd of Han tourists observing them. I thought I recognized them as the same group from the previous evening, just wearing matching light blue dresses today instead of red.

It didn't take much longer for me to find what I was looking for. Just across the highway, at the top of a short hill, I saw a group of buildings that looked much older than the others. They appeared to have an earthen quality to them, exhibiting less uniform, more natural, shades of brown—clearly distinct from the Uyghur/European fairy-tale hybrid architecture of the New Old City. This could certainly be the Old Old City; the *real* Old City.

As I approached, I saw how decrepit this neighborhood was. It appeared as if no building had been lived in for years. Perhaps this was by design, as the CCP's justification for razing the Old City was to improve the infrastructure.

I walked half way up the dirt road before seeing a slimly-built police officer with buzzed black hair, stationed by himself in a vacant lot next to the entrance to the neighborhood. His assignment was obviously to prevent anyone from venturing in there, and I thought it'd be too risky to try to sneak past him. Reluctantly, I decided it would be best for me to give up.

"Ayyyy!" I heard him shout, just as I had turned around to leave.

I turned back around to see him jogging toward me. He was refreshingly unarmed, and the expression on his face seemed one of interest rather than hostility.

"Hi!" I responded in a cheerful tone, when he got close enough to hear.

After asking me a question in Mandarin, to which I just shrugged my shoulders, he took out his phone to type something into the translation app.

"Why are you trying to go here?" the text read.

"I want to see the older part of Kashgar Old City. I have read a lot about it," I responded. I corroborated this by showing him my Genghis Khan book.

He scanned the book for ten seconds before handing it back to me.

"There isn't anything to do here. All of the attractions are in the New Ancient City." He seemed unaware of the inherent irony in the phrase "New Ancient City."

"Yes, I was going there next. Thank you."

"You should try the lamb kabob that Uyghurs make there. Xinjiang's best food!" He smiled, and held on to his phone after showing me, suggesting this was the end of our conversation. I gave him a thumbs-up and headed back down the road toward the highway.

I was disappointed in not being able to see the real Old City from the inside. Spending so much time immersed in the fakeness of the New Old City made me wish even more that I could have had the chance to see just how different its authentic version really was. But I accepted that seeing something of it, at least from the outside, was better than never having seen it at all.

The next place I wanted to go was the Kashgar "Night Market." It wasn't very far from where I was, but it wouldn't open for another few hours, so I decided to rest up at Sue's apartment until then. I took the long way back—through the New Old City—just in case the police officer was still keeping an eye on me.

\* \* \* \* \* \* \*

I left the apartment around seven, ready to make the most of the night. I had read that this market had the widest selection of freshly made foods of any place in Kashgar, and Sue had confirmed this before I left. I asked whether she and Li wanted to come with me, but she said the place was too loud for her. I wasn't sure what that meant.

The Night Market was on the far end of the New Old City, almost across the street from Id Kah. I had become familiar enough with the layout of the New Old City that I was now able to get there in a straight shot.

As I neared the end of the street, I began to pick up on the aroma of grilled meats, mixed with an assortment of unfamiliar smells. The stalls were now selling naan and pastries instead of clothing and souvenirs. One vendor offered pomegranate juice and pomegranate popsicles. Another was hawking an impressive selection of dried fruits and nuts. Two others were selling, side-by-side, a variety of different colorful hard candies, and equally colorful stones—a placement that I thought might have been ill-advised.

A large crowd was gathered around what looked like it could be the last stall in the dessert section. Through an opening I could see a Uyghur man about my age, holding a steel pole, maybe three feet long, that had a scoop of vanilla ice cream in a waffle cone attached to the end of it. A young Han Chinese boy stood there laughing as the ice cream vendor presented him the cone, still attached to the steel pole. Just before the boy could grasp it, the vendor would twist the pole with impressive speed to another, still-not-quite-accessible angle. He playfully taunted the boy, using a high-pitched clownish voice. This went on for almost a minute, until the vendor finally relented, and smiled as he handed the boy the ice cream cone (with his hand), giving him an affectionate pat on the head.

The crowd of Han tourists cheered, and the next kid stepped up to have her go at him. There were probably a dozen other children waiting in line behind her, with more drifting in every minute or so. It seemed like an impossible job, but the vendor was every bit as entertaining with this child as he had been with the previous one. He even switched up some of his maneuvers, in case the girl had taken note of the routine that had so outwitted her predecessor. I was craving some more substantial food right then, but I knew I would have to return later to see just how quick this sorcerer really was.

Ahead and to the left of the ice cream vendor, the street opened to the main part of the Night Market. When I had passed this area that morning, on my way to Id Kah, it was empty. Now it contained at least thirty different food stalls, and was teeming with people. Luckily, there were multiple kabob stands positioned right at the entrance. I picked up a couple to help give me the fortitude to decide what to have for dinner.

Sue certainly wasn't exaggerating when she described this place as loud. But I was honestly surprised by how loud. The sounds reverberated off the surrounding buildings to make the collective noise a few orders of magnitude higher, creating a sort of noise gestalt.

Most of the foods that lay in front of me I'd never seen before—unusual types of noodles doused in bean paste and vinegar, fried fish with a mysterious black substance spread over it, a stand that claimed to be selling peacock, and plenty more that I couldn't even hope to guess. Many of the stands had signs in English, but many did not. Some didn't much need a sign, like the stand with a row of lambs' heads placed in front of a large cauldron.

The heads didn't exactly look appetizing; but they definitely stood out. And that's what can sometimes matter most in these sorts of moments. I approached the stand, and indicated to the cook with my finger that I wanted one of whatever this was.

I was surprised upon being handed my bowl to see that the head was included as part of the soup—not just the meat from the head. To be honest, I hadn't even expected that the meat would be head meat. I'd thought that the collection of lamb skulls on the table was simply to indicate the freshness of the product. Nope. The vendor just leadenly handed me a large bowl of broth, a lamb's head smack in the middle of it—as if I were supposed to know what to do after that.

A drink vendor next to the lamb's-head stand was selling two sizes of Wusu beer. I bought a pair of large ones for good measure, in case I'd need help washing down my main course.

(Wusu is the generic beer in Xinjiang—boasting a full 85 percent of the region's beer market. "It's popular for its delayed effect that easily gets you drunk," Chinese state media CGTN explains.[56])

The seating was plentiful, but not private—composed of long wooden picnic tables, where everyone sat communally. I went for the open spot closest to me.

When I sat down, I was immediately met with some audible gasps from the diners around me—almost certainly for being a Westerner.

"Hello!" I announced with a smile to everyone, acknowledging that I noticed their staring at me.

The portly Han man sitting next to me didn't hesitate for a moment to grab my shoulder and pull me closer for the optimal selfie. His face was covered with some sort of shining meat grease; but he didn't seem too self-conscious about it.

After taking the picture he looked down at my meal and let out what I interpreted to be an approving grunt. I laughed and gave a thumbs up. He seemed like the type of guy who would know good meat, so his positive review made me somewhat more optimistic about my unconventional choice.

I won't get into how I managed to get the meat off the lamb's head and into my soup. It wasn't the easiest dish to figure out. But once I actually got to eating it, it was pretty satisfying. The gaminess of the skin and outer layers of the head mixed with the mushy, mild-tasting brains to create an indelible texture. The taste of each component was interesting, and taken together, they were an arresting combination. The addition of some spicy red pepper flakes, available at the center of the table, made for the perfect finishing touch.

Many people believe the lamb's head (the brain, specifically) is the tastiest part. Based on my own experience, I can't say they're crazy for thinking so.

"Hello!" I heard from the end of the table, interrupting my feast.

I looked over to see a Han man in a black ribbed tank top, signaling for me to come sit with him and his two friends. One of the friends was also Han; the other looked South Asian. They all appeared to be in their early-to-mid-thirties. I couldn't think of a reason to decline, so I moved over to join them.

"How's it going, my man, do you want a drink?" he asked with a heavy Chinese accent, inviting me to sit down next to him.

I was happy that he spoke English, and that we would be able to interact with more than single words. He seemed not to care that I was already working on two large-sized beers, but I didn't want to be rude.

"For sure. Thank you, man!" I replied.

He turned around and asked the drink vendor behind him for more Wusu beers, and handed one of them to me.

"Cheers, mate!" he Britished, as we two and his two friends took long chugs.

"Are you from America?" he asked.

"Yeah, I am, how'd you know?"

"You just look like an American. I've never seen an American here before. Why did you come?"

"I'm a student and I'm interested in the Silk Road, so I wanted to travel to Kashgar to see the history here."

"Silk Road?" he questioned.

"Like the ancient trade road," the South Asian friend chimed in. "The one that China traded with the Europeans on."

"Ah, yes, okay." He didn't appear to actually have come to any realization.

"Have you guys lived in Xinjiang for a while?" I asked.

The Han friend raised his hand. "I've lived here for five years. He moved here last year," he said, pointing to the friend in the tank top.

"I moved here this year," the South Asian friend said.

"Oh, cool. What made you guys move here?"

"We work for an oil production company," Tank Top said, taking a swig of his beer. "There is a lot of opportunity in Xinjiang now, especially with the oil industry."

At the time, I had a feeling that "oil production" in Xinjiang was likely to be exploitative, given everything else I knew and had seen thus far. But I had no idea how deeply ingrained the economic exploitation runs.

---

To understand the ways in which Uyghurs have been shut out of their own economy, you need to know about a one-of-a-kind, amorphous entity called The Xinjiang Production and Construction Corps, also known as the Bingtuan. The Bingtuan is difficult to define in a comprehensive way, but the best succinct description I have seen is "a vast farming militia that cultivates cotton, tomatoes, and lavender, and dabbles in mining and textiles—when it's not fighting terror."[57]

The Bingtuan was established by Mao in 1954, in order to keep peace in the region and to promote the CCP's rule. It was originally composed of slightly fewer than 200,000 Han Chinese who came from throughout China. Today, it has about 2.7 million members—11.9 percent of Xinjiang's entire population.[58]

It operates at the expense of the Uyghurs in a variety of ways. Most directly, its members are almost entirely Han,[59] and it actively encourages further Han Chinese settlement in the region. In fact, according to the CCP Organization Department, its explicitly stated mission today is to promote Han settlement in Xinjiang.[60]

It also monopolizes all aspects of the most lucrative industries in Xinjiang, locking out Uyghurs from participation on any worthwhile levels. Farming, for instance, has been made almost impossible for Uyghurs to engage in profitably, due to their inability to compete with the massive, state-subsidized farms of the Bingtuan. In 2012 the Bingtuan controlled 31 percent of all arable land in Xinjiang, and, as Nick Holdstock notes, "given that it often also manages the water supply, in practical terms it controls far more."[61]

Even more disturbingly, the Bingtuan has an active role in the direct oppression of Uyghurs. It operates and oversees factories and plantations where Uyghurs are forced to work for little or no pay (more on this in a later chapter). It operates many of the regular prisons in Xinjiang—which, as you would expect, are disproportionately filled with Uyghurs. And it runs many of the re-education camps as well.

I tossed my second empty Wusu beer into the recycling bin behind me and started on my third.

"Yeah, I know some people who have gotten into the oil business back in America. It's definitely a good place to make money," I replied.

"When I came here from Pakistan, I knew that I would find very good opportunities here for me," the South Asian friend said.

"Yeah, it looks like it really worked out for you. Were there not many oil production jobs in Pakistan?" I asked.

"There were some, but the opportunities in Xinjiang were better. Plus, I had also heard about how safe it was. In Pakistan I would have fears about terrorist attacks all the time. But here I have no fear of that sort of thing at all."

His answer struck me. It was so specific—by rote, reciting the difference in the risk of terrorist attacks between Xinjiang and Pakistan. My question was about his job, and yet he chose to tell me how safe Xinjiang was. While I had heard this many times before, he was the first to explicitly compare terrorism in Xinjiang to terrorism in China's neighboring countries.

"It certainly does seem safe here. I see police officers everywhere," I replied, testing how he would react to this insertion.

"Yes, they are everywhere. And they are so helpful. Despite me being a practicing Muslim from Pakistan, they treat me with total respect."

At this point, I was a bit skeptical. This guy seemed fake—almost like a prop. It would have been believable enough that this guy might spontaneously mention "safety" as part of his story. And I might have even understood that in the course of a longer conversation, he would say something about his positive feelings toward the Chinese police, given the risks involved in being a brown-skinned Muslim in Xinjiang. But he seemed too quick and eager to bring up such a sensitive subject with someone he had just met, in words that would be indistinguishable from a CCP propaganda paper. I knew then that it was time to find a way out of there.

I entertained their small talk for a few more minutes, finishing off my last beer and the remnants of my lamb's head potion.

"Thanks so much for the drink, guys. I'm going to head back to my hotel now. It was great to meet you all!"

"Oh, don't you want to stay?" Tank Top asked.

"I wish I could, but I have to wake up early tomorrow morning," I said, truthfully.

"Okay. It was nice to meet you, man!" He said, as the others waved goodbye as well.

I was ready to put some distance between me and my drinking partners. But as I was walking back, I remembered the mission that I had postponed earlier: I needed to challenge that Uyghur ice cream vendor. And there he was, directly ahead of me, up to his usual tricks.

It was getting late, and there were only a handful of children waiting. The vendor pretended not to notice this six-foot-tall white man who had just stepped in line behind the Han kindergartener wearing light-up sneakers. I figured he was trying to stay in character.

When I got to the front of the line, I was preparing to make eye contact with him for the first time. I hoped my friendly countenance would indicate that I wanted him to do his routine on me, but that it would also reassure him that he and I would just be kidding around together. The first look he gave me made it abundantly clear that we were not on the same page.

He was smiling at me, but not at all in a friendly way. It was a mix of condescension and resentment; the kind of smirk that you might get from a conflict-averse friend who is angry with you, but doesn't want to express it outright. I interpreted it as his way of snapping me out of my stupid supposition that maybe this guy, unlike other Uyghurs who worked in the New Old City, was doing this job because he actually wanted to. He was selling his whole charade so flawlessly that he had made me forget the context that came wrapped around every interaction in Xinjiang. His look told me: This is a prison. I'm playing my part because I have to—to survive. What are *you* doing here?

He fixed my cone and did a shortened version of his normal routine, acting it out just as perfectly. It was now difficult for me to play along, but having begun this mess, I did my best. I waited for him to finally hand me my cone when he had finished his act. I thanked him and promptly slinked away to contemplate how much of a piece of shit I was.

As I searched for a solitary place to eat my ice cream, the lights at the market suddenly went out, all at once. Everyone around me stopped what they were doing and began to immediately disperse. I was concerned there might be some serious problem at first, but everyone seemed to treat it as a routine closing. I decided to follow their lead, and joined the crowd that was exiting down the road I had taken from Sue's apartment.

I walked for several minutes until I began to hear a commotion coming from farther up the road. The noise was faint at first, but it grew progressively louder, eventually becoming clear that some of it was aggressive shouts and grunts. In anywhere not a police state, I would have been convinced it was a brawl. I considered turning around to find another route, but none of the people around me seemed to be disturbed, so I stuck with them.

I soon came alongside a small open space next to the road, where eight police officers were being overseen by a superior officer. They were divided into two teams of four officers each, and faced each other roughly ten feet apart. One team were armed with riot shields; the other four appeared to be unarmed (but were fully armored in SWAT gear). The four unarmed officers charged the officers carrying the riot shields, feign-grunting and making attacking noises as they collided into their colleagues. One of the pretend-attackers was knocked over onto his back by the counter-force of the shield. His commanding officer marched over to him, shouting what must have been a string of derogatory curses, pulled him up by his collar, and threw him back into line to try again.

I looked around at the crowd to see if anyone was showing interest in this histrionic police exercise; if maybe it *wasn't* totally routine to come across while walking home after a night of boozing and socializing in the most popular tourist district in the city. But most were not even looking in the officers' direction. Those who did look, swiftly turned their heads away.

I kept walking along with the rest of the crowd, as the sound of cops smashing against one another faded into the night behind me.

Chapter 11

# Kashgar, Day Three
## —The Livestock Market

"Good government obtains, when those who are near are made happy, and those who are far off are attracted."

—Confucius

When I emerged from my room the next morning, I saw Li stretched out on the couch, fully dressed, doodling in a black composition notebook. "Grayson, you're coming with us still?" he asked as I brushed the sleep from my eyes.

"Yeah, definitely. Are you guys planning on leaving soon?" It was just past eight in the morning, which struck me as a bit early to go to a livestock market.

Sue entered from the kitchen, wearing a straw summer hat, with a red bow tied across it, and a similarly colored red sundress.

"Grayson! You should get ready, we are about to leave," she announced.

Admittedly, I hadn't asked what time we were leaving when I had agreed to come.

"Okay, give me five minutes." I rushed back to my room, threw on some clean clothes, and re-emerged in well under three.

"Sorry if you guys were waiting on me. I didn't think we would be leaving until later."

"That's okay. We wanted to get breakfast at the market, so we decided we should leave earlier," Sue said. "Let's go now?"

I nodded in agreement. Li was buried in his phone, but voiced no protest, so we were off.

Sue had called the local equivalent of an Uber, and we waited for the car on a curbside bench outside her apartment complex. There seemed to be very little traffic, so Sue commented that we would probably get to the market before nine. This reassured me that I would have plenty of time for the other things I wanted to do on my last day in Kashgar.

## The Livestock Market

Li and I were in the middle of discussing what kind of kabob might taste best at the market, when I was startled by the blare of a siren.

A convoy of about a dozen armored police trucks was approaching us from down the street. They were driving slower than the other cars on the road—suggesting that they weren't responding to a pressing emergency. I figured it was just another performative action, same as the kind I'd seen regularly the last couple of days.

Neither Sue nor Li seemed to be concerned by it either.

Our Uber driver arrived minutes later in a sleek black sedan. Sue took shotgun, and Li and I hopped into the back. The Uyghur pop music playing on the radio prompted me to look at the driver, to note that he was Uyghur as well.

As we set off, I made the bold decision to conduct a social experiment I'd had in mind since arriving in Kashgar.

"Salam alaikum!" I said to the driver. This is Arabic for "peace be upon you," but Muslims throughout the world use it to greet one another.

The driver completely ignored me. His eyes, which I could see through the rear-view mirror, never moved from the road in front of him. Li was similarly silent. The only one in the car who reacted was Sue.

"You can't say that here, Grayson," she informed me. She chuckled uncomfortably after she said it, as though she were pretending that my saying this must have been a joke.

"Oh, I'm sorry."

After an uncomfortable silence, Sue shifted to talking about how excited she was to see the livestock market. This would be her first time going there, she said, even though she had lived in Kashgar for a few years. I stated my own excitement about going there as well, although I knew that some of my reasons were different from hers.

Out the window, I saw three Uyghur men sitting on the side of the road, a pair of police officers standing over them. Behind them was an armored police vehicle, like the ones we'd seen just minutes ago. They brushed past my window and out of view behind us. I wondered what transgression had put these three men in that position, and what might happen to them.

As we drove farther outside the city, the buildings and storefronts had all but disappeared, replaced by an overgrowth of gnarled shrubs and poplar trees, and continuous white stone walls bordering either side of the highway, peppered every so often with unpaved side streets leading elsewhere.

The Uber driver let us off in a huge dirt lot that was marked with more hoof tracks than tire tracks, leading up to a large rusted building about a hundred feet ahead. We could see sheep and cows being unloaded from trucks and corralled through a gate that I assumed led into the market. The herders lined either side of the mass of animals, ensuring that they stayed the course. I watched as one of the herders slapped a cow who was hesitating to walk through the gate.

"Oh my goodness, look at their butts!" Sue exclaimed as she burst into laughter, pointing to a couple of sheep that passed in front of us on their way to the market gate.

"They are so big!" Li added.

I laughed along with them, mostly out of politeness, but also because their butts really were comically large (look up "fat-tailed sheep" if you'd like an idea). As they continued laughing, I noticed another herder closer to the gate, who was yanking the leash of an insubordinate goat, trying to get it into the market. The goat was on the ground, refusing to cooperate, and bleating to the herdsman in protest. But this didn't seem to matter to the herdsman, who began dragging the goat through the dirt behind him until, after an unsettling number of seconds, it finally rose in compliance.

"Let's eat right away and then look around. It's already past time for breakfast," Li proposed as we approached the large building.

The potent smells of smoked meats and spices that emanated from it were familiar, in the best sort of way. I already sensed that these would be the best kabobs I would have in Kashgar, perhaps in all of East Turkistan.

There were dozens of kabob stands spanning the width of the building, all appearing to be operated by older Uyghur women. I could tell they were seasoned veterans in the kabob game; light-years ahead of those pretenders in the New Old City.

"What kind do you want?" Li asked. "I can order them for us."

"Two of every kind. I'm starving," I requested, handing him enough yuan to surely cover all of us. "Use that to get yours and Sue's, too."

Li came back with an array of kabobs that he told me were lamb, chicken, and goat. We decided against sitting down at the wooden tables next to the stands; that instead we'd snack on our kabobs as we entered the market.

The market was divided into sections according to species—goats and sheep were at the front, near the entrance; cows and bulls were in one back corner; horses were in the other back corner.

I decided to take a lap around the entire market, while Sue and Li stayed in the sheep area, captivated by their still-ongoing butt jokes.

The inside of the market was hectic, with traders walking swiftly between the various sections: some herding animals, and some on their own, trumpeting what must have been their practiced sales pitches to attract the attention of prospective buyers. The animals kicked up clouds of dust from the loose dirt on the ground, all of it accumulating into a thin haze that suffused the entire space.

"Bosh bosh!" I heard from behind me. I turned to see a herdsman grimacing at me, as he struggled to get his two cows to the correct area across the market. I promptly moved aside. (I have since learned that "bosh bosh" means "watch out!" in Uyghur.)

What was most refreshing about this place, ironically, were the disgruntled expressions on the faces of the Uyghur herders. It was clear that they felt no obligation to pretend to be happy about anything. Every one of them who made eye contact with me indicated unambiguously how uninterested, even mildly annoyed they were with the presence of a white tourist in their midst.

Some of the animals were put into pens that appeared to be reserved for those that were in the best shape and would sell for the highest price. The cows, bulls, and horses were tied separately along posts, with comfortable space between them. The sheep and goats, though, were tied together tightly, cheek-to-jowl at their necks, in groups of thirty or forty, forcing their squirming heads and bodies onto each other. It looked incredibly uncomfortable, and their continuous strident bleating, echoing throughout the market, seemed to confirm that.

It was quite strange that this livestock market, where the practices of animal treatment seemed archaic and inhumane, was one of the few aspects of Uyghur culture that the CCP was not cracking down on, evidently not considering it to be inconsistent with its goals for remaking Xinjiang. And yet the CCP views any expression of religious faith to be grounds for imprisonment. I wouldn't necessarily advocate that this sort of market be banned—the wet markets in southern and eastern China make these look like petting zoos. And I've seen too many documentaries about factory farming in the United States to be that hypocritical. But it was interesting to think about the mental gymnastics required for some career Party member to decide that animal cruelty is an acceptable cultural practice, while anyone who grows a beard or vocalizes an Arabic greeting must be cured of "the virus of religious extremism."

I roamed around for maybe an hour before circling back to look for Sue and Li. I found them outside, sitting at one of the tables, eating from a small basket filled with samsas (probably my favorite Uyghur food—essentially lamb and onion Hot Pockets).

"Hey! What did you guys think?" I asked.

"There isn't very much here. Since I don't want to buy an animal, I don't see the usefulness of this place for me," Sue replied.

"I liked the sheep, but other than that, I thought it was overwhelming," Li said. "So much 'bosh bosh!'"

Per usual, I largely agreed with Li.

"I'll get us a taxi now to go back," Sue offered.

"I think I'm going to look around here for a little bit more," I said, taking a bite of a samsa that Li had gifted me. "Later I was going to go to the central market in Kashgar to check that out."

"You haven't seen enough of the livestock yet?" Sue asked, perplexed.

"I want to spend some more time looking at the horses," I said. "I'll be able to find a taxi to take me back, and I still have your apartment's address in my phone to show the driver."

"Okay, we'll see you later then. Enjoy the horses!"

I waved goodbye to them as they walked toward the end of the dirt lot to wait for their ride, knowing full well that I had no intention of going back to look at the horses.

Chapter 12

# Kashgar, Day Three
## —A Uyghur Neighborhood and the Bazaar

"Why should the Muslim people alone be provoked and made the subject of criminal charges?"

—Yongzheng Emperor, 1722–1735

I returned to the dining area to buy more samsas while I waited for Sue and Li to get their ride. Once I saw them drive off, I began my walk.

My true reason for staying behind was to explore one of the neighborhoods I had seen just down the road as we were making our way in. I knew this would be a rare chance to see what the real Kashgar is like.

The highway—the same one we had come in on—looked freshly paved, as did the sidewalk next to it that I was walking down. The sidewalk was lined the entire way with pristine street lights, many of them decorated with surveillance cameras.

All of this gleaming development couldn't have stood in starker contrast to the deeply rutted dirt side streets that jutted off it. They looked like they hadn't undergone any serious maintenance for years, and had simply been left to languish there, bumping right up against a fine example of the type of refurbishment they desperately needed themselves. I turned onto one of the first side streets I came to, checking both directions of the main highway to see if someone might be observing me (aside from the cameras, of course) before beginning to walk down it.

It was eerily quiet. The only noise I heard, besides the buzz of the occasional vehicle driving by on the highway behind me, came from a couple of stray dogs who were playing with each other beneath a flat-bedded tuk-tuk parked next to a large mud brick wall. An identical wall lined the right side as well, but without the stray dogs. I chose that side to walk on.

Fifty feet past the tuk-tuk, I came to a set of large wooden double doors built into the wall on my right. The left door had a small white sign hung on a nail that showed the ID pictures of four Uyghur women and one Uyghur man; descriptions next to them were written in Chinese. A QR code was printed on the right-hand side of the sign.

*Could this family be under investigation for something?* I wondered, before reminding myself that every Uyghur is essentially under investigation, all the time. I noticed a tiny white surveillance camera in the upper right corner of the doorway, looking straight at me. I didn't know exactly what any of this meant, but I got the strong feeling that sticking around this place wouldn't be a great idea. My Silk Road traveler story would be useless in trying to explain myself to a police officer if they saw me there.

I turned back to return to the highway.

---

After getting back to the United States, I learned that these QR codes are common on the doors of Uyghur households, particularly in more peripheral neighborhoods, where the blanketing of high-tech surveillance is less extensive. Every few days, a team of government officials comes to scan the QR code, which brings up the number of people who are registered to the house, along with their personal information. This enables officials to monitor the comings and goings at each Uyghur house, and whether any unregistered people are staying there.[62]

---

I had no desire to go back to the livestock market at that point, and I didn't remember seeing many taxis waiting there. I decided to just continue walking down the highway sidewalk in the direction of the city, and hope to get the attention of a taxi driver passing by.

I did see several taxis drive past me as I walked, and I tried a variety of hand signals to convince them to pull over for me, but none of my attempts were successful. I couldn't blame them much. I imagined that, after looking me over, they concluded I might cause more trouble for them than the fare was worth.

After I'd walked for maybe thirty minutes, and had come to terms with the fact that I would probably have to make it back to the city on foot in the punishing desert heat, a bus pulled up alongside me and opened its doors. I looked at it, somewhat confused, since I had seen no signs nearby for a bus stop.

"Do you need a ride, sir?!" I heard in perfect English from inside the bus.

"Uhhh, yes! Thank you!" I replied, after deciding that this was not a hallucination from the early onset of heatstroke.

I approached the bus to see a Han Chinese man in a sweaty grey T-shirt, grinning down at me from the driver's seat.

"Come on, it's hot outside!" he said, as I hurried onto the bus.

"Where are you going?" he asked, as I inserted a blindly chosen amount of fare into the machine.

"The bazaar," I told him. "Does this bus go there?"

"Yes. You get off at the last stop and it will be close. Easy to walk there," he said, putting the bus in drive and heading down the road again.

"Great. Thanks so much for stopping for me. I thought I was going to have to walk the entire way!"

"That would have taken the whole day," he laughed. "You might not have even made it there in this heat." The bus didn't have air conditioning, but the electric fans placed throughout gave some relief.

"Yeah, maybe not. Where did you learn to speak English?" I asked. "You speak very well."

"I went to school for business, and in Xinjiang many people learn English to work with investors," he replied, gruffly. "You should find a seat. The bus usually gets very crowded after the next few stops."

I was curious as to how he'd ended up driving a bus after going to business school, and having mastered what seemed like an impressive amount of English, but I couldn't think of an inoffensive way to probe him on this question. And it was clear that he didn't want to make further small talk.

"That's cool. Thanks again for picking me up!" I said, as I went to find a seat.

The bus had only a few other people on it—all of them were Uyghurs, and none of them were interested in making eye contact with me. I chose a seat toward the back.

The driver's advice to find a seat proved to be helpful. After the next four stops, the bus was standing-room only. It remained that way until we got to the last stop, where the bus emptied out onto a cramped sidewalk in front of a convenience store.

"Thanks for the ride! Should I just follow all those people to get there?" I asked as I was getting off.

"Yes, probably. Enjoy the bazaar, sir!" the driver replied with a wave before closing the doors behind me.

This area of town was distinct from the parts I'd seen before. The modest storefronts that lined the sidewalk were a fairly even split between those with Uyghur script on their signs and those in Chinese only. The sidewalk was packed with both Han and Turkic people, many of them flowing in and out of the various businesses, but the patrons seemed to be segregated by ethnicity. It struck me as a sort of inchoate borderlands, where the ever-expanding synthetic Kashgar of the CCP's creation clashed and combined with remnants of the city's former authentic self.

I followed the horde of people from the bus for a few blocks until we arrived at a large line, leading into a small room that then spilled out into the bazaar. Metal bars on the perimeter separated the bazaar from the outside, but through them I could see and hear the goings-on of a small close-up section.

That section was packed with a row of stalls, where sellers were proffering knock-off sportswear products labeled as Nike, Adidas, and other notable brands. To be fair, I couldn't be certain that *all* of the products were knock-offs. But when I spotted a basketball on display with "Spadats" written on it, in the same style as the Spalding I had back home, I felt pretty confident that the rest of the inventory was probably similarly sourced. In the same stall, I saw a man with his son, haggling with the shopkeeper over a pair of "Nike" tennis shoes that were made with the swoosh facing the wrong way.

It took me about thirty minutes to reach the room separating the bazaar from the outside. Predictably, it was a security room staffed by police officers. I was asked to put my daypack through an x-ray machine, while an officer with a metal detector frisked me. I then had to show my passport to another officer, who asked me the usual questions through a translation app on his phone. This process took longer than it had for me to get through customs at the Beijing airport.

When I finally made it inside the bazaar, I got a feel for how enormous the place was. The smooth concrete avenue that I was on continued straight for as far as I could see, filled with swarms of browsing customers, and buttressed on either side by a rainbow of different shirts, dresses, and rugs hanging from the sides of stalls. There were more shops on numerous side paths that each appeared to extend from the main avenue for a hundred yards or so. I eagerly began my own browsing, leaving the knock-off sports apparel shops behind me.

I admittedly had a great time at the bazaar, and I was in awe of the incredible selection of products being sold there. But I didn't realize at the time that the majority of products made in Xinjiang are produced by what is essentially Uyghur slave labor, integrally connected to the CCP's broader "re-education" strategies and to the regional economy in its entirety.

"Re-education through labor" camps began under Chairman Mao, where they were used for petty criminals and political dissidents to correct behaviors that didn't align with CCP ideology. The system was officially abolished by the Standing Committee of the People's National Congress in 2013, and the detainees were allegedly released. (Although there is evidence that some of these facilities were simply reconfigured to serve the same purpose, often under the guise of being drug rehabilitation centers.[63])

This pre-existing framework of re-education through labor was a convenient way for the CCP to justify its intensified exploitation of the Uyghurs. Today, Uyghurs who "graduate" from the re-education camps are routinely sent afterward to work in factories for little-to-no pay, where they live in dormitories in conditions strikingly similar to those in the re-education camps they came from. This system of forced labor extends far beyond the territorial borders of Xinjiang. A report published by the Australian Strategic Policy Institute (ASPI) in March 2020 estimates that, through the government policy known as Xinjiang Aid, "80,000 Uyghurs were transferred out of Xinjiang to work in factories across China between 2017 and 2019, and some of them were sent directly from detention camps."[64] The report also notes that this estimate is a conservative one, that the actual number is likely far higher.

At these factories, the workers live in "segregated dormitories, undergo organised Mandarin and ideological training outside working hours, are subject to constant surveillance, and are forbidden from participating in religious observances." The employers gush over the positive effects of this program on the workers, stating that it helps to "transform them into 'modern' citizens, who, they say, become 'more physically attractive' and learn to 'take daily showers.'" The report also notes that there is significant economic incentive for local governments and private companies to find places for these Uyghur slaves, as they are "paid a price per head by the Xinjiang Provincial government to organise the labour assignments."

Moreover, this system of Uyghur slave labor reaches extensively into global supply chains. The same ASPI report found "eighty-three foreign and Chinese companies directly or indirectly benefiting from the use of Uyghur workers outside Xinjiang through potentially abusive labour transfer programs as recently as 2019." The companies listed included the likes of Adidas, Nike, Apple, Amazon, Calvin Klein, Google, H&M, Sony, Victoria's Secret, Polo, Ralph Lauren, and other globally recognized brands.

To reiterate, this is a description of only the forced Uyghur labor *outside* of Xinjiang. Based on the present conditions in the region, it is reasonable to assume that any factory operating in Xinjiang is complicit in this system.

Cotton, for example, has long been a lucrative cash crop in Xinjiang: eighty percent of the cotton produced in China, and twenty percent of the world's total, comes from the region.[65] Naturally, the CCP has implemented schemes to capitalize on Xinjiang's cotton production abilities at the expense of the Uyghurs. In a December 2020 report, Adrian Zenz finds that:

> [I]n 2018, three Uyghur regions alone mobilized at least 570,000 persons into cotton-picking operations through the government's coercive labor training and transfer scheme. Xinjiang's total labor transfer of ethnic minorities into cotton picking likely exceeds that figure by several hundred thousand.[66]

Chances are, you have probably benefited personally from Uyghur slave labor. If your cotton clothes are made in China, there's a solid chance they were made under the pretextual auspices of re-educating innocent Uyghurs. If you like ketchup with your french fries, or tomato sauce on your pasta, then you have probably been consuming part of the one quarter of the world's tomatoes that come from Xinjiang.[67] Whatever car you drive probably includes parts that have been sourced through factories using Uyghur slaves.[68] If you get energy from a solar panel, it is likely that parts of it were produced in Xinjiang.[69]

Almost everyone in the West has a smartphone. Indeed, since the COVID pandemic began, we have become even more dependent on our smartphones for all our necessary connections—family, friends, shopping, medical services, news, and everything else. It is virtually certain that at least some piece of your smartphone was installed in or originated from a factory that operates in this system.[70]

Apple, for instance, is active in Xinjiang.[71] And along with other prominent companies including Nike and Coca-Cola, Apple has actively lobbied *against* legislative efforts in the U.S. Congress that would require companies to demonstrate that their supply chains in China are free from this system of slave labor.[72]

In a surely-coerced interview with state media, one Uyghur woman says about her new factory occupation, "Like President Xi has said, happiness is always the result of struggle."[73]

Perhaps Nike could consider adopting this as its new slogan.

I spent the better part of the afternoon in the bazaar, and came out with a small Kashgari rug with pale blue overtones, a pair of thick black drawstring pants, a baggy, collared white shirt, and some binoculars. I was quite proud of myself, having negotiated the price of each of them down to less than half of the initial offering.

I got out my map to check where I was. It appeared that the distance to the New Old City was very manageable on foot, so I decided I would head back over there.

When I made it back to the entrance archway of the New Old City, the main square was less crowded than on my previous visits. The same food stalls were still open, and some of the dancers were still performing. But the torrent of Han tourists that had been there the past couple of nights was now reduced to a stream.

This allowed me to get a better sense of the area without having to peer over crowds of other people as I had the previous two nights. Most of the tourists were walking toward a pedestrian road that straddled the top of the New Old City perimeter wall; a road that I somehow hadn't seen until now. Clearly there was something over there that was worth checking out, so I decided to follow them.

After walking only a few dozen feet, I saw why it was so popular. The whole street had been fashioned into one big cocktail lounge and dining emporium. Tables were set up along one side of the street, overlooking the top of the perimeter wall, providing a jaw-dropping view of the Tumen River as it shimmered in the late afternoon sun, and of the less-touristy parts of Kashgar across from it. The other side was lined with restaurants, each with its own upscale design, but all seeming to offer largely the same kabob-heavy selection of foods. It didn't look like it mattered where you sat, since waiters were serving tables several restaurants away from their own.

I knew this seating and serving system was too byzantine for me to hope to comprehend. So I just found a table, and hoped the waiters would see the confused Westerner sitting by himself and know that he would need assistance with placing an order. It took thirty seconds for a waitress from the closest restaurant to spot me. She did a double-take before flitting over, wide-eyed.

"Menu?" she asked.

"Xie xie," I replied. She spun around and headed off to retrieve one for me.

"Piju!?" I called, trying to sneak in my drink order despite her already being halfway back to the restaurant. It was louder than I'd intended, enough to disturb the conversations of customers at surrounding tables. When she turned back around to see me, I smiled and quietly held up one finger. She nodded, giggling at my clumsiness.

*Piju* means beer, by the way. Although I know hardly any Mandarin words, I felt it would be irresponsible not to educate myself on that one.

Sitting alone at the next table over was a thin Han man in a white poplin shirt and finely pressed khaki pants, working on what looked like a generously sized sampler plate of every kabob they sold. After he heard my order, he called out to the waitress in Mandarin, then looked at me and gave me a thumbs up. I had no way to know whether he was mocking my uncouth drink request or paying for it. I was thrilled to have closure on this when my beer arrived with no check.

Along with my beer, the waitress handed me the menu, which was only in Chinese, and had no pictures. I pointed to the plate in front of the man at the next table. She appeared confused at first, but eventually understood after seeing me trying to mime myself eating a kabob.

As she went through the door and into the restaurant to place my order, I noticed that right beside it were a couple of black amplifiers, along with a guitar, a microphone, and three metal stools. I didn't see any musicians, but from my limited knowledge of live music culture, I didn't think it was common for musicians to leave their instruments lying around unattended *after* the performance.

A cold beer, an exquisite view, and soon enough, fresh kabobs and live music. What more could a guy ask for on vacation?

The waitress brought out my platter of kabobs twenty minutes later, along with a complimentary large circle of naan. She asked me to take a selfie with her, to which I of course agreed.

Before she had finished, a trio of Uyghur men around my age emerged from the restaurant. Two sat down on the stools, while the other began fiddling with one of the amplifiers. The man on the stool by the microphone had long black hair, slicked and parted on the side, and wore a baggy plain white T-shirt and black skinny jeans that looked unbearable for even the relatively mild evening heat. The two others were dressed in similarly plain clothing, but had chosen shorts.

A waiter placed a small wooden table in the middle of the three stools, and an ashtray on top of it, before re-entering the restaurant. One of the three musicians got out a pack of cigarettes, handed one to each of the others, and they all lit up. After the guitarist did a ten-second tuning, they began to play.

I enjoy pretty much any type of music performed live. But this song—for all the musicians' evident talents—fell into a genre that I did not particularly care for. It sounded a bit like how I would imagine the live version of my Guangphone ringtone might sound, with its overly-ambitious blend of pop, alternative rock, and some kind of Chinese folk music.

It was easy to tell that the vocals, which were all in Mandarin, carried the band. The bassist and the guitarist played simple, almost redundant chords, while the singer changed pitch seamlessly.

They began to attract a small crowd of Han tourists. Much to my embarrassment, some tourists stopped initially to ask *me* to take a picture with them, and only later turned their attention to the talented Uyghur musicians. Of course, once they did, they turned their phones to film the performers. Some had the flash on, and one especially irreverent man got within a couple of feet of the singer's face for a better shot. The singer somehow soldiered on, unfazed.

After about an hour, two of the musicians stepped away from the stage, leaving just the singer, on his stool, holding the microphone. The guitarist cued an instrumental track, with a beat that sounded substantially different from what I had just been hearing. Moments later, the singer began his solo performance; for the first time that night, he was singing in Uyghur.

Even though I could not understand the words, his passion shone through in every one of them. I couldn't imagine it was possible for him to separate the emotion he conveyed with his singing from the sorrow he felt for the state of his community. While the lyrics certainly couldn't have been advocating anything too rebellious, I sensed that the jarring intensity of his performance was itself a small form of resistance. Listening to it in that moment imbued in me a deeper sense of the true feelings of the Uyghurs in Kashgar than anything else had—or perhaps could have.

But before I was even able to hear him finish his song, this moving experience was suddenly interrupted.

"Hello, are you from America?" I heard from my right.

I turned to see an older Han Chinese man with an easy smile, just across the table, wearing glasses with large, square lenses and a white polo shirt. He had his left hand on the top of the chair next to him, seeming to anticipate that I would invite him to sit down.

"Yes, I am," I replied.

"I am a Chinese journalist. Would it be alright if I ask you a few questions about Xinjiang?" he asked, slowly pulling the chair out so he could sit down when I agreed to the interview, which he presumed was coming.

I felt I had no choice but to agree.

"Yes, of course," I said, pointing to the seat he was already preparing to take.

"So what news agency do you work for?" I asked him.

"I am a freelance journalist." he said, as he got out a small notepad from his pocket. "Why did you choose to come to Kashur?"

"I'm a student interested in the history of the Silk Road. Kashgar played an important role in that history, so it seemed like a great place for me to visit." This guy spoke very good English, so I chose to skip showing him the Genghis Khan book.

"Ah, yes, of course. What do you think of the Ancient City?" he asked. I assumed by this he meant the tourist attraction, not the actual ancient city it has replaced.

"I like it a lot, the food here is really good, and the live music makes it even better."

"Yes, I agree," he said flippantly, as he jotted a few things down on his notepad. "It was not always as safe as it is now."

I paused for a moment to make sure he had finished speaking.

"Yes, it feels very safe." I recited.

"Thank you. Could I get your name as well, for my article?" he asked eagerly.

"I would actually like this to be a background interview, if that's alright," I replied, hoping that the concept of background interview would be familiar to him.

"Oh, . . . that's alright. Thank you for your time," he replied, disappointed. "Enjoy the rest of your stay in Xinjiang!" With that he got up from his seat, and walked off toward the archway.

I had a strong feeling he wasn't really a freelance journalist.

The Uyghur singer had finished his song soon after my "interview" began, and I was disappointed to see that the trio were now packing up their equipment. I needed to wake up early to get to the train station the next morning, so I chose to call it an early night and head back to Sue's. It would also give me the opportunity to thank her in person for her hospitality, which I was determined to do after all that she had done for me.

I paid my outstanding bill and got up, taking one last look at the view of Kashgar over the wall, before starting what would be my final walk through the New Old City theme park.

When I arrived back at the apartment, Sue, Li, and Sue's mother were sitting around the kitchen table laughing, with a large bottle of rice wine in between them.

"Hello, Grayson!" Sue exclaimed, clearly inebriated. "Would you like to join us?"

"Of course!" I answered as I took a seat. "What did you guys do tonight?"

"We just had some fresh lamb and rice pilaf. You wouldn't have been interested," Li said. I couldn't tell if he was teasing or serious.

"Ha ha. Well, I did have some lamb in the Old City," I replied. Sue's mother poured me a tall glass of rice wine. "Have you been to the street next to the archway, where they play live music?"

"Yes, the performers there are so good!" Sue declared.

Her mother poured herself another glass of wine, and Sue caught her a second after her glass began to overflow, spilling a small amount on the tablecloth. They yelled at each other excitedly in Chinese, while Li was giggling to himself. He kept looking over to see whether I shared in his amusement. He could tell that I did, even though I was less open about it.

The yelling subsided after thirty seconds or so, and Sue picked up where she'd left off.

"There is this one Uyghur band that I see there a lot. They play the best rock music! I love their singer!"

"Yeah! I just saw a Uyghur band there. It might have been the same one you're talking about," I said, as I took a swig of the rice wine.

Sue's mother made a comment in Mandarin, at which Li erupted in laughter. Sue's face got bright red, and she slapped her mother lightly on the arm.

"What did she say?" I asked Li.

"She said that you would be a good husband for Sue," he managed to get out.

I chuckled awkwardly, and I'm sure my face got bright red as well. Judging by the reactions of Sue and Li, and the wide smile on her mother's kind face, it didn't seem like it was entirely a joke.

"Ha ha, I'm sure Sue would be a great wife, but I have a girlfriend," I confessed, falsely, hoping to alleviate Sue's embarrassment.

Sue had her head down, staring at her phone screen, but my comment seemed to help her get comfortable again.

"Sue, I've been wanting to ask you, why did you and your mother come to Kashgar?" I asked.

She perked up, and slid her phone back into her pocket. This question seemed to really interest her.

"Well, we came to visit when I was younger, like fifteen, maybe. And we loved it so much that we decided we would move here," she replied.

"What do you love most about it here?"

"Well, we really like the food—and the warm weather is very nice. But the most important thing to us is the people. When we first moved here, we didn't know anyone. Our Uyghur neighbors in the next apartment invited us over for dinner all the time, and became our good friends."

Li translated this to Sue's mother, who smiled, and nodded in agreement.

"That's such a great story. Do your neighbors still live there?" I asked.

"No, they don't." Sue said.

I sensed that she did not want to say more.

I knew that to inquire further might not only be rude, but potentially dangerous for everyone. Although I had known Sue for only these couple of days, her affectionate words for her Uyghur neighbors came off as genuine and heartfelt.

The four of us continued talking for a while longer, until it became clear that everyone was getting tired.

"I should get to sleep. I have to wake up early to get to the train station," I announced.

"Right! You definitely don't want to miss it," Sue affirmed. "Do you remember how to get there?"

"Yes, thanks. Will I see you guys in the morning?"

"Probably not, it's our off day tomorrow," Sue said matter-of-factly. "It was great having you stay with us, Grayson."

"Thank you so much for having me, Sue," I responded, smiling at her mother as well. "It was wonderful to meet you. It was great to meet you, too, Li."

"Yes, great to meet you, Grayson. I hope you enjoy Ürümqi," he said.

"Will you stay in touch?" Sue asked.

"Yes, definitely." I gave her my WhatsApp number, and asked her to message me so that I would see it once I got back to America "where my American phone is."

Sue did send that message, and I received it. But I still haven't replied, and I doubt I ever can.

I truly would like to know how she and her mother are doing. Not only did they accept me as a guest when nobody else was willing to, but they also sought to connect with me personally during my stay. They were incredibly generous hosts, and they seemed like wonderful people. But nobody is safe from government surveillance in today's China, including Sue and her mother. The mere publication of this book, notwithstanding all of the precautions I've taken to obscure their real identities and to emphasize their complete ignorance of my true purpose for traveling to Xinjiang, could put them in serious danger.

I have come to terms with the fact that, because of the ruthless nature of the CCP, the best thing I can do for them at this point is to never contact them again.

# Chapter 13
# Train to Ürümqi

"There is no such thing as the re-education centers."

—Hu Lianhe, Deputy Director General of the
United Front Work Department of the Central Committee,
address to a United Nations panel in August 2018

My train wasn't scheduled to leave until two p.m. But I was a unilingual foreigner, who wasn't always great at travel logistics even in my own country, so I made sure to arrive at the train station a full five hours early, just to be safe.

When I got off the bus at the train station stop, I followed the other passengers in the direction of the massive clay-colored brick building.

I say "in the direction of" because, as usual, the actual entrance to the station was obscured by a security checkpoint building, with a line stretching outside and weaving around a zig-zag of metal barriers.

That it felt hotter outside than on any of the previous mornings, with the sun beating down in a cloudless sky, made me dread what looked to be a prolonged wait. I retrieved my fisherman's hat from my bag.

After forty-five minutes of moving slowly along the security line, I was inside the checkpoint building. It took about twenty minutes more to hand over my passport, have my bag x-rayed, get patted down, and give the officers the usual explanations, before I was finally cleared to enter the train station. Now I could wait in the actual ticketing line. This took another hour, plus an additional thirty minutes to explain to the woman behind the booth why I was taking a train rather than flying. She seemed skeptical of my admittedly misleading reason—that I was trying to save money. Eventually, I was cleared to go through to the terminal.

My expectations for what I would find in the waiting area turned out to be overly optimistic—to put it mildly. Instead of a slightly smaller version of Kashgar airport, this was essentially a large warehouse with long rows of steel benches. There was no air conditioning, and three of the four giant fans on the ceiling were either broken or not turned on.

There was a solitary food stand in the far corner, selling mostly chips, candy, soda, and water. The only protein on offer, from what I could see, was vacuum-sealed whole dried fish. Only a few were on display, suggesting that they must be selling fast.

I had skipped breakfast that morning, counting on getting a big lunch at the terminal during my long wait. And, anticipating that meals might not be served on the train, my plan was to buy some extra noodle dishes to-go from the selection of restaurants I imagined would be there.

Instead, I bought five bags of chips and three vacuum-sealed fish, unhappily cramming them into my backpack for later.

One bright spot was that the terminal contained at least twice as many benches as there were people waiting to board, allowing me to convert part of one row into a makeshift bed. I tried sleeping, but I was not really tired, and I didn't want to leave my bags vulnerable to snatching. So I passed the time reading my book, learning about Genghis Khan's unlikely rise to power; his incredible military acumen; the fascinating religion of Manichaeism (the official religion of the ancient Uyghur Empire) and Genghis's adoption of some of its key tenets; and his surprising predilection for philosophical and theological discourse with all the most renowned figures he could find throughout his expansive empire.

It would be unrealistic to attempt to fairly compare the ruling styles of Genghis Khan and Xi Jinping, their lives being separated by almost a millennium. But one striking difference was their attitudes toward other cultures. Genghis, while certainly not a committed cosmopolitan by today's standards, exhibited a worldview that not only left room for minority cultures in his empire, but recognized that no culture has a monopoly on the best way to live, and that by incorporating wisdom from these other cultures, it would strengthen his empire as a whole. Xi, on the other hand, seems uninterested in all non-Han cultures in China. And to any culture, like that of the Uyghurs, that he deems to be at odds with his efforts to build national cohesion around the dominant Han culture, he is unconscionably hostile.

At quarter past two, a scratchy voice came over the intercom, and everyone stood to form a line in front of the double doors at the far end of the terminal. I had been concerned that I might not know when my boarding group was called; but apparently there was only one group.

The boarding process was unexpectedly quick. To confirm that I had a ticket, the conductor seemed satisfied to simply look down in the direction of my hand, to see that I was holding a piece of paper of a proper size and color. Since he didn't appear interested in the information on the piece of paper, he allowed multiple people to walk past him at once. I suppose, after the long and tedious process we had endured getting through the gauntlet of other security checkpoints, it was not unreasonable for him to assume that everyone who'd made it that far was supposed to be there.

The line led outside and along the station platform. The train was at the other end of the platform, about a hundred yards in front of us. Its cars were gleaming silver, with twin lines, bright red and blue, painted horizontally along the side; and two rows of windows, indicating there were two levels of seating. There was nobody else on the platform except our group, and a pair of armor-clad police officers standing at opposite ends. Steel benches were positioned in the middle of the platform, closer to the train, all of them empty—remnants of a less security-obsessed time in the past.

A conductor greeted me as I got on board: an older Han man, with thinning, grizzled hair and bright eyes. He was missing maybe half his teeth, and several of the remaining ones were tarnished silver. He glanced at my ticket, and directed me to the right, smiling intensely.

There were three levels of tickets. The top tier was "soft sleeper," which included a two-person bunk bed and some space to move around. The middle tier was "hard sleeper," which included a bunk in a room with three other bunks, its name suggesting it would be somehow less comfortable. The bottom tier was "hard seat," which came with a predictably firm seat, to be shared with another person.

Those who had purchased either of the two types of sleeper tickets were directed to the upper deck of the train. The hard seats were located on the first level. I never got to see the upper deck.

As I made my way along the crowded aisle, every eye in the car was on me. Lively conversations stopped, so they could all get a look as I walked past. Of all the public places that I'd been in Kashgar, this was where I felt the most conspicuous.

The seating was organized in groups, in a similar fashion to some Amtrak trains, but more tightly packed. There were two hard seats—more like benches—facing each other, each fitting two or three passengers, with a shared tray-table in the middle small enough to frustrate even a single passenger. The seats were unpadded cream-colored plastic benches—and fully lived up to their "*hard* seat" designation. The overhead compartments were just thin platforms, with a slight upward bend at the end in place of any barrier that actually secured things placed on them. Miniature fans, spaced along the center of the ceiling for the length of the aisle, told me there would be no air conditioning. They weren't turned on, at least not yet, and the temperature inside was stifling. A strange, rosy scent pervaded the place, like an acrid fabric softener, which only partially masked the lingering smells of cigarette residue and sweat.

About halfway down the car, I arrived at my seat. A young Han Chinese man with a chiseled face, wearing an authentic-looking Gucci T-shirt and brown cargo shorts, was sitting in the aisle seat, entranced by the *Mission Impossible* movie he was watching on his phone. Across from him sat a tall, burly Uyghur man in a pressed black collared button-down shirt, and his young son, who I guessed was about eight years old, wearing a long-sleeved green T-shirt and blue jeans. The boy's mouth was fully agape in astonishment from seeing me, but his father seemed unfazed. He simply looked at me for a second, smiling, and then waved his hand at the Han man to get his attention for me. The Han man looked up at the Uyghur father, then over at me, then back to his screen, as he adjusted his body to create a path for me to get to my seat. He seemed much too taken by Tom Cruise to give me any attention.

Despite my having been one of the last passengers in line, the train still hadn't started moving after I'd been seated for fifteen minutes. Unsure of how much longer it would take, and wanting a break from reading about Genghis Khan, I decided to make some notes in my journal.

I was in the middle of detailing the events of the previous night when I was interrupted by the nearly-toothless conductor. He was standing in the aisle, looking at me sternly, with an outstretched hand. He wanted to look at my journal. *If this guy reads English, I'm done for.* I hesitated for a moment, but I knew that my refusal to hand it over would only heighten his suspicions. I closed it nonchalantly before placing it in his hand, hoping for the best.

I was relieved when he opened it to the first page, which had innocuous notes from a previous trip to Thailand, instead of to the page where I had just been relating my vivid thoughts on the dystopian faux-Kashgar.

"Travel journal," I announced, as if that would have any effect on the man, even if he could understand me. He examined it for a few more seconds, and handed it back with a shrug.

"Xie xie," I said. He tipped his cap and gave me another beaming smile, before moving on down the aisle. I kept the journal in my bag for the remainder of my time on board.

Finally, I felt an abrupt lurch forward, and the train began to move. In twenty hours, I would be in Ürümqi, Xinjiang's capital city. But until then, I would have to find a way to occupy myself.

Since the station was on the outskirts of Kashgar, the scenery outside soon shifted from the vestiges of an urban center to the vast wasteland that surrounds the city for miles in every direction: the Taklamakan Desert.

The Taklamakan, meaning "place of ruins" in Uyghur, is a brutal and treacherous place. Although its average annual temperature is relatively cool, as far as deserts go, it is among the driest, due to its significant distance from any large bodies of water. Much of the scarce water that is in the Taklamakan is groundwater, which "can be saltier than blood."[74] It is bordered by the Pamir and Himalayan mountain ranges to the south, and to the west and north by the Tian Shan range, which translates to "Godly Mountains" in Chinese (the Uyghurs call it "Tengri Tagh," meaning the same thing), separating China from Kyrgyzstan.

Out the window, I could see the front range of the Tian Shan, a string of desert-tan mountains, with their rocky ridges speckled in different shades of grey, stretching out past the horizon. Out the opposite window, on the other side of the train, all I could see was flat, harsh desert, with occasional pockets of mudbrick homes, most looking like they'd been unoccupied for some time.

As it is roughly the size of Germany, one can imagine the difficulties crossing The Taklamakan on camelback—the preferred method for most of recorded history. But countless traders made the trek anyway. Their doing so created a crucial link in the network of trails and paths that together made up the Silk Road.

Soon after we had left, I spotted something potentially significant out my window. Roughly a quarter mile from the train, standing off by itself, was a complex of buildings, with no other structures anywhere near them. We were no longer in Kashgar city, but I thought we were probably still in the greater prefecture, or barely outside it. This place *could* be a re-education camp. I quickly pulled my binoculars from my bag to get a closer look. The complex was surrounded by a grey concrete wall with what looked like razor wire at the top; at the corners I could make out what appeared to be guard towers.

Unfortunately, even with my binoculars, this was the full extent of what I was able to see. The train was moving too fast, and the complex was too far away. It certainly fit the mold for a re-education camp—it was outside of the city, it appeared to have guard towers and razor wire, and it had large monochromatic buildings that looked like they could be dormitories.

---

When reports of the re-education camps began to garner the attention of Western media in 2018, CCP officials categorically denied their existence. Since then, as more information has emerged, making outright denial impossible, CCP officials have pivoted to justifying the existence of the camps with two obfuscatory and shifting explanations. When a security-based justification is useful, CCP officials characterize the camps as places to de-radicalize citizens who have been corrupted by the "Three Evil Forces": terrorism, separatism/splittism, and religious extremism. When justification based on poverty alleviation is more convenient, officials claim that these facilities are used to teach Xinjiang's ethnic minorities essential job skills to boost their economic prospects. They claim that the "students" are at these camps voluntarily and are grateful for the opportunity to learn valuable skills, comparing the camps to standard boarding schools.[75]

All available evidence indicates that these characterizations are flagr9antly dishonest. Instead, the evidence demonstrates that what is happening in Xinjiang is the most abhorrent abuse of human rights anywhere in the world today.

What emerged first were accounts from formerly interned Uyghurs who had been released and had managed to escape China. These firsthand accounts have been surfacing since 2017, when the camps were first established. The former detainees describe the general "curriculum" as consisting mostly of being forced to learn and recite CCP propaganda, to sing CCP propaganda songs, to learn and practice Mandarin, and to renounce Islam and most other core parts of their Uyghur identities. Some of the abuses that detainees must endure in the camps include squalid and severely overcrowded living conditions,[76] constant interrogation,[77] forced sleep deprivation,[78] starvation,[79] physical torture,[80] rape,[81] forced abortion,[82] forced sterilization,[83] forced organ harvesting,[84] and unexplained deaths.[85]

Beyond first-hand testimonials, we now also have reports—the majority of them authored by Adrian Zenz—corroborated by the PRC's own official documents, that prove conclusively that the CCP's characterizations of the camps are malicious falsehoods.

One Zenz report, titled "'Wash Brains, Cleanse Hearts': Evidence from Chinese Government Documents about the Nature and Extent of Xinjiang's Extrajudicial Internment Campaign," draws on open-source research as well as leaked government documents to provide a vivid picture of how the camps are intended to operate.⁸⁶ The name used for the camps in the government documents is "Vocational Skills Education Training Centers." Zenz refers to them in his report as "Vocational Training Internment Camps" (VTICs).

His report thoroughly discredits the claim that the "students" are there of their own volition. Zenz notes that the very first item in the classified government document he used for his report was "security measures," and that "of the 'five preventative measures,' 'escape prevention' was discussed first." He adds that these are the same "escape prevention" measures used at regular prisons throughout China.

He illustrates the CCP's emphasis on making sure that the "students" cannot leave, by comparing the budgets of different counties in Xinjiang to reveal how many police officers are assigned to VTICs. In one county, he notes, "a stunning thirty-one percent of the county's entire assistant police force is tasked with guarding VTIC detainees."

Zenz also describes what happens to detainees who aren't sufficiently enthusiastic about being re-educated. The classified document counsels the administrators of VTICs that students who exhibit "'a vague understanding, negative attitudes or even show resistance' are to be dealt with through an 'assault-style transformation through education' to 'ensure that results are achieved.'" The report explains that students are given a classification while in the camps that determines which of the four "management areas" they are to be sent to, ranging from "lenient" to "forceful."

Shockingly, according to Zenz's research, VTICs are only *one of eight* different types of extrajudicial internment facilities in Xinjiang. He estimates that "the region has probably somewhere between 1,300 and 1,400 extrajudicial internment facilities (excluding prisons)," and that "it appears that broadly speaking, 10 to 30 percent of the rural Uyghur adult population are typically in some form of extrajudicial internment or formally sentenced to prison."⁸⁷

The number of Uyghurs sentenced to prison for harmless expressions of their faith or culture is more difficult to determine. Stories abound from those whose loved ones have been sentenced to lengthy prison terms for vague violations like "gathering chaos to disrupt social order" or "illegally using superstition to break the rule of law";⁸⁸ and Chinese prosecutors only have to provide "basic truth" and "basic evidence" to secure a guilty verdict.⁸⁹ But there are measurements that can provide some insight. One particularly illuminating (and depressing) statistic is that "in 2017 and 2018, [about 136,000] people were prosecuted through the legal system in Xinjiang, while in previous years, the figure had been less than 30,000 annually."[90]

Zenz concludes his report with what may be the most incisive one-sentence summary of the crisis in Xinjiang to be offered by anyone, describing it as "nothing less than a litmus test for the world's most basic shared values."

Right now, most of the world is failing this test.

Chapter 14

# Train to Ürümqi
## —New Friends

"The happiest Muslims in the world live in Xinjiang."
—Gheyret Saliyup, Deputy Director of the
Xinjiang Party Committee
Foreign Propaganda Bureau

The "Game of Slaps," as it is colloquially called, is an under-appreciated activity. Its unfortunate name can conjure up images of belligerent bearded men in the back rooms of dimly lit bars, testing their fortitude by taking turns slapping each other until one of them loses consciousness. (That game also exists, for those who are interested.) This Game of Slaps, by contrast, is actually an ideal game for playfully forging a connection with someone.

The rules are as follows: Two players face each other. Player One extends their arms toward Player Two, palms facing up. Player Two, arms extended, places their hands on Player One's hands, palms facing down. This is the starting point. Once each player is in position, Player One quickly flips their hands out from under Player Two's hands and back down again on top, in an attempt to slap Player Two's hands, before Player Two can pull their hands away. This continues until Player One succeeds, at which point the players switch roles.

The game is designed so that the "slap" is intended to not be a painful blow, which is what makes it an effective ice-breaker.

The Uyghur boy across from me could not sit still. His father tried repeatedly, but futilely, to convince him to relax. Each time, moments after the dad had slipped back under the spell of his smartphone, the boy would begin again to kick and bounce on his seat.

We had practically a full day until we would arrive at our destination, and it seemed unlikely that the boy would tire himself out before driving his father and the rest of us insane. Recognizing how unsustainable this continuous cycle was going to be, I got to thinking about ways that I could help to keep him occupied. The Game of Slaps quickly came to mind.

I would need to figure out how to communicate this proposal to the man and his son. I needed to be cautious—to convince the boy, and even more so, his father, that I was a totally normal guy just trying to make the ride more bearable for everyone.

I waited another minute for the cycle to return to the quieter point, where the father would remind his son about what he had requested just minutes earlier. That was when I made my move.

"Ni-hao," I inserted. The father and his son both looked up from their negotiation and over at me.

I reached out my hands in the direction of the boy, with my palms facing up. I made sure to smile calmly the entire time, shifting my attention from father to son, to nonverbally ask the dad's permission to have a go at getting the boy to settle down.

The dad grinned and nodded at me to go ahead, but in a way that suggested an understandable curiosity as to what I had in mind. I turned further toward the boy as the dad told him something in Mandarin, which I imagined maybe went something like "he looks safe enough, son, go ahead." The boy still wore the same amazed expression that he had when I first sat down, as if I were some sort of playful apparition.

I placed one of my hands on top of the other for a moment as I looked at him, trying to convey that this was what I wanted him to do with *his* hands. He slowly stretched out his arms and placed his hands on top of mine. They were small enough to fit neatly into just the palms of my own.

"Okay," I said. He looked up at me with a glassy gaze, entirely unprepared for what would happen next.

1 . . . 2 . . . *thwap*!

"Aaa!" he yipped, pulling his hands back quickly. He looked down at them intently, as if to confirm that they were still intact. But it became clear that his initial reaction was of surprise rather than offense when, a moment later, a bright smile appeared on his face.

I took this to mean that he would want a second chance, so I put my hands out again in the same position. Normally, we would switch places, since I won. But it was only fair that I give him a fresh shot now that he had seen how the game worked.

He exhaled a slight cough, followed by a giggle, and placed his hands on mine again.

The moment he put them down . . . *thwap!*

This elicited a full-throated laugh. He looked at his father, who couldn't help but chuckle himself, and immediately put his hands back to go again. The father and I looked at each other and nodded, demonstrating our shared understanding that I would be taking his restless son off his hands for a while. He slouched back into his seat and slowly closed his eyes, entering a state of tranquil repose at a speed I could only wish to know for myself.

I hoped that in such a state, he might be granted a temporary escape from what must have been an unfathomably stressful life. Not only did he have to take care of himself in this prison state; he also had to look out for his boy.

I couldn't imagine what raising a child in Xinjiang must be like for a Uyghur.

How much does he tell his son about what's going on in their society? If their family members, their neighbors, or the boy's classmates are sent away, where does the father tell him they've gone? When the boy asks if they're ever coming back, does the father truthfully say that he may never see them again?

I felt lucky that I had never needed to ponder such questions for my own family or friends. If the trajectory of my relatively privileged life held, I would never have to. The least I could do was to keep the boy occupied for a while, and allow his father to get some extra sleep.

It took the boy several rounds to get the hang of it. The attack role was particularly difficult for him to grasp, judging by how he would grab my hands from beneath before trying to slap them. But he eventually came around to playing by the rules.

I had never actually played more than a dozen rounds of this game in a single sitting. The Game of Slaps wasn't designed to be a long-term engagement. And on previous occasions, there were plenty of other activities to switch to. After what must have been a hundred rounds, it became increasingly difficult to restrain myself from shaking his father out of his sleep, so he could save me from being caught in a game with no end.

Thankfully, the boy grew tired of playing after I'd allowed him to win a number of times in a row. (In retrospect, I can't say how I hadn't thought of this idea at an earlier point during the first hundred games.) He turned toward his father, who was still fast asleep, and began to push on his chest—lightly at first, then more forcefully—to get him to wake up. The dad lethargically peeled open his eyes, slung himself into a semi-upright position, and proceeded to address his son's flurry of comments—all of which it seemed were about how he had just trounced me at my own game.

The dad turned his head toward me and smiled.

"Xie xie." His voice was surprisingly alert for a man who had woken up moments ago.

I smiled and nodded back at him, and pulled my book from my daypack, settling in for what I hoped would be a solid block of time immersed in the world of Genghis Khan.

I saw out of the corner of my eye that the boy was slowly approaching me with his hands out, palms facing up. A part of me admired his persistence, but I knew I would surely fling myself off the side of the train if I was forced to endure any more of the Game of Slaps. His father gallantly interjected, admonishing him to leave me alone.

I pretended to be too deeply focused on my book to notice.

Over the course of the next hour, the boy's condition deteriorated markedly. It began with an increase in the frequency and harshness of a cough, which I had heard a few times as we were playing our game. But now it came every thirty seconds or so, and instead of a single dry cough, it was a fit of multiple coughs, during which I could hear fluid building up in his throat. A film of sweat covered his small face, and he was shivering, despite his father having cloaked him in a thick, adult-sized cotton blanket.

A miniature bottle of Korean hand sanitizer, which I discovered had tagged along with me at the bottom of my travel bag, was a welcome surprise. I tried to apply it discreetly, so as to not embarrass the boy or his father.

I wasn't the only passenger to take notice of the boy's exploding coughing fits. The Han man sitting next to me, whose eyes had not left his phone screen since I had first sat down, was now staring reproachfully at the boy, as if this sudden illness were somehow the boy's fault. Other passengers around us were peering over at him as well, but I was heartened that they appeared more sympathetic to my young friend than my seatmate did.

The father was gently rubbing his son's back, and whispering reassuring words in his ear as he looked around nervously at the assorted eyes that were fixed on the two of them. Passengers from the distant ends of the car were now craning over the rows of seats between us to see what the commotion was. Conversations continued, but grew quieter. It wouldn't be long before a conductor caught wind of the situation.

With my focus on the scene playing out in front of me, I hadn't realized that the train was slowing down. Out the window, the vast expanse of cracked desert had been replaced by an industrial skyline, with smokestacks billowing their black discharge into the thin desert air. The train slowed to a crawl as we pulled into the station, coming to a complete stop with my window almost directly in front of the station sign. *Aksu,* it read.

I turned to see that the father had already begun pulling down their bags from the overhead compartment. Other passengers in our car were getting ready to disembark as well, which, I hoped, would allow the man and his son to attract less attention. The boy was standing to the side of his father, still wrapped in the cotton blanket.

I waved to the boy when he looked in my direction. He feebly waved back, his face mostly hidden by the blanket. His father took his hand, and the two of them headed down the aisle and off the train. I watched them through my window, the father striding forcefully toward the intake building, leading his sluggish son close behind him.

Their hard seats were promptly refilled by a sexagenarian Uyghur woman and her granddaughter, who looked about eight, the same age as the boy had been. The girl had an androgynous bowl haircut, nearly identical to the boy's, but she was given away as female by her violet-colored T-shirt with white flowers stitched onto the sleeves. I pretended not to notice her unflinching stare, just like the boy had given me earlier.

Soon after we had passed into the outer reaches of Aksu and re-entered the interminable sands of the Taklamakan, I made use of my binoculars, still draped around my neck, to see if I could spot anything of interest.

One thing that made searching for the camps especially difficult was the generalized high security in the region. A structure surrounded by barbed wire with police stationed out front might be solid proof of a prison in most other parts of the world; but it was becoming the norm for many buildings in Xinjiang to have some prison-like features.

I was able to spot one or two such buildings as we left Aksu; buildings with barbed wire, but not an unusual amount of barbed wire, just an ordinary modern-day-Xinjiang amount.

I lowered my binoculars and sank into my seat, frustrated that it would be unlikely for me to know if I had spotted an internment facility. As I turned my attention away from the window, I saw that the Uyghur girl sitting across from me was still staring at me, in the same position she had been in before, her hands resting on her knees.

She wasn't staring at my face, but at my shirt. I was perplexed, until I realized it was the binoculars hanging *in front* of my shirt that had piqued her interest.

I took the binoculars in my right hand and held them out in her direction, with an expression that I hoped would communicate that I was asking if she wanted to use them.

The girl understood, and she wasn't timid. She jumped from her seat and came over to claim them, burrowing her way into the space between me and the window. It was amazing that she hadn't woken her grandmother, who, barely out of the station, had somehow already curled up in her hard seat and was fast asleep.

I removed the binoculars from around my neck and slipped the strap over the girl's head.

She didn't hide her disappointment at her first look out the window.

"Auuuuhhh?" Her melancholy look and puzzled voice told me the binoculars were not working for her. I directed her attention back out the window to try again as I adjusted the focus.

"Oooooo!" she exclaimed, followed by a jubilant string of Mandarin. She was hooked, scanning intently back and forth across the sparse landscape. It was touching to see how much enjoyment she was getting from scenery that she had probably been surrounded by for her entire life; now viewing it through a novel lens.

After several more minutes of her fascinated survey, she suddenly stopped. She looked at me and smiled, in what I thought meant, "Thank you, but this is boring now." But as I extended my hand so she could return them, she hopped off the seat and bolted down the aisle, my binoculars swinging on her neck.

Mindful of the ways in which my chasing a school-age Uyghur girl down a train aisle could be misconstrued, I elected to stay seated.

I didn't think she had pilfered them—her grandmother was still snoozing away in the seat across from me. More likely, she had run off to some other part of the train in search of a better view. I accepted that there was a good chance they'd be broken or lost by the time she returned.

But the girl came back just minutes later, my binoculars still around her neck, followed by a parade of five other Uyghur children. She had taken it upon herself to inform other similar-age kids on our monotonous train ride that she had found an activity for all of them to pass the time. She had apparently concluded that because I had allowed her to borrow my binoculars, the same offer would apply to every other child on the train.

The adorable expression on the girl's face, and the gleeful anticipation of the young regiment behind her, disarmed me of any ability to say no. My cinephilic seatmate had become aware of the situation, and, without so much as a glance in my direction, or ever taking his eyes off the movie on his smartphone screen, he stood up and went to occupy the girl's seat across from me.

"Xie xie," I said in his direction, expecting no response, and not receiving any.

The kids crowded onto his hard seat. They made a commendable attempt to all squeeze in together, but two of them soon accepted having to stand. I tried my best to stipulate that they needed to each wait their turn at the binoculars, and to be careful with them, because they were mine.

My effort at establishing order was quickly followed by the largest of the kids, a Uyghur boy with a black knock-off Adidas soccer T-shirt, shoving the girl next in line for the binoculars off her seat and onto the floor. I glared in his direction, ensuring that the other children could see it as well. This convinced him to allow the girl to reclaim her spot.

Having proven myself against the strongest of them, I had earned their respect, and I was able to maintain a cooperative atmosphere from then on.

We established an informal system: one of the children looked out the window through the binoculars, while the next one in line stood alongside to point out interesting objects; the rest of the group hung with me as they waited their turns, teaching me how to say various Mandarin words (and laughing hysterically at my attempts). Every few minutes, I would direct them to rotate positions.

Everything was running smoothly, and the kids all seemed to be having a good time. Then I noticed something. As I looked in the direction of two of my young Mandarin instructors who were kneeling on the aisle seat, I saw the face of a slightly older Uyghur girl, about eleven or twelve, in the seat on the opposite side of the aisle, peering curiously at me through the gap between their heads.

She was wearing a knee-length black dress, with baggy sleeves that almost covered her forearms. On top of the dress she'd added a semicircular white drape, with a meticulous eyelet design stitched along its bottom perimeter that reminded me of a fancy lace tablecloth. Her dark brown hair, frizzy from the heat, was gathered into a single braid down to the middle of her back. Her bright purple earphones couldn't have contrasted more with the rest of her persona.

Every time I looked in her direction, I would see the same pair of dark brown eyes looking over at me, and then immediately look away and back at her phone when we made eye contact.

It was obvious that she wanted to be included in the child social club I had inadvertently founded, but she was just too shy to take the initiative. I tried to come up with some way to make her comfortable joining the group.

After ruling out more Games of Slaps, a plan came to mind fairly quickly. My iPhone had a sizable selection of music on it, and I had earphones in my daypack. Maybe she'd be interested in hearing what American music sounded like? The music was downloaded, so I wouldn't have to connect my phone to a potentially invasive Chinese cell tower.

But I knew that even bringing out my iPhone was risky. If an official asked to inspect it, I'd be powerless to prevent their scouring my message history and turning up evidence of the questionable intentions behind my trip. I also couldn't be entirely sure that there wasn't a way for the government to access my phone's contents remotely, even if it was disconnected from the internet.

Nevertheless, I went ahead with this idea, judging that a surprise phone inspection was unlikely on a train barreling through the middle of the desert.

After a few lackadaisical tries at pronouncing the Mandarin word for "fingernail" for the kids, I instructed the two sitting on the seat next to me to stand. They obliged, and I saw the girl staring at me again, then swiftly turning her head down and away.

I took out my iPhone, unspooled the earphones wrapped around it, and extended the left earbud across the aisle toward her. I knew she'd look up again in seconds, and when she did, she was predictably startled that I was reaching out to her.

I made a circular gesture toward her with my extended hand, hoping this was a universal motion that she would grasp. It took a moment, but once she understood, her eyes lit up with excitement. A bashful grin came across her face as she stepped across the aisle and slid into the seat.

She wouldn't take the earphone from me, perhaps afraid that she had misinterpreted my invitation. So I placed it in her hand.

"Grayson," I said, as I pointed to myself. I hoped that some basic introductions might put her more at ease.

She looked quizzically at me.

"Hmm . . ." I dug around in my daypack and found my Chinese-English translation dictionary. I flipped through the pages to find a simple word that I might have a chance to pronounce intelligibly.

"Uh. . . Wo. Wo Grayson."

*Wo* is Mandarin for "me"—the easiest term I could think of for this purpose.

The girl snickered lightly. Apparently even this two-letter layup of a word was impossible for me to say without sounding like a clumsy foreigner.

"Ayyy-nuur," she said in a gentle voice, pointing to herself.

"Ayyy-nuur," I repeated, as closely to her pronunciation as I could muster.

She nodded her head to confirm I'd said it correctly.

I later discovered that Aynur is a relatively common name for Uyghur (as well as Turkish and Azerbaijani) females. It translates to "moonlight," deriving from the Turkish word "ay" meaning "moon" and the Arabic word "nur" meaning "light."[91]

I had no clue what kind of music Aynur liked, of course, but I was pretty confident that she wouldn't recognize any of the songs in my library. So I put it on shuffle, making sure to skip past the heavier stuff. I chose not to expose her to the raw eloquence of 50 Cent, for instance.

I can't recall the first song that played, but I do remember her total lack of reaction. She showed no change in activity or facial expression. After thirty seconds or so of watching this stoicism, I skipped to the next track.

"Ohhhhh," Aynur commented, turning her head toward me for a moment, smiling, and then back down toward the ground.

I couldn't tell if her eyes were fixed on the floor because of shyness, or because she was focusing on the music—or both. I detected a hint of a rhythmic foot-tap. She certainly seemed to be into this track, and I now had a way of knowing what she liked, and what she didn't. Complete non-reaction meant skip, anything else meant stay. Easy.

Naturally, the younger kids became interested in what we were doing. One of them carefully inched her hand closer to my earphone, trying, it would seem, to dislodge it and place it in her own ear without my noticing. Detecting her plan, I turned toward her and shook my head. I could accept the risk of harm coming to my binoculars (which weren't all that expensive), but my headphones were a bridge too far.

I was pleasantly surprised when Aynur boldly inserted herself into the dispute, seeming to tell the kids everything I would have, and in Mandarin. Her directive seemed to work, as the children returned their focus out the window. With Aynur as my lieutenant, Hardseat 36 E/F was shaping up to have the makings of a viable, governable micro-city-state.

But alas, these high aspirations were quashed when the younger kids' fathers showed up. Apparently they had organized a search, wondering where their kids had gotten off to, and worried whether they might be in some kind of trouble or danger. Their initial expressions suggested that maybe half of them were happy enough to see them with me.

There were four fathers in the group. Two of them looked merely astonished; the other two looked appalled. One of the more protective fathers yelled something in Uyghur at his son, who was using my binoculars at that moment. The boy handed them off to the next kid and ran over to join his father. I expected the man would have some words for me as well, or at least give me an aggressive stare to convey his displeasure, but he never even looked at me. He and his son walked off.

The other fathers began to discuss the situation, and consulted the surrounding passengers to confirm, I supposed, that I wasn't any threat to their kids. It was one of those moments when I would have found it useful to speak the language.

They eventually seemed to decide that they weren't upset with me, but that they wanted their children returned to their care.

I gave the five youngsters a final opportunity to snicker at my mangled Mandarin, and I was relieved when the fathers laughed, too. The kid holding my binoculars gave them back to me, and I draped them back around my own neck.

"Goodbye!" I said to them all as they returned to their parents.

"Bye bye!" two of them answered back.

One of the fathers waved at me, as they headed along the aisle to return to their seats. The first little girl, whose grandmother was somehow *still* passed out in her seat, ran along with them.

Now it was just Aynur and me, jamming out to music together to escape the tedium of this train journey. The more songs we listened to, the more comfortable she became. Her slight foot tap from earlier was now unrestrained, and she was moving her head from side to side in tandem with the melodies she enjoyed most. We even developed a "secret handshake," consisting of two quick sideways high-fives, followed by two quick back-handed and sideways high-fives, and an elbow bump to top it off. I had repurposed the high-fives from my signature handshake that I used to do with one of my former basketball teammates. The elbow bump was entirely Aynur's idea.

Things were already going very well. But even then, I couldn't have predicted what would happen next, when Aynur found her new favorite song.

Or, rather, I should say that she found her favorite thirty seconds of a song. She seemed to enjoy the entirety of the Grateful Dead's *Sugar*

*Magnolia*; but it was the concluding half-minute that she immediately became enamored with.

Fans of the song will not be surprised by this. There's an extended finale, with a chorus sung by Bob Weir, and Jerry Garcia adding a repeating rhythmic background stream of euphonious "doot–doo-doot"s, eventually fading into the conclusion. It makes for a very catchy song ending, one of my favorites.

The instant that the finale started, Aynur radiated excitement. She looked up at me, at first with her mouth wide open, and then with a delighted smile. It was as if she had just then been exposed to an angelic sound that she had always known intuitively existed out there, but had yet to discover for herself. Every music fan knows the feeling of hearing a tune that hits our preferences in all the right spots so perfectly that it seems as though it had been created just for our enjoyment. Aynur had found *her* tune.

When the finale was over, she unilaterally decided that we were listening to it again; she reached over and pressed the "back" button. And so we listened to it again . . . and again . . . and again . . . and on each play she reacted to the finale as if she were hearing it for the first time. I really like the Grateful Dead, and *Sugar Magnolia* specifically, but I have never had the desire to listen to it a dozen times on repeat. I went along, though, seeing how ecstatic she was.

Then, I began to hear her faintly whispering along with the doot–doo-doots. She would start to whisper with the track, and slowly get a bit louder, only to suddenly fall silent again. I knew that she wanted to sing along, but she was just too timid.

In that moment I did something I had never imagined myself doing; anywhere, in any part of the world. The next time the finale began, I began to sing the lyrics—out loud. "Sunshine daydream, . . . " I had sung in public only once before in my life, the result of losing a sports bet. And now, Aynur's enthusiasm had moved me to sing in front of an audience of every stranger on this train car.

I looked over at Aynur, as I continued in my coarse, cracked singing voice, expecting a look of embarrassment. But it didn't come. Instead, she was laughing. I'm sure it was a fairly hilarious scene; I saw a number of passengers around us who agreed, as they hastily pulled out their phones to film us.

*Perfect, now everyone on Chinese social media will get to hear my awful singing voice.*

I was contemplating stopping to avoid further embarrassment when, as I had hoped, Aynur joined in with the doot–doo-doots.

She wasn't much better than me, truthfully. She fluctuated erratically around the pitch of the doot–doo-doots, and sometimes veered off on a different tempo altogether. Obviously, though, I was not one to criticize; and my purpose had been to give her confidence enough to do it.

We sang the finale together three times, until she finally pressed skip to move on to the next track. I let out a furtive sigh in relief, knowing that we were finally giving that song a rest—though I would have been willing to go on for longer, had she wanted to.

By then, I was pretty exhausted. I'd spent almost all of my time on the train interacting with kids, despite my expectation for this to be an opportunity to re-charge a bit before the second half of my journey. So after Aynur and I had listened to a couple of more songs, I hit the "pause" button. She looked at me as I pointed to myself and angled my hands together on my cheek, miming my desire to sleep.

She smiled and nodded her head. We performed our secret handshake another time, and she headed off down the aisle.

I tried to actually get some rest, and I succeeded for some short intervals. But the bumps and jolts of the train's movement along the track were far more noticeable now that I was only focused on falling asleep. I positioned myself with my head leaned against the window, and continued listening to my music.

With the exception of a few brief bathroom breaks, I cozily stayed in that position until late into the night. At around midnight, as we arrived at another stop, I felt a tap on my shoulder. I turned to see Aynur looking at me, smiling softly through her tired eyes.

We did our handshake one final time, waved goodbye to each other, and she headed off down the aisle with her mother, her single braid bouncing against her back.

---

I often think about Aynur nowadays. When I do, I like to imagine that she's living happily with her mother and other family members; that she's finding new music to listen to, and maybe even some songs that she'll sing along with in that adorable voice I heard on the train; that she has caring, lifelong friends who she feels she can trust with any problem; that she'll continue to grow into a beautiful woman and find a kind and loving husband someday; that she will have beautiful children who she nurtures into successful and ethical adults; that when she finally succumbs to illness or frailty in her old age, she'll be buried in a cemetery in accordance with traditional Uyghur burial practices, surrounded by the people who love her.

A more realistic prediction for Aynur's future would read differently.

When I met Aynur, her father was probably not with her because he was unjustly imprisoned in one form or another. If and when he is released, he would probably be sent to forced labor, either within Xinjiang, or elsewhere in China. Her mother might have been struggling to make enough money on her own to provide for Aynur, having to rely on some form of government subsidy to give them any sort of decent living standard.

The CCP could have replaced her father with a Han "relative," as part of the "Pair Up and Become Family" initiative, where Han Party cadres are assigned to live in the homes of Uyghur families to ensure that they aren't exhibiting signs of "extremism." During the day, the "relative" might supervise Aynur's studies when she got home from school, would eat "family" meals with her and her mother, and would quiz them on questions related to CCP history, or "Xi Jinping Thought," to have them demonstrate their conformity to the proper Chinese way of living. "Relatives" are encouraged to sleep in the same beds as their female hosts, where the women are frequently sexually abused. This could be a nighttime routine that (hopefully) only Aynur's mother would be forced to expect and endure.[92]

Aynur might live this way with her mother until she enters her teen years. At that point, one of several things might happen to her.

Very likely, she will be forcibly sterilized. According to Adrian Zenz's research, "comprehensive new evidence from government documents reveals a systematic state campaign of suppressing minority births"—a campaign that Zenz convincingly argues fits squarely within the definition of genocide.[93] The following quote from the report captures the thrust of this research:

> In 2018, a stunning 80 percent of all newly placed IUDs in China were fitted in Xinjiang, even though the region only makes up 1.8 percent of the country's population. By 2019, Xinjiang planned to subject over eighty percent of women of childbearing age in the rural southern four minority prefectures to "birth control measures with long-term effectiveness."

Another possibility is that Aynur will be claimed by one of the many Han Chinese bachelors who exist in China today, largely as a product of the CCP's ill-considered "One Child Policy" instituted from 1979 to 2015. The CCP heavily promotes inter-ethnic marriage in order to "promote ethnic unity." Tellingly, there are an abundance of examples of the CCP encouraging Uyghur women to marry Han men, but very few of the opposite arrangement. Would-be Uyghur brides who refuse to marry Han grooms are readily labeled as harboring sympathy for religious extremism or ethnic separatism.[94]

Aynur could also end up in a re-education camp herself. This would be a likely outcome were she to resist any of the previously noted abuses. But she could also be sent there for a casual conversation with one of her friends or relatives, had that person been deemed "suspicious" without her knowing. She could be sent there for missing too many public flag-raising ceremonies, thereby failing to demonstrate a sufficient amount of patriotism. She could even be sent there for downloading new music on her phone, if those songs originated from the "wrong" website.

Considering the practically endless number of innocuous actions or inactions that can send a Uyghur away for re-education in Xinjiang, it will be difficult for Aynur to avoid them all.

I'd like to be able to picture Aynur living a happy life. But, as of now, I can't see much hope for that. Instead, I see her dressed in prison garb, sitting at a desk in a cramped, windowless classroom filled with a few dozen Uyghur women just like her. I see her face, macerated from a lack of nutrition, emotionless, as she and her classmates are forced to sing ballads to the greatness of the Chinese Communist Party, and its beneficence and generosity to its many subjects.

Chapter 15

# Overnight and Arrival in Ürümqi

"The striking hand needs to be hard, and the educating hand needs to be hard as well."
—Zhang Chunxian, Xinjiang Party Secretary
2010–2016

The remaining eleven hours on the train before we arrived in Ürümqi were restless and red-eyed. I split the time between reading my Genghis Khan book, which I felt bittersweet to finish shortly after dawn; watching the Chinese version of *John Wick 3* with Movie Guy, who generously offered to share his earbuds so I could enjoy it with him; and mingling in the smoking areas at either end of the train car.

The mingling was mostly uneventful, aside from one interaction.

At some time in the very early morning, after wolfing down an early breakfast of my last vacuum-sealed fish (they tasted every bit as unpalatable as you'd expect), I got up from my seat to stretch my legs.

I wandered to the rear smoking area, past the rows of sleeping passengers, where I found a lone Han Chinese man of about thirty casually scrolling through his phone as he leaned against the wall, enshrouded in a cloud of his cigarette's making.

I'd been here several times already that morning. Each time there had been a group of four or five men, who cordially invited me into their gathering. (It's not common for Chinese women to smoke.) I would check each time to see whether any of them spoke English, by asking a simple question. "Are you from Ürümqi?" was the one I used most. It hadn't worked yet, but I didn't let that stop me from trying.

"Ni-hao," I said to the man, barely in time before being smacked in the face by the perimeter of his smoke cloud. I took out my box of Chinese cigarettes to offer him one.

(I'm not typically a smoker, but I thought it would be useful to become one for this journey, to be able to offer cigarettes as an icebreaker. The Game of Slaps isn't very popular with grown men.)

He looked up from his phone, doing the usual double-take, which he followed with an affable smile. He finished what was left of the cigarette he already had in his hand, tossed it to the floor, and grabbed a fresh one from my box.

"Hello! English?" he asked, as we lit up.

"Yes! Well, American, but I speak English."

"Oh wow! What are you doing on a train in Xinjiang?"

"Trying to get to Ürümqi, just like you." I responded with a friendly smirk.

"Ah, of course. Nothing strange about that," he chuckled.

I'd finally found the first person in Xinjiang to get my dry humor.

"I'm a college student on vacation," I added. "I wanted to see Xinjiang because I'd read how cool of a place it is."

"It's very cool—the most beautiful place in all of China." He stomped out the cigarette I had given him, having somehow burned through it already, to light up another of his own. "I've lived here for my entire life."

"Really? In Ürümqi?"

"Yes, it's a great city. I'm sure you'll like it a lot."

I felt comfortable with this guy—more so than with any other stranger I had spoken with in Xinjiang. Obviously it had a lot to do with the fact that he was fluent in my language, but he also gave off a positive vibe.

So, I ventured into a sensitive topic, to see where it might lead.

"Yeah, I've heard great things about it. I also heard that I'll be stopped a lot while I'm there, though."

I knew where I wanted the rest of the conversation to go from that point. I wanted to see, carefully, if this guy might be willing to open up a bit about what was happening in Xinjiang. I thought that this statement would come off as benign ignorance.

I was fiddling around in my pocket for another cigarette—mostly so I could avoid eye contact for a moment after pitching that statement. When I looked back up at him, his smile was gone. It had been replaced by a hollow expression, which I was able to glimpse for only a split second, before he flicked his quarter-finished cigarette onto the floor and walked away. He went back into the next train car, without another word.

*Well, that couldn't have gone worse.*

I had no idea who that guy was, or who he suspected me of being. Most likely, he was just a normal citizen of Xinjiang, aware of the potentially devastating penalties for speaking negatively about the situation there. But it was possible that he might feel compelled to report our conversation to the police.

I finished off my cigarette before returning to my seat.

\* \* \* \* \* \* \*

At some point overnight, we had made it out of the Taklamakan. We were in Zungharia, the historical name for the northern half of East Turkistan.

Instead of vast expanses of dry unicolor desert and mountains, I now saw rugged green steppe, dotted with agricultural fields, idyllic pastures, and grazing animals out my window. The mountains that surrounded everything were still present, but much closer, colored a mixture of granite grey and brown, with birch and pine trees running up their slopes. On the more distant mountains, multiple layers back, I could make out snow-capped peaks—an especially surreal sight considering that the last time I could see anything out the window, we were still traversing what was probably the hottest environment I'd ever been in.

---

The name Zungharia is derived from the Zunghar (also spelled Dzunghar) Khanate, which refers to "a confederation of Oirat (Mongol) tribes . . . that coalesced under Zunghar tribal leadership in the early seventeenth century in northern Xinjiang."[95] The period of Zunghar control in the northern half of the region—and, for a time, most of the southern half as well—was important for a variety of reasons. But, most important, in terms of their relevance today, were their agricultural policies. In order to develop irrigation and to maintain the land in Zungharia, and particularly in the areas around modern-day Ürümqi, the Zunghars relied heavily on the taranchis—predominantly Muslim captives taken from the Tarim Basin to the south. As historian James Millward explains, "This policy marks the beginning of the process by which Zungharia came to be inhabited by non-nomadic Muslim Turkic-speakers from the south—a group that by the twentieth century would be called the Uyghurs."[96] (Some claim that Uyghurs inhabited Zungharia prior to the relocation of the taranchis. This is an ongoing debate that I am far from qualified to engage in.)

In other words, the Uyghurs are a distinct group of people who had lived throughout East Turkistan for at least fifty years prior to when the

Qing dynasty became the first to consolidate the region under Chinese rule, when they conquered it in 1755—in the process slaughtering or enslaving every Zunghar living there, what is known as the "Zunghar genocide."

---

We pulled into Ürümqi Station around 11:30 that morning. By then, the only passenger left with whom I had begun the journey was Movie Guy, who had finally given himself a break from his taxing work to doze off for a bit. I had to gently tap him on the shoulder repeatedly to rouse him when it was time for us to get off. After he'd dragged himself out of his drowsiness, he gave me a formal, firm handshake as a show of thanks, which I thought was an unexpectedly charming way to say goodbye.

I retrieved my Osprey bag from the top compartment, and followed the other passengers off. I took my first, refreshing step off of the train in almost a full day—all the more refreshing for the bracingly cooler temperature than what I had left in Kashgar.

We headed toward a stairway just down the station platform from the train. It was flanked on both sides by a police officer in black riot gear, with full body armor and a massive assault rifle. They were more heavily armed than most of the other police officers I had seen in Xinjiang, although this didn't strike me as totally out of the ordinary at a train station.

At the bottom of the stairs, everyone emptied out into a capacious uncovered concrete enclosure, leading into a security checkpoint building on the far side. Dozens of riot police, dressed and armed in the same way as the first two, corralled us into two different groups. From what I could tell, the Han Chinese passengers and I were being directed to the left-hand line, while Uyghur and other Turkic passengers were sent to the right.

I decided to check how fast the two lines were moving relative to each other. I estimated that there were about forty people between me and the entrance to the security checkpoint. I looked over to the Uyghur line and counted back to the fortieth person—a grey-haired woman in a long yellow dress, who was about parallel with me. According to the clock on my Guangphone, it took me twenty minutes to reach the front of the line. As I entered the checkpoint building, I looked back to see that the Uyghur woman had hardly moved at all.

Inside the building, as I placed my bags on the x-ray conveyor belt, I was taken off to the side by a Uyghur policewoman in a more casual uniform. There was a small desk set up just to the left of the line, and behind it were two male Han officers.

"Passport, please," the younger of the two requested, in an ornery voice.

As the younger officer flipped through it, his comrade was munching on what looked like a pork version of the vacuum-sealed fish that had been my last three meals. Being reminded of that fact, I began to crave for a meat that I wouldn't need to unseal first.

"Why are you in Xinjiang?" He asked after a minute.

"I'm a student and a tourist."

"What are you studying?"

"Silk Road history. I wanted to come to Xinjiang because of how important it was to the Silk Road," I replied, unsure of how much of my practiced cover story I needed to deliver.

I also handed him my Genghis Khan book, just for good measure. He took one look at it and gave it back to me, along with my passport.

"Enjoy your time in Ürümqi," he commanded, as the Uyghur policewoman escorted me back to the metal detector.

After I'd walked through without issue, and picked up my bags from the conveyor belt, I looked down to the other end of the building, to the Uyghur line. Now I could see why their side was moving so much slower. Not only did they have an x-ray for their belongings, and a metal detector for their person. Each of them was also made to take an iris scan, and was physically patted down by a police officer after coming through the metal detector. Several of them appeared to have been taken off to the side to be questioned by other police officers.

I continued on toward the exit.

---

The use of the extensive security measures I saw at the Ürümqi train station may have been the least surprising of any place I visited in all of East Turkistan, given what had taken place there not too many years before. On the fourth and final day of a trip that Xi Jinping took to Xinjiang in April 2014, two Uyghur militants carried out a suicide bombing at Ürümqi Station, killing one person and injuring nearly eighty others. This followed a similar terrorist attack at another train station, just weeks earlier, in the southern Chinese city of Kunming, where Uyghur militants armed with knives killed thirty-one commuters, mostly Han Chinese. And less than a month later, after another bombing, at Ürümqi's vegetable market, President Xi decided that he had seen enough.[97]

In an accounting of secret, closed-door speeches given by Xi to top Party officials during this period, and other Party directives that followed, all gathered and reported by the New York Times,[98] it becomes clear how the "Strike Hard Campaign Against Violent Terrorism," the campaign that birthed the prison state that exists in East Turkistan today, was first conceived and took hold.

In these initial speeches, Xi directed officials in Xinjiang to unleash the tools of "dictatorship" to eradicate radical Islam in the region and to "show no mercy" doing so. He likened Islamist extremism to a virus-like contagion and a dangerously addictive drug, and proclaimed that remedying it would require "a period of painful, interventionary treatment."

In another of these secret speeches, given on a trip to southern Xinjiang, Xi told Party officials, according to the Times, "Ensuring stability in Xinjiang would require a sweeping campaign of surveillance and intelligence gathering to root out resistance in Uighur society." Specifically, he said, "There must be effective educational remolding and transformation of criminals . . . and even after these people are released, their education and transformation must continue."

Surprisingly, Xi also stated in these speeches that he did not want officials to "overreact" to natural frictions between Han Chinese and Uyghurs, and that he wanted the Uyghurs' right to worship freely to be respected. These statements are difficult to square with the rest of his totalitarian rhetoric, which bears far more resemblance to the policies that have been enacted in Xinjiang since then.

Two years later, in 2016, Xi installed Chen Quanguo as Party Secretary of Xinjiang. Chen had won a reputation as Party Secretary in Tibet (2011–2016) for the brutal security state he had constructed to quell unrest in that region. Within a few months of his arrival in Xinjiang in August 2016, Chen quickly went to work on what might fairly be described as the most brutal overreaction to terrorism in history.

The first "re-education" camps began to appear in early 2017.[99]

# Chapter 16

# Ürümqi, Day One
## —Settling In, Hongshan Park

"The central goal of China's diplomacy is to create a peaceful and stable international environment for its development."

—PRC White Paper on Peaceful Development, September 2011

When I exited the station, a horde of hopeful taxi drivers descended on me, each vying for my attention.

"Taxi!?" they called out over each other, incessantly, all seeming keen on getting the patronage of the one Western tourist in the crowd.

Still recovering from the day-long train ride, I couldn't summon the energy to bargain over the fare, so I chose the least aggressive driver, a slovenly man leaning against the front door of his cab, with an almost-comically disinterested look on his face.

I hopped in the back, handing the driver a printout of the address of the Airbnb I had reserved almost a month earlier, just before leaving Korea. This was the first time I had taken the sheet out of my bag since leaving, and I was concerned to see that it had sustained some water damage. Luckily, it appeared to still be legible to the driver, and he started his engine after giving it just a quick look.

We turned out of the station parking lot onto an elevated highway. As soon as I saw the view, I was grateful that the driver had picked this route.

The Tian Shan mountain range, with its snow-capped peaks and craggy contoured ridges, presided as an epic backdrop for the city's glistening skyscrapers, high-rise apartment buildings, and impressive number of construction cranes. It was like a miniature version of Beijing placed in the middle of a mountain fortress; an interesting contrast that I had never seen anywhere on such a dramatic scale.

Ürümqi is an undeniably beautiful city—beautiful enough, without a doubt, to live up to its Dzungar translation: "beautiful pasture." Or to the first half of that translation, at least. Despite its being among the most geographically isolated large cities in the world, Ürümqi's population is more than three and a half million according to China's 2017 census, making it more populous than any American city besides New York and Los Angeles.[100]

Every leader in the PRC's history has sought to invest in the modernization of Ürümqi, viewing the city as an essential outpost for ensuring stability throughout all of East Turkistan, as well as to present it as a selling point to convince more Han Chinese to feel comfortable enough to relocate there. Recently, however, Ürümqi has also become a critical piece of the CCP's globally ambitious development plan.

In 2017, Xi Jinping announced plans for the creation of the "Belt and Road Initiative" (BRI). The official Party line is that the BRI seeks to create a modern version of the old Silk Road trade route, stretching from Beijing across Eurasia to Western Europe on land, and to all southern Asia and Africa by sea. In the words of economic analyst Tom Miller, in his book *China's Asian Dream*, the BRI is "the diplomatic arm of China's broader quest for economic, technological, and international leadership."[101]

Xi's BRI ambitions have expanded on the proposal, first voiced by former CCP Premier Wen Jiaobao, to transform Ürümqi into "the gateway to Eurasia." The freight train network that serves as the principal component of the land portion of the BRI (or the "Silk Road Economic Belt") uses Ürümqi as its central hub, which makes the city instrumental to the larger success of the project.

The CCP has provided constant reassurances to the international community that the BRI is simply an economic initiative built around benign infrastructure and development opportunities for underdeveloped countries. However, evidence suggests that the BRI is designed to be a front for the CCP to beguile vulnerable nations into accepting one-sided development contracts, trapping them into debt and inescapable obligation by conditioning the financing on future repayments that the CCP knows they will be unable to afford. This, in turn, makes these countries more dependent on Beijing, and furthers China's ambition to supplant the U.S. as the world's leading economic and political power.

An unspoken component of the BRI is that all signatory countries must maintain silence about what China deems to be its "domestic affairs"—a euphemism for essentially anything that China chooses to do within the borders of what it proclaims is rightfully China's territory.

That includes Taiwan, Hong Kong, and the South China Sea—as well as East Turkistan. This silent agreement explains why so many countries, and most notably the majority Muslim countries, remain supine as the CCP carries out its systematic ethnic cleansing in East Turkistan. While it is safe to assume that leaders throughout the Muslim world are appalled by these policies, they recognize that the fallout from criticizing China could be catastrophic for their economies. They also know that calling out China's human rights abuses risks inviting more scrutiny into their own flawed human rights records.

As of March 2021, the number of countries officially signed on to the BRI was 140.[102]

---

The taxi driver eventually dropped me off—requesting an exorbitant number of yuan, which should not have surprised me, since we hadn't discussed the fare—on the sidewalk at a busy intersection, in front of the closed metal gate to an apartment complex. I texted my new Airbnb host, who I'll refer to as Nancy, to let her know that I had arrived.

The area was fairly gloomy. The elevated highway we had just exited ran directly overhead, shadowing the main street, as well as much of the sidewalk where I was standing. Everything was further darkened by a haze of air pollution, which carried a slight metallic taste. But just inside the gates of the apartment complex, out of reach of the highway's overcast, sunlight broke through the haze and washed over well-trimmed hedges and cleanly cut lawns that surrounded a group of light brown brick apartment buildings. I even saw a young couple enjoying a picnic on the front lawn of the building closest to me.

It wasn't long before I saw a young, slightly-built Han woman scurrying toward the gate. She wore a large purple T-shirt that reached down to cover the top half of her grey knee-length jean shorts. She had a thin, serious face, and her black hair was tied in a taut ponytail.

We waved to each other as she approached to open the gate.

"Hello, Nancy?" I asked as she let me inside.

"Yes, Grayson," she replied in a delicate voice, declaring my name instead of asking it.

I nodded in agreement, and followed her as she walked back along the main sidewalk toward the inside of the complex.

"Thank you for coming to get me. I'm excited to see the place," I said, as we passed the picnicking couple, who were in the process of gathering up their things.

"Yes. You're welcome." She glanced up at me for a split second, and then quickly back down to the ground in front of us.

We passed several buildings before arriving at hers—situated, just like Sue's had been, all the way in the back. The foyer had no reception desk, but there was an open space to the left that suggested that the builders had originally intended to install one. We walked to the back and waited for the elevator.

"Ürümqi looks so beautiful," I said in an attempt to break the silence.

The elevator doors opened and an older Han man exited swiftly.

"Uhhhh . . . English not good," Nancy replied uneasily.

She took out her phone as I moved in front of the elevator to prevent it from closing on us. When we entered, she handed me her phone with the WeChat translation app on the screen. I typed my original statement and handed it back to her once she'd pressed the button for the sixth floor.

She smiled softly when she read it and typed out a response. The elevator doors opened again as she handed her phone back to me.

"Yes. I'm happy that you think so already," it read.

I tried to smile at her in confirmation, but she didn't face me.

We walked a short distance down a white marble hallway, covered by a red and yellow carpet of distinctly Chinese design running through the center, before arriving at her door. She took out a small black keychain.

"Uhhhh," she began typing into her phone again. It took about a minute before she handed it to me.

"The key is to open this door. The dark circular one is to get in the gate. If you have trouble with them ever, you can text me and I will help you."

"Xie xie," I replied simply, intent on avoiding the WeChat app. I used the key to open the door, demonstrating to Nancy that I would be competent enough to enter the dwelling without needing her help.

The photographs that Nancy put on Airbnb were probably what the place had looked like when she first began renting it out. In those photos, the contents of the apartment had looked sparse—a single leather couch in the living room, with a coffee table in front of it, and a dinner table with some wooden chairs were all that her place appeared to be furnished with.

But the apartment I saw when I walked inside looked like something closer to the condo of an eccentric Wall Street executive, or maybe a more chic-minded Bond villain.

What jumped out as soon as I entered—surely by design—was a gargantuan fish tank built into what was at least two-thirds of the back wall of the living room. The kaleidoscopic assortment of fish inside it were captivating, and made only more so set against everything else in the room—from the tables, the chairs, the couch, the TV—all of which were either black or white or a combination of the two. The floors were a glossy white tile, so spotless that they looked slippery.

"Wow—this place is incredible!" I exclaimed.

Nancy gave me a brief, confused look. But I managed to get the basics of my message across with a thumbs up before she'd taken her phone out again. She gestured at me to follow her down the hallway, past the fish tank.

"Your bathroom," she said after opening the first door to my left. It was similarly luxurious, with a roomy standing shower with glass walls, and an electronic toilet. I nodded and smiled to show that this would certainly be acceptable.

We continued to the end of the hall and she opened the last door on the left.

"Your bed."

It was queen size, with what appeared to be silk sheets carefully folded halfway over the pillows, hotel-style. A selection of different sizes of towels, and even a bathrobe, were strategically positioned on the center of the bed, so as to optimize their impression on me.

I looked over at Nancy to tell her how impressed I was, but she was too busy furiously typing away on her phone.

"This all looks great! Thank you. Xie xie," I blurted out anyway.

She handed me her phone.

"I hope this will all be suitable for you. Thank you for choosing to stay with me. And let me know if there is anything you need," the text read.

"Yes, this is much better than suitable. Thank you so much for letting me stay in your home! I was wondering, if it wouldn't be too much trouble, if you could tell me how to get to these places." I handed her phone back as I took out my notebook, where I had made a short list of the main sites I wanted to visit.

She handed it back after just typing "????" into the text box. It wasn't the first time this app had failed to work properly.

I revised my message to read "Can you help me get to Hongshan Park, Erdaoqiao Bazaar, and [I named a particular mosque I wanted to visit]?"

She looked at her phone quizzically and tilted her head, like she was thinking about how to respond.

"I can text you the addresses and names of those places in Chinese if you'd like. Why do you want to go to that mosque? I've never heard of this place before."

I wasn't surprised by Nancy's reaction to the mosque, which I am not naming, for security reasons. Based on what I had read about Xinjiang before leaving for this trip, I expected that many of the iconic Uyghur and Islamic sites would be shells of their original selves; my time in Kashgar had proved this to be heartbreakingly accurate. Therefore, in my planning I had searched Google for a mosque that wasn't near any tourist attractions, so that I might be able to see one of the remaining unsullied landmarks of Uyghur Islam in East Turkistan. It didn't take long to find one—an architecturally pretty but otherwise typical mosque on the outskirts of Ürümqi.

"I read about it online, it's supposed to be particularly beautiful."

She still looked puzzled, but her response was reassuring.

"Okay, I will text them to you. When will you be going to these places?" She asked.

"I want to go to Hongshan Park now if I can, and Erdaoqiao Bazaar tonight. I think I'll save the mosque for tomorrow."

"Okay." She showed me her response on the phone without handing it to me, turned around, and entered the room across the hall, hurriedly closing the door behind her.

I had only just met Nancy, but it was already clear how very shy she was. I could count on a single hand the number of times we had made eye contact. My strong sense was that her reserve was not an indication of suspicion or animosity; the substance of our communications had been pleasant. And, like Sue had been, Nancy was the only Airbnb host among more than a dozen I'd contacted in Ürümqi who took no issue with my being a foreigner.

I left my Osprey bag on the floor next to my bed, holding on to my travel backpack, since I planned to be heading out as soon as Nancy texted me the directions. I chose to wait for Nancy's text in the living room instead of testing out my new sleeping quarters. Having gotten a full zero hours of sleep that night, I knew all too well that even a few minutes on that bed could be a quick route to undermining all of my ambitious plans for the day. Plus, sitting in the living room allowed me to marvel at Nancy's entrancing fish tank.

Soon enough, Nancy sent the text. I was pleasantly surprised by how much detail she gave me. She had included the full English name of each place, its distance from her apartment in kilometers, and the name of the district it was in. She sent all of this information in English, as well as the Chinese characters, and their transliteration into the English alphabet, for me to show or attempt to speak to any taxi driver. She added some of her own suggested places to the list as well, which she insisted I should "certainly visit, but only if there is time."

"This is great, Nancy!" I replied. "Thanks so much for your help. I'll definitely try to make time for the suggestions you've added. I'm getting a taxi to Hongshan Park now, and I'll be sure to text you if I have trouble with anything."

With that, I headed out to make the most of my first day in this new city.

\* \* \* \* \* \* \*

The taxi let me out at the edge of the park, at the base of a steep, forested pathway. I didn't know at the time that Hongshan means "Red Mountain" in Chinese. But I could have deduced as much upon seeing the climb that lay ahead of me.

A small ticketing building between the sidewalk and the entrance doubled as another security checkpoint. Two Uyghur police officers asked to inspect my bag and passport, and instructed me to sign in on a list attached to a clipboard on their desk. Judging by the only two other signers, it was a list specifically for foreign visitors. The first was a man from Poland; the second, a man from Pakistan.

It was interesting how visiting East Turkistan seemed to be popular with Pakistanis, thinking back to the oil man I had met while enjoying my lamb's-head soup at the Night Market in Kashgar. I was even more interested in the Polish man—the prospect that I might encounter the first Westerner in the region other than myself.

The officer handed back my passport and bag, and after I paid him the park entrance fee, I was on my way.

The cool mountain climate was especially palpable as I began my upward trek. It still felt like summer, of course. But even before I had entered the shade of the trees, it was evident how much less taxing it would be to walk around here compared to doing so in the sweltering heat of Kashgar.

I was soon disappointed to discover that this park was designed primarily for taking my money rather than for showcasing its natural beauty.

I had come to a row of carnival games, the first of many that lined the path at various intervals all the way up the mountain as far as I could see. The first game had a long line of maybe a dozen Han Chinese people, mostly couples, stretching back to almost block the entire width of the path. The game they were waiting to play was the classic ring-toss seen at county fairs in the U.S., in which the player pays too much money for the chance to throw a barely-large-enough ring around the top of a soda bottle. In the unlikely event that he succeeds, he has impressed his date by demonstrating that he is really good at throwing small rings over empty bottles, and he gets to allow her to choose a prize. I stopped for just a moment to watch the guy at the front of the line come up short, before he was pulled away by his date as he tried to talk her into letting him have another go.

I eventually came across a game that I couldn't resist trying—a miniature basketball shooting game. It had only a few people waiting, and it wasn't obviously rigged—no slightly-pressed-to-oval hoop. Having a modestly successful background in basketball, and not being shy about showing off, I decided to give it a go.

I made two out of the three attempts. (The third one was the wind, obviously . . . ) The few others waiting in line cheered, and the guy behind me congratulated me with an unnecessarily firm slap on the back.

For my prize, I had my pick between a sizable stuffed cow and a real rose. Having no desire to lug around a stuffed animal, and thinking it would look bad if I refused to accept a prize, I chose the rose. The young game operator's face lit up in amusement when he handed it to me. I placed it carefully inside my bag, and continued up the hill.

The crowds seemed to get thicker around the carnival games the farther uphill I went. I sometimes had to move sideways through them, something I never once had to do in Kashgar. It was disheartening to think that I might be the only person who actually wanted to appreciate the park for its natural qualities.

Eventually the covering of trees and the carnival games abated, giving way to a stunning hundred-foot pagoda—bright red, with green and blue shingles layering the top of each of its three layers of roof. It was guarded by a stone wall colored in the same scheme as the pagoda, with flowers planted along the bottom.

The main attraction was the view from beyond the pagoda—a rock jutting out behind it where tourists were ascending to a scenic overlook, marked by a red obelisk. This appeared to be the actual "top" of the mountain. Predictably, it would only be accessible if I paid an additional park fee. But off to the side was a separate (and free) overlook, where I still got a sufficiently picturesque view of the city. It was the best view of the city that I had seen thus far—although it paled in comparison to the view of the Tian Shan through my taxi window that morning.

I didn't stay very long before turning to head back down, deciding that my time would be much better spent at the bazaar.

As I neared the path down the hill, I was approached by an attractive Han woman, maybe a couple of years my elder, wearing a tan pressed pantsuit and holding a microphone, a cameraman trailing behind her.

"Hello! Pardon me," she declared, her voice brimming with professional confidence. "Would you be okay with doing an interview?"

Ideally, I wouldn't have chosen to participate in a Chinese state television segment that would surely end up being about how wonderful and safe tourists say Xinjiang is. I could already picture its chyron: "Americans love the authentic cultural charm of China's Ürümqi." But I didn't feel comfortable declining, thinking that it might come off as having something to hide.

"Yeah, okay."

"Great!"

The woman said a few words to her cameraman in Mandarin, upon which he began counting down from three with his fingers.

"Hello!" The woman said vigorously in the direction of the camera. "We are here in Hongshan Park, on a busy summer day. We've found one of the many tourists here visiting the park, and he has agreed to speak with us."

Her emphasis on the word "many," as if I would be a spokesman for every foreign tourist who had come to the park that day, made me even less enthusiastic about where this might be headed.

"So how do you like the park?"

"I love it. The view from over there is beautiful," I replied, pointing in the direction of the overlook.

"Yes, absolutely. Where else have you been to in Ürümqi on your visit?"

"This is the first place, actually. I just arrived here this morning." I thought it best not to get into where I'd just come from, since I wanted this interview to be as quick as possible.

"Ohhhh, nice! You should visit the Xinjiang museum next! That will give you more interesting information on the history of Xinjiang."

"Yeah, I'd love to learn more about the history," I replied, pretending to be convinced that a museum recommended to me on state television would give me a truthful understanding of regional history.

"So what did you like most about the park?"

This question gave me an idea—and, for a change, one that I couldn't imagine would put me in any danger.

"I liked the view a lot, but my favorite part was winning this basketball game earlier," I said as I took out the partially crushed rose from my backpack. "This was the prize I got for winning. Would it be okay if I give it to you?"

I thought this would be a fun way to dispose of this rose that I had no need for. And I hoped that she would find it amusing, at least.

She accepted it, and giggled just a bit. But it trailed off quickly, into almost a sigh. She didn't seem very happy with the gesture. Perhaps, by making it while the camera was rolling, I had taken her off her professional stride—a factor that I'll admit had not occurred to me.

"Ohhhh thank you!" She had gathered herself back into her giddy on-camera persona.

"You're welcome." I managed to squeak out.

"I hope you enjoy the rest of Ürümqi. Thank you for speaking with us!" She said cheerfully, waving goodbye and cutting the interview off.

"No problem. Thank you."

She turned away and strode off with her cameraman, in search of another of the "many" tourists in the park.

*At least she never got to ask me about how "safe" I felt in Xinjiang*, I said to myself as I walked back down the hill.

Chapter 17

# Ürümqi, Day One
## —Erdaoqiao Bazaar and M-Plex

"Political power grows out of the barrel of a gun."

—Mao Zedong

A heavy rain began to fall during my taxi ride to Erdaoqiao Bazaar. We were trapped in standstill traffic on one of the old roadways that run beneath the modern elevated highway, very much like the street outside Nancy's apartment. Beyond the protection of the highway overhead, pedestrians on the sidewalk darted to wherever they might find shelter from the downpour. Among them was a Han man in a business suit pulling a rolling travel bag, trying frantically to reach some nearby refuge, while having to stabilize his luggage from rolling over with every few steps he took.

We reached an intersection where I noticed an enormous electronic billboard on a nearby building.

I had seen this type of electronic billboard twice before, in Kashgar. Like those, it displayed an image of Xi at a construction site with a majority-Turkic workforce smiling behind him. The specific image was different, though. It appeared to have been taken in or around Ürümqi, based on the mountain peaks in the background. Instead of Xi pretending to give the foreman advice on the construction blueprint, he had advanced to pretending to identify a flaw in one of the structures that had already been built. He was pointing up at it, with a stern, paternalistic expression, like he was generous enough to correct the supposed error, yet irritated that it had been made in the first place; the foreman standing beside him was looking up as well, appearing to value Xi's insight.

The billboard transformed into a different picture, this one of Xi standing behind a dark mahogany podium, displaying his characteristically reserved, soft smile, against the backdrop of a large PRC insignia. He appeared to be giving a speech at an assembly of Party officials.

Then it morphed again, into a picture of Xi crouching in front of a crowd of joyful uniformed Turkic children, at what was surely one of the "boarding schools" or "orphanages."

I pondered what the reasoning might be behind this selection of images, and why they were arranged in that particular order. Was the choice to insert the photograph of Xi speaking at an official Party event between the two other photos meant to emphasize his, and the CCP's, love and respect for ethnic minorities? Was it meant to convey that Xi was exalted and powerful, and a true Party man, but simultaneously a relatable man with working class roots?[103] Or maybe it was simply another reminder to Ürümqi's Uyghurs of the unbridled power that Xi holds over them?

After being stuck in that same line of traffic for an hour, we finally turned off onto a less congested street, the driver letting me out shortly thereafter.

The sidewalk was bustling with consumers, flooding in and out of the generic streetwear clothing stores that lined this block of the street, their inventory of knock-offs resembling those I saw at the bazaar in Kashgar. At the end of the line of stores stood a giant sand-colored minaret, overlooking a clearing and a cluster of similarly colored stone buildings.

Just behind the minaret was a building with four smaller minarets at its corners, each adorned with three white balconies encircling it at different heights, and a green dome at its center—and a green wooden sign in front of it, reading "Erdaoqiao Mosque." To the left of the sign, I found the entrance to the Erdaoqiao Bazaar.

In order to gain entry to the bazaar, I waited in the usual security line, where my bag was inspected, my passport was examined, and I was questioned about my reasons for being in Xinjiang by police officers who looked greatly over-equipped for their post. This security line had a novel feature: a massive armored police vehicle guarding the entrance. I'd seen others like this in Kashgar, parked at police stations or out on the street. Judging by the accumulated dust around its wheels, this one had been sitting there stationary for some time. It was another example of how integral the display of control in East Turkistan is to the CCP, not just the reality of it.

---

Erdaoqiao Bazaar featured prominently in an event in July 2009 that damaged Han-Uyghur relations profoundly, planting seeds that influenced Xi's more recent genocidal escalation. (The summary that follows is based on a more detailed account presented by Nick Holdstock in his book, *China's Forgotten People*.[104])

The 2009 event began with an unsubstantiated rumor circulated online by a former worker at a toy factory in Guangdong Province, nearly 2,000 miles away from Ürümqi. In the online post, the former worker claimed that six male Uyghur workers at the factory—who had arrived there from Kashgar the previous month—had raped two female Han Chinese coworkers. Although no such crimes were ever officially reported, these accusations spurred a mob of Han workers into seeking revenge, and invading the factory dormitory where the Uyghur workers were lodged. The official account claimed that two Uyghurs were killed and more than a hundred people injured, but judging by graphic videos taken by some of the Han mob members, these numbers appear to be significant undercounts.

After a week went by with no statement from the government that the killers were being held accountable (officials claimed that one of the "rumor mongers" had been detained, but there was no further word), Uyghur internet message boards blazed with outrage at the inaction. A call went out for a massive demonstration in People's Square in Ürümqi on July 5th.

The demonstration began peacefully, with many of the marchers carrying Chinese flags to preempt any attempt by the CCP to paint them as separatists or Islamists. When the demonstrators attempted to march into majority-Han neighborhoods, they were met by a blockade of police and People's Liberation Army (PLA) soldiers, who used aggressive force to push them back—making arrests, using tear gas and warning shots, and by many accounts, beatings and shootings as well. At some point during this stage of the altercation (it's unclear exactly when, according to Holdstock), the demonstrators began throwing stones at the soldiers and police officers.

It was after the protestors had been pushed back farther into the Erdaoqiao district, where there was little police presence, that things got completely out of control, and the killings indisputably began. As noted, many accounts claim that the bloodshed had begun earlier, by police and PLA as they repelled the crowd away from the Han neighborhoods. But other accounts, most prominently the official CCP narrative, claim that the protestors had been first to attack—police officers and PLA soldiers, as well as Han citizens. Either way, what followed, and continued throughout the night, was widespread destruction of property, and many deaths and injuries. The Uyghur protesters indiscriminately targeted Han Chinese, even setting up roadblocks where they forced Han Chinese drivers from their vehicles to violently attack them. The violence and destruction is documented in numerous publicly available video clips,[105] widely disseminated by Chinese state media. Holdstock notes that, "The whereabouts and actions of the police and army during this period remain unclear, though many residents reported hearing gunfire during the night."

The CCP ultimately declared the official number of casualties to be 197. This number, however, does not include any of the deaths at the hands of police during that night, or the countless "forced disappearances" of Uyghurs over the following weeks—none of which were ever acknowledged. The official reports also make no mention of the organized Han crowds that marched through Uyghur neighborhoods with weapons two days later, seeking "revenge," or the video evidence of PLA soldiers, who were supposed to be keeping the peace, instead colluding with the Han vigilantes.

Perhaps most tellingly, the CCP acknowledged none of the grievances that had motivated the initially peaceful protest, claiming instead that the bloodshed had been "instigated and directed from abroad, and carried out by outlaws in the country." This is the same deflectionary tactic regularly employed by the CCP in response to any evidence of civil dissatisfaction with the system. It was used to deflect investigation of the crackdown against pro-democracy Umbrella Protests in Hong Kong, and even the Tiananmen Square massacre in 1989, for which the CCP blamed the American CIA.[106] The Ürümqi incident was similarly and conveniently blamed, without evidence, on the largest Uyghur diaspora organization, the World Uyghur Congress, and their then-leader Rebiya Kadeer. The Party Secretary of Xinjiang at the time, Wang Lequan, claimed that the event revealed "the violent and separatist nature of the World Uyghur Congress."

Tragically, but predictably, the CCP mis-characterized this at-first entirely peaceful expression of Uyghur discontent as pre-meditated, calculated violent extremism.

For many Uyghurs, as well as for Han Chinese and CCP officials, the 2009 incident in Ürümqi and its immediate aftermath snuffed out all hope for improved ethnic relations in East Turkistan. Along with earlier examples of peaceful Uyghur demonstrations being violently suppressed in the towns of Baren and Yining (known as the "Ghulja massacre" to Uyghurs), it proved to many Uyghurs that they would never be granted a fair hearing by the CCP to voice their legitimate grievances. The CCP took it as a sign that the relatively tolerant religious and cultural policies of the 1990s would need to be hardened. Though, in earnest, it also likely revealed to many Party officials that the long legacy of CCP and Chinese dynastic mistreatment of the Turkic peoples in East Turkistan had ingrained in them a deep antipathy toward the Chinese that was easier to forcefully quash than to try to remedy.

The first area of the bazaar contained mostly Ürümqi-specific souvenir shops. There were T-shirt and hat stands selling casual apparel featuring the iconic "I [heart] _____ " design; some shops specializing in trinkets with depictions of popular Ürümqi tourist destinations, including Hongshan Park and its multicolored hilltop pagoda; and others that sold various spices and clothing items native to the region. One of the stands, run by a bubbly, rotund Han woman, sold packages of black tea leaves that allegedly could be found only in the foothills of the Tian Shan. The free samples I accepted were satisfyingly strong and earthy enough that I felt compelled to purchase a small pack to take home.

As I continued on, the variety of the types of shops grew a bit, but not much. They sold basically the same contrived cultural items that had been ubiquitous in Kashgar's New Old City; and all of it apparently being sold by Han Chinese shop-owners. The light posts on either side of the path were strung with PRC flags, as miniature hand-held versions were being hawked by street vendors just below them.

Admittedly, I should have expected to find that this kind of culturally bereft tourist-focused commercialism had also overtaken Erdaoqiao. But part of me had wanted to believe (being ignorant to most of the history at that time) that the cultural destruction I had witnessed in Kashgar would not be so pronounced this far north, where the Han population is much larger in relation to Uyghurs, and displays of Uyghur culture might be more accepted, and not viewed as potentially threatening to Han-centrism.

I later found out that this wasn't the real Erdaoqiao Bazaar. As with so many other places I visited, the real one had been demolished, in 2002, replaced by this supposedly more tourist-friendly "International Grand Bazaar."

I drifted along the main avenue awhile, until I spotted an entrance to a covered area of the bazaar, inside a brown brick building behind a couple of the mobile street-side shops to my right. I sprang toward it, eager for the possibility that it might hold some variation.

It was much more diverse—both in the items being sold and in the ethnicities of the shopkeepers. At least three-quarters of the owners were Turkic. And although there were still stalls selling the same tourist-targeted souvenirs, as well as some trafficking in suspect electronics and cheap wristwatches, most of the items in this section I hadn't seen before. A rainbow of fragrant spices and herbs greeted me at the stall beside the entrance; another stall a bit farther down was filled with a selection of high-quality leather coats; another had stacks of what looked like used Uyghur and Kazakh cookbooks; and one had several walls covered in textiles, with a diverse array of colors and designs from paisley to polka-dot.

The most interesting stall I spotted, after browsing for some time, was near the opposite entrance.

A young Uyghur man was selling beautiful ornate blades, ranging from pocket knives to machetes. Each was decorated with a unique pattern and design on the handle, as well as its own inscription on the blade. Some of the handles bore intricate artwork that depicted people, some of them with animals; others were less detailed, with only entrancing geometric patterns imprinted atop a golden-handled base.

I had no intention to purchase one of these blades—I shudder to imagine the reaction of a police officer at the next security checkpoint reaching into my bag to find a fancy meat cleaver. But I thought it would be interesting to view them up close.

"Can I look at these?" I asked the man as I approached the stand.

He stared blankly at me, still seated on his stool.

"Okay to look at your knives?" I repeated, pointing to the display case.

Nothing.

"How much?" I rephrased, thinking he might be more familiar with this question.

He remained expressionless—not hostile in any way, just apparently uninterested. He shook his head slowly at me, returning his attention to a game on his phone that I had interrupted.

"Are they not for sale?"

He looked up again, now visibly annoyed.

"No." he stated firmly.

"Then why are they here?" I persisted, taking unreasonable offense at his terse reply.

He looked down the aisle of shops in each direction, then back at me.

He rose from his stool and stepped over to the closest point to me behind the display case.

"No," he said again, this time in a softer, more diplomatic tone. His eyes were bright, and serious, silently conveying an unmistakable anxiousness.

I was ashamed that it took so long for me to understand. Why would he risk selling a lethal item to a foreign stranger when such major consequences could befall him for doing so? For all he knew, I could even be part of a baiting trap by the CCP, to trip up Uyghur salespeople into committing a transgression that would justify their being imprisoned.

"Xie xie," I replied, nodding my head at the man to clarify that his message had been received, before exiting the enclosed area through the opposite side.

The section of the bazaar that I emerged into was just more of the usual—entirely Han-owned shops selling folksy souvenir items to exclusively Han tourists. This division between the outside and the inside areas of the bazaar was striking, and it made me wonder whether the Han storekeepers were being given the more favorable, accessible locations, while the Uyghurs were relegated to places that were less visible and harder to reach.

I wandered around for a while longer, and soon happened upon a sort of pop-up food court, which appeared to just be opening up. I checked the time on my Guangphone, and I was surprised to see that it was already almost six. I had been hoping to come across some local cuisine options—I'd skipped breakfast, and had eaten only a couple of quick kabobs I grabbed on my way back down the hill at Hongshang Park. But all I had seen here until now was a large, out-of-place KFC sign plastered to the side of one of the buildings abutting the bazaar.

The setup here was much like the Night Market in Kashgar, but spread over a larger area. And every food stall helpfully provided English translations on its signs. Some of the stalls were still in the process of being erected, but the place was already buzzing with patrons.

There were plenty of enticing dishes to choose from. The longest line by far was in front of a stall offering platters of neatly sliced Peking duck, the crispy brown skin glistening with oil. At the stall beside it, an older Han man was selling bowls of fresh-made steamed dumplings in soup. Nearby, I spotted another tempting offering of lamb's head stew; by the looks of it, just the meat this time. In lieu of these options, I decided on the sparsely patronized stall farther down, to try a serving from the mountain of polo overflowing from a giant steel drum.

Polo is a Uyghur rice pilaf dish, traditionally served with mutton as the protein, and mixed with diced onions and carrots, as well as a crucial pinch of cumin (or a few pinches, depending on the cook). It was the aroma of cumin that had fortuitously led me to this stall, under the mistaken impression that it was coming from cumin-seasoned kabobs that had by then become my staple food.

I had wanted to try this legendary Uyghur dish at an authentic Uyghur restaurant. But by that point I had come to terms with the fact that it might be impossible for me to find a restaurant that met all my uncompromising notions of authenticity. This food stall looked like it would be close enough, and might be my best opportunity to try it.

I ordered a hearty bowl of polo with a large Wusu beer, and found one of the few open spots, at the end of one of the long wooden picnic tables spread within the circle of food stalls. Immediately after the obligatory *ni-haos* I gave to all the diners nearby, I was greeted by the group I'd sat down next to.

"Hello! What is your name?" the Han guy next to me asked, smiling through tobacco-stained teeth.

"Grayson. What's yours?" I replied, after taking a few seconds to finish chewing the mutton chunk in my first rich bite of Polo.

"Zhang" he replied, as he shook my hand. "These are my coworkers, Chen and Fang."

He pointed to a Han man and woman sitting across from him, who waved at me, their facial features so similar that I assumed they were probably siblings.

"Nice to meet you!" I announced, raising my beer bottle slightly toward the two of them, which they reciprocated. "What kind of work are you guys in?"

"Business," Zhang answered nondescriptly. "Are you a businessman?"

"No. I'm still a college student." Zhang translated this to his coworkers.

"Oh really?!" Zhang exclaimed. "Do you go to university in Xinjiang?"

"No, I'm just visiting here. I go to college in America."

The siblings' faces lit up when they heard the word "America." Chen excitedly said something to Zhang—seeming like he wanted Zhang to ask me a question.

"He wants to know where in America you are from," Zhang conveyed in a much more measured tone.

"Oh, I'm from Colorado."

Upon hearing Zhang's translation, Chen's face shifted to a look of confusion. Maybe not knowing where Colorado was, he was disappointed that I hadn't said somewhere more notable, like New York or Los Angeles.

"Did you come to Xinjiang by yourself?" Zhang asked.

Interestingly, this was the first time anyone had asked me if I was traveling alone, instead of asking me the question I was now used to, why was I in Xinjiang.

"Yeah, I did."

He translated to Chen and Fang, who each let out "ooooos" in response.

"You are very brave." Zhang replied, taking a swig of his own Wusu beer.

"I'm not brave!" I countered, chuckling. "Why would I need to be brave to come here?"

"You're right, Xinjiang is really safe," he said with a grin, translating this for Chen and Fang, who nodded their heads in agreement. "It's now the safest region in China."

These declarations were becoming so predictable as to be boring. Xinjiang is the best; there aren't any terrorists here anymore; don't you love the dancing Uyghurs?

I wolfed down my Polo as quickly as I could without appearing to be in a hurry, and I got up to finish off the last of my Wusu.

"It was nice to meet you all," I announced, smiling at the three of them.

"It was nice to meet you too, Grayson. I hope you have a good time in Xinjiang," Zhang said.

I left the food court and headed down the bazaar pathway toward the main street, in search of a taxi. I hoped that maybe one of the places Nancy had recommended to me would be more enjoyable, and offer more interesting company. A second dinner wouldn't be so bad, either.

\* \* \* \* \* \* \*

"M-Plex" didn't sound very Uyghur to me. It didn't even sound Chinese. But that was the place that Nancy had recommended in her text. She described it as having "the widest selection of foods and shops in all of Ürümqi," and that was all I really needed to know.

When my taxi dropped me off, her recommendation revealed itself to be a paragon of the failures of digital communication. M-Plex, as it turned out, was a huge Western-style shopping mall. (I later discovered that this place is literally called "United States Shopping Mall." Where Nancy got the name "M-Plex" from remains a mystery to me.) But judging by its sheer size, I had no doubt that it did, in fact, contain the greatest number of foods and shops in the whole city.

Apparently, Nancy had pegged me to be the type of cloistered Westerner who would choose to travel to Ürümqi, the most remote large city in the world, on the opposite side of the world from the United States, only to eat and shop exactly as I would back at home. It was more amusing than anything else, not least because her intention was to make me feel more comfortable.

I had the lowest of expectations. But since I had already taken the taxi ride to get there, I decided I might as well see what it had to offer.

The first part of the inside was precisely what I had anticipated—rows of designer-brand stores on either side of white marble-tiled floors. Dividing the two store-filled aisles was a small garden sprouting with ferns and flowers. Above me were four or five additional floors of shops, all contained beneath a giant sunroof that provided a healthy amount of natural light.

Lots of the stores were popular Western brands: Adidas, Calvin Klein, Apple, Puma, and numerous others, many that I now know utilize Uyghur slave labor in their production lines.

One that still features vividly in my memory was a sleek Nike store, prominently displaying a large black and white photograph of Lebron James, at the zenith of his rising up for a tomahawk slam dunk, with the word "WITNESS" inscribed above his head in bold white text, and the Nike swoosh underneath it. Looking back on it now, I sometimes imagine what one of the Uyghurs who was forced to assemble countless of Lebron's most recently designed shoes would think if they saw this picture—should they ever be released from the prison-factory where they assembled these shoes. Would they think of Lebron as someone who is "educated" on China's record on human rights?[107] Would he strike them as someone who is unwavering in his support for social justice? What if they wandered inside the store and recognized one of the kinds of shoes they had assembled themselves, bearing a price tag they'll never be able to afford? Would they be proud to see the fruits of their labor valued at such a high price? Or would it make them feel angry, and disdainful of those who turn a blind eye, who seek not only to profit from the Uyghurs' hopeless situation, but to do so in part by selling their products back to the wealthy, well-connected families in Ürümqi who are directly involved in the system that is slowly eliminating Uyghurs as a people? This might be the sort of thing that Nike's executives and signed athletes should think about more often in regard to their relationship with Xinjiang and the CCP.

Soon after passing by the P.F. Chang's, I turned through a set of automatic doors to be confronted by a giant sign that read "Ürümqi

World of Beer Festival this way," with an arrow pointing down a smaller hallway. *Maybe Nancy's recommendation wasn't so bad after all.*

At the end of the hallway, I arrived at another set of doors that led out into an expansive concrete atrium. It had been repurposed into a food court, laid out in the same way as the pop-up food court in Erdaoqiao, with seating arranged within the center space, and the food and drink stalls lining the perimeter. But this place had something completely unexpected: a boxing ring in its very center.

The ring was empty. But the possibility that this night might contain a live boxing match, along with another dinner, and several internationally acclaimed beers to go with it, was enough to revive my previously dampened spirits.

I wanted to take my time choosing what to drink—as is customary at beer festivals—so it made good sense to just order six kabobs from the first food stall I came to. After placing my order, I was given a numbered card to put at my table, and was informed that someone would bring my food out to me.

The beer selections turned out to be less impressive than I had expected. It seemed that the "World" in the World of Beer Festival actually meant "American," as every one of the admittedly wide variety of "exotic foreign beers" was an American brew that I could get back home for a fraction of the rapacious price it was on offer for here. To make matters even more disappointing, the line to buy one of these twenty-five-dollar bottles was at least that many people long. I retreated back to the kabob stall, where I sought the warm embrace of Wusu.

I found the closest table I could to the ring, hoping to get the best view of the fight once it began. Meanwhile, I was a bit at a loss for how to entertain myself. I felt a strange sensation come over me: boredom. It was one of the only times during my trip when I had nothing to do. I'd finished my book—which had previously been my antidote in similar situations. There wasn't any scenery to admire. I had nobody to talk to. I had my journal in my daypack, but this was too conspicuous a place to take it out; and sitting by myself making diary entries wasn't the sort of red-blooded debauchery I'd come to the Ürümqi World of Beer Festival to partake in.

After about fifteen minutes, a party of elegantly dressed Han Chinese couples, around my age, sat down at a table two down from me. The women were wearing silk dresses with diamond and pearl necklaces; the men, designer suits. None of them seemed aware of how overdressed they were for a boxing and beer event; or they didn't care. As they were settling in, one of the members of the party, a stocky, good-looking guy, who had just finished smoothing out his expensive-looking hairdo, waved to me to come join them. He must have noticed that I was sitting by myself.

"Hey, man!" the guy nearly shouted to me when I was just feet away. He grabbed a chair for me from the next table. "What are you doing sitting over there alone?!"

"Um, because I came here by myself," I replied, unsure what sort of answer he might be expecting. "I'm an American student traveling for my summer break."

"That's crazy, man!" he declared, loudly again, running his spread palm across the front of his coiffure, in an exaggerated expression of shock. "Where in America are you from?"

"Are you from California?!" he asked, before I could answer.

"No, I'm from Colorado."

"You've seen California before though, right?!"

I had noticed that the others at his table were looking toward me. In particular, the stunningly beautiful woman sitting across from the guy I was chatting with, who I supposed was his date, appeared to be waiting for him to introduce me—or for him to be done with me and get back to their group. It was unclear whether he noticed.

"Uh, some of it, yeah," I replied.

"Like Los Angeles, of course!"

"No, actually I've just been to northern California. Like around San Francisco."

"Oh. How are the chicks there? Still hot like L.A.?" he inquired, loudly enough for it to have been impossible for his date to miss, if she spoke English. Nobody else in his posse seemed to pay any mind to his boisterous macho performance. Evidently this was just a typical night out with him.

"Oh yeah, definitely, man." I replied, trying to humor him before changing the subject. "So when is this fight happening?"

"Who fight? Us?"

I pointed over to the boxing ring that he somehow hadn't noticed. "Yeah, you and me. When are we getting in the ring?" I was assuming he would catch that I was kidding. But I smiled after a second just to make sure, and this led him to it.

"Ha-ha-ha, oh yeah. Let's not fight, man."

Considering he was at least twice my size, I readily accepted his decision.

"You need more to drink!" he informed me as he called over a server, despite my nearly full Wusu that I had just opened. But I didn't want to object to his generous offer. Thankfully, my plate of kabobs arrived just then, so I'd have some substance to balance the beers out with.

He seemed to be getting more relaxed—and not so loud. I was unsure whether this was because he was becoming more comfortable with me, or if perhaps he had been on some kind of uppers earlier.

When the next round of beers arrived, it came with a colorful plate of what appeared from a distance to be jello shots. When they got closer, I couldn't pretend to guess what they were.

"I got us fermented duck eggs to share," he said as he put the plate between us.

How thoughtful.

"I've never had fermented duck eggs before. What do they taste like?"

"You will see," he replied, ominously.

The eggs looked utterly inedible: cut into halves, like deviled eggs, but each colored with different green, blue, and yellow hues, and all with the same repulsive gelatinous texture. Their scent reminded me of ammonia, but somehow worse. When I picked one up, feeling its slimy exterior on my fingertips, it made me even less enthusiastic, as did my new friend's unrestrained look of sadistic anticipation. But I was a good sport, having tried similarly repulsive foods in my life and survived. I took the plunge and ate it in a single bite.

I was barely able to choke the thing down without hurling it back out. But it wasn't the taste that did this, to my surprise. In fact, it didn't taste so different from a typical hard-boiled egg. My struggles were with the combination of its texture and its malodorous scent; and eating it all at once couldn't have helped much either. I quickly went for a gulp of Wusu to wash it down.

Unsurprisingly, my drinking partner thought this to be hilarious, announcing to the rest of his group—for the first time speaking in Mandarin—what I had said and done, to which they all burst out laughing.

"Ha-ha, do you not like it, man?"

"It's not my favorite," I admitted, still fighting to quell my angry stomach. "Thanks for letting me try one, though."

He popped two in his mouth at once, swallowing them both without even a hint of distaste. "No problem! That means I get more now."

He was beginning to grow on me. His coarseness took some getting used to at first. But he seemed to embody precisely the sort of unvarnished authenticity that was so lacking in most of my previous conversations in Xinjiang.

We continued our carousing for another hour or so—mostly swapping stories of our wildest nights out, which he possessed far more of than I did—until I remembered what I was planning for the next day. I looked at my Guangphone to see that it was getting close to ten o'clock.

I needed to get back to Nancy's.

"I've got to wake up early tomorrow, man," I said as I slowly stood up, noticing then the cumulative effect of the many beers I'd consumed. "Thanks for inviting me to join you all."

"Of course, man! It was nice to meet you," he chirped as I stepped back from the table, waving to all of the rest of his group, with whom I had had barely any interaction. "You must promise me you'll try the eggs again sometime!"

"Maybe once more, 'cuz the ones you got me this time were so good," I joked, waving to him for a final time as I stumbled away toward the mall exit, to hail a taxi back to Nancy's place.

I never learned his name, but my conversation with that guy might have been the best I had throughout my entire journey. It was an unexpected, refreshing reminder of the sort of friendly drunken engagements I would have at a typical bar back home—or anywhere outside of a totalitarian police state.

Had I known what would be in store for me the following day, I might have chosen to stay a little longer.

# Chapter 18
# Ürümqi, Day Two
## —The Mosque

"Among all the conservative nations on the globe there is probably not a single one which has been kept intact. . . . It will not be long until we become Turks and Negroes."

—Kang Youwei, Chinese Philosopher and Politician (1858–1927)

I woke up early, just as the first rays of morning sunlight infiltrated my room. The exquisite bed in my Airbnb was every bit as comfortable as I had anticipated. Paired with the fully-immersive experience I'd had at the beer festival the night before, it made for the sort of morning where I might prefer to sleep in. What was on my itinerary, though, rendered me near-sleepless.

Today I would visit the mosque.

I left the apartment at around 10:30, daypack in hand, and went outside to hail a taxi. It was a beautiful day. Scattered clouds lingered from the rain the day before, but the radiance of the sunlight overpowered them, leaving me confident enough to travel without my jacket. I figured that I would have to take it off inside the mosque anyway.

I walked to the main road and stuck out my hand. Within thirty seconds I flagged down a cab. Getting in, I showed the driver the name of the mosque in Chinese characters, which Nancy had been so helpful in providing. The driver laughed and asked me a question in Mandarin—probably something along the lines of "are you crazy?"—in that I was asking him to take me to the outskirts of town, where there was nothing for a tourist to see. I offered to pay him double what I knew to be a reasonable fare for the trip, expecting that he'd almost certainly be coming all the way back by himself. He agreed, still chuckling to himself as we started down the road.

As we drove along the highway, my focus was fixed on the gradually declining number of buildings I saw out the window. I was well aware that every mile between me and the city's plausible tourist attractions would add significantly to my conspicuousness.

After a while, we exited the highway. The mosque soon came into view, and the taxi driver pulled up in front of it to let me out. As I paid him, he still made no effort to hide his amusement at my chosen tourist destination. He grinned at me and sped off back in the direction of the highway.

The mosque was the lone structure on its side of the road, with a basalt ridge that loomed behind it like a natural wall. It was surrounded by a black iron fence topped with razor wire and a pair of white security cameras. The center of the front-facing side of the fence doubled as a gate, which served as the entrance to the mosque. Posted on the fence, just to the left of the entrance, were various propaganda posters. One was a cartoon image of men laboring in a field, supposedly to laud the virtue of hard work. Another included photographs of Uyghurs and Han Chinese laughing together, depicting a harmonious relationship between the two ethnic groups.

Inside and to the right of the gate, almost as high as the top of the mosque, was a PRC flag, drooping down flaccidly around its pole in the still air. On the left side of the gate was a small, unmanned ticket booth with several notices written in Chinese posted on its front window.

Directly across the street from the mosque were a couple of vacant office buildings, their windows and doors boarded up, and small piles of concrete debris stacked beside their tattered front steps. On one side of the vacant buildings was a grocery store, which was connected to some drab grey high-rise apartment buildings. On the other side, there was a police station.

As I stood alone in front of that mosque, I knew I was looking at the real, unmasked version of Xinjiang. The version that the Chinese Communist Party has tried so determinedly to hide from the world.

The gate was locked and I saw no one inside. So I walked around the side in search of another entrance that might be accessible.

I soon heard a familiar "pat-pat" sound: someone was dribbling a ball on pavement. I turned the corner and saw a partially constructed basketball court and three men shooting hoops, presumably workers on their break. I hadn't played on a non-carnival basket for weeks now—a lengthy hiatus by my standards—so I walked over to see if I could join in.

One of the men spotted me as I approached—his jaw dropped. The others turned quickly to see what had diverted his attention from their game.

I might as well have had little green antennae coming out of my head the way he and his friends were gawking at me. Of course, I understood why—I had yet to see another Westerner in East Turkistan, even in the city tourist centers, and here I was, farther away from a city than I had been at any other time during my visit. I didn't think it was out of the question that I may have been the first Westerner that any of them had ever encountered in their lives.

Two of the men were clearly Uyghur. The third appeared to be Han, but it wasn't easy to determine due to his dark complexion. His white shirt was much cleaner than the stained white shirts worn by the two Uyghur men, indicating to me that he was their supervisor. The Han-looking man's initially gobsmacked expression changed to a smile as he passed me the ball. It took a moment to sink in, that I really was being invited to shoot hoops on a court behind the first mosque I'd ever seen surrounded by razor wire. Then I dropped my pack and dribbled over to the basket.

I'm happy to report that I was feeling it that day, and all of my first shots went in. I noticed that the others had stopped playing and had taken out their phones to film me. I pretended like I didn't notice.

"Step back three!" yelled the supervisor in passable English. I turned back and grinned, full of myself for having impressed them. After allowing their filming session to go on for a few minutes, I invited them to join me in shooting.

We played together for a while before they stopped to ask for a picture with me. I posed for several, and asked for one myself, thinking that this was too cool a moment to pass up. Then I pointed to the supervisor's phone and made a typing gesture, trying to ask him to use his translation app.

I asked him if I could go inside the mosque to look around. He respectfully declined, informing me that it was only open during prayer hours—from four to six. *What a peculiar schedule,* I thought to myself, knowing that most Muslims pray five times a day. But it also occurred to me how little the posted "prayer hours" would matter in actuality, since any Uyghur who sets foot inside a mosque runs the risk of being sent to an internment camp. I thanked the men for the game and said goodbye.

It was a little before noon, and it wouldn't be worth it to wait around the mosque until four. It was far from certain that I would be allowed to enter freely as a foreigner, even if I did adhere to their deliberately inconvenient hours of operation. I decided instead to walk farther down the road, to see what more I could of the area.

There was a highway overpass, about a hundred yards down the road from the mosque. After I'd passed under that, all I could see in front of me at first was barren rocky terrain. But once I'd walked a bit farther, something crossed my line of sight. Off in the distance straight ahead, what I estimated might be a mile or so down the road, I saw the faint outlines of what looked like a small cluster of buildings. *Could that be a re-education camp?* It was impossible to tell from that distance.

I never made it close enough to see.

# Chapter 19

# Ürümqi, Day Two
## —Encounter on the Road

"Secret ruses are not incompatible to but hide in open acts. Utmost openness conceals utmost secrecy…"
—Thirty-Six Stratagems
(Ancient Chinese text on politics and war)

Not long after the outlines of the distant buildings had first come into view, a Chinese police truck drove past me, abruptly turned around, and pulled up alongside me. Five officers with assault rifles exited the vehicle.

Given the number of militarized police officers I had encountered in the preceding days, I wasn't particularly startled when these officers got out to confront me. I thought I knew what to expect.

Before any of them could speak, I handed my passport to the driver of the truck—a bespectacled Han man of about thirty, with a pale face and bushy eyebrows—who I took to be the highest-ranking of the group. He took a second to look it over and gruffly asked me, "Chinese?"

"No, only English," I replied.

His laugh reminded me of the taxi driver's: hoarse and strained, like someone whose lungs had already endured a lifetime of unapologetic heavy smoking. He knew how difficult this interaction was going to be. As he got out his phone to pull up the translation app, he commented something in Mandarin to the group that got them laughing along with him.

"Why did you come to Xinjiang?" his cracked phone screen read.

I gave my Silk Road student cover story—though maybe in a bit more detail than I had before, since this was obviously a more serious encounter than the routine security checkpoints where I'd used it previously. I also handed him my Genghis Khan book for good measure, but he seemed entirely uninterested.

He ran through the predictable follow-ups—Where are you staying? Where are you headed right now? What do you think of Xinjiang? When will you go back to America?—and I answered all of them plainly.

I told him (of course) how safe I felt, and that I would be leaving China in a couple of days. I also told him that I had come to visit the mosque up the road, and was venturing along here in search of a taxi back to my Airbnb in the city.

He moved swiftly on to what I knew was the question he most wanted an answer to:

"Why did you choose to come to this particular mosque? There are many more popular ones closer to Ürümqi."

"I saw pictures of this mosque online. I thought its architecture was very beautiful," I explained. It really was an attractive structure, notwithstanding its "security" renovations.

It was soon obvious, though, that the officer didn't share my appreciation for the mosque's aesthetic.

"It is inconvenient to be questioning you on the side of the road like this," he said dryly. "Come with us to our station and we will finish there."

As I thought about what this officer's idea of "convenience" might be, a feeling of helplessness began to twist in my stomach.

I climbed into the back seat of the truck, followed by three of the officers—at least two officers too many to fit comfortably into the space, particularly with the commando uniforms they were wearing. The officer next to me reeked of cigarettes and ginger, and had his assault rifle draped haphazardly across his lap. He didn't seem to notice or care that the barrel was poking into my ribs.

After about a minute of driving back down the road, we pulled up at the police station I had noticed earlier, across the street from the mosque. While I had guessed that this was the station they had come from, I wondered what had alerted them to me. Did they spot me outside the mosque when I arrived? Did one of my basketball buddies report me as suspicious? Did someone driving past me call to notify the police of the strange bearded white man walking down the road? Or did these officers just happen by while on patrol? Not that any of that mattered now.

We entered the main room of the police station. There was a receptionist at a desk in the center, with three chrome benches facing her, one of which I was told to occupy. None of the lights were turned on—the only light sources being a small, circular window next to the receptionist's desk, and the thick glass of the automatic double doors at the entrance—creating a shadowy, foreboding atmosphere. The walls were uniformly grey, with a single exception: a huge framed photograph was mounted on the back wall. It was strikingly similar to the electronic propaganda billboards I had seen in the two cities.

It depicted Xi Jinping, smiling superciliously, shaking hands with a Uyghur man, and a sea of Uyghur laborers behind them. They were standing in the middle of what looked like a cavernous textile factory—a common "job placement" for Uyghurs after they have been deemed sufficiently re-educated. The Uyghur man shaking President Xi's hand wore a pressed button-down shirt with khaki pants, suggesting a managerial position, or that he was playing one for the camera. His smile appeared to reflect his enthusiasm at the opportunity to meet the Dear Leader.

The receptionist waved at me and extended her hand.

"Passport please," she requested.

As I handed it to her, the senior officer from the truck came out of the back room to offer me a cup of tea, which I accepted graciously. He then went behind the receptionist's desk to assist with whatever she was doing with my passport.

For the next hour, I sat in my seat, waiting. The officer spoke to the receptionist in Chinese every few minutes as she typed away, while I sat across from them, wondering what it was they were trying to find out about me. A simple Google search of my name would have led them to articles I'd published—articles that would have immediately blown my claim of merely being a tourist. That thought was front-and-center in my mind.

Eventually, the officer came back over to resume his questioning. He began by asking for my phone, presumably to check it for sensitive photographs. I presented him the Guangphone, which he seemed suspicious of initially, judging by his hesitant, confused reaction. He handed it to the receptionist without comment.

He retraced the same questions he had asked me on the side of the road, typing them into the app translator. I interpreted this as a tactic to search for inconsistencies in my responses, or to signal skepticism and see if I would falter and change my story. I took care not to misstep.

After cycling again through those questions, he got more personal.

"What is your religion?" he asked.

"I was raised Christian, but I'm agnostic now," I told him.

"Agnostic?"

"I don't know whether there is a God or not. I don't follow any organized religion, but I believe there could be some sort of higher power."

He still appeared confused. I assumed that something got lost in the translator, knowing the trouble it sometimes had with even simple sentences. I expected there might be some slip-ups now that our conversation had graduated to metaphysics.

"So you are not a Muslim?"

"No, I am not. I just went to the mosque to admire the architecture."

No response.

He got up and returned to the receptionist's desk. It dawned on me not only how suspicious it must have seemed for me to visit this mosque, but also how my personal appearance might have added to his suspicion. My face was hairier than usual, after going more than three weeks without a shave. And the baggy collared white shirt I had on somewhat resembled the top half of an Islamic prayer robe. They might not just suspect me of being a journalist; they might think I'm a Western Muslim on a proselytizing mission, here to radicalize Uyghur worshipers.

Another forty minutes passed before the officer got up and came over to me again, handing me his phone.

"Our station chief wishes to speak with you now," it read. His face was expressionless.

"Okay," I replied, looking over at the door to the back room, awaiting his entry.

Instead, the officer gestured for me to get up. He led me outside the police station and into a smaller, unmarked and windowless grey building next to it. We entered, and made our way down a short, narrow hallway. He opened a door at the very end and let me inside, immediately closing it behind me.

Standing just feet away from the entrance was a paunchy man with a round, slightly florid face, smiling brightly at me while holding two cups of tea. Without the tightly-fitted police uniform, and the pair of black aviator sunglasses propped on his forehead, he would have made an outstanding depiction of the Buddha.

"Hello Gerg!" He was trying to say "George," my legal name, the one on my passport.

"Hello sir," I replied as I accepted my second cup of tea.

Despite the warm welcome, I could tell that I'd been taken to an interrogation room. In contrast to the intake room I had just come from, the lighting here was uncomfortably bright. There was a metal folding chair for the chief, facing a smooth wooden coffee table with a porcelain teapot, a lighter, and packages of Chinese cigarettes propped up on a large silver ashtray. On the opposite side of the table, next to the door, was a brown leather couch with thick cushions, and embroidered silk pillows placed in each corner. Just as in the police station next door, three of the walls were plain grey; but this time, taking up the top half of the fourth wall, to the right of the couch, was an opaque glass screen. I'd never seen one in person before, but it seemed like it could be a one-way mirror masking an observation window on the other side.

"Please," he said, waving in the direction of the couch. As I took a seat, he grabbed one of the packs of cigarettes on the table and handed it to me. We each lit one up.

(*Note:* The chief spoke almost no English. Unless otherwise specified, the conversation reported here took place using a translation app.)

The chief began by repeating the same questions I had already been asked twice by his deputy. Some of them he re-worded—"Are you a Muslim?" became "Do you follow Islam?"—but the gist was the same. He also seemed to be taking a more relaxed, conversational approach than his deputy had, which I appreciated. I was still careful not to stray from my original responses.

"What do you think of China's relationship with America?" We were more than thirty minutes in, and this was the first fresh question he asked.

"I hear it's not that great right now, but I don't really keep up with that stuff," I said, intent on convincing him of my general disinterest in politics.

"Have you heard about troubles in Xinjiang?"

"Some, but I figured I would be safe as long as I didn't behave disrespectfully."

"Yes, of course," he reassured me. "What have you heard about the Muslims here and the security problems they bring?"

"Not much, I really just care about the history here," I replied, leaving aside the presumption that was embedded in his question. I took out my book for the umpteenth time to present to him as grist. "I'm studying the Silk Road and Genghis Khan, see?"

He took the book and examined it, handing it back in seconds.

"There have been terrorism problems in Xinjiang," he declared. "But now we have protections in place. Xinjiang is the safest area of China now."

"Yes, I have felt very safe for my whole stay here."

"We just want to know some things about you. You are not in trouble," he said. Perhaps he sensed the vacuousness of my statement.

He got up and left the room, giving me a bro-ish pat on the back as he headed out.

I was alone again for a surprisingly long time, maybe forty minutes. Left to my thoughts, I meticulously ran through all the possible negative outcomes in my head. I had been at this police complex for almost three hours, with no indication as to when (or if) I was going to be allowed to leave. The only person on earth who knew where I had gone that day was Nancy; and if I were arrested, there would be nothing she could do to help me without putting herself in danger—which, of course, would be too much to hope for from an Airbnb host.

The police chief returned, this time holding two noodle-filled plastic containers, one in each hand. He placed one on the coffee table in front of me, then poured me another cup of tea. He also opened another pack of cigarettes and handed me one, noticing that I had finished off the contents of the first.

"Foreign affairs police wishes to speak with you. We will wait here until they arrive."

It felt like a hard punch to the gut.

"Why? Have I not answered all of your questions?"

"Yes. They still would like to ask you some questions. It is for your own benefit, they will speak English." Somehow this explanation didn't give me comfort. "We can eat together until they get here. Do you like spicy noodles?"

"Yes, they're very good." It was cathartic to give a completely straightforward answer to one of his questions.

I opened the container and began to dig in. Surprisingly, these were some of the best noodles I'd ever eaten. Though I do recognize that my assessment of their quality in the moment may have been enhanced by the stressful circumstances.

As we ate our lunch, the chief handed me his phone with another question typed out.

"So, who is your favorite NBA team? I like the Los Angeles Lakers."

I stared at the text, then looked back up at the chief, catching his boyish smile. *Is he seriously asking me about professional sports right now?* I didn't even know for certain that I wouldn't be spending the next NBA season inside a Chinese prison cell.

"I like the Dallas Mavericks," I typed back.

"Oh! Dirk Nowitzki! He is a very good shooter! We will be better than you this year, though. Dirk is old and we now have Lebron James."

I tried to think what angle he could have for broaching this topic. I guessed that he might have seen me playing across the street earlier, or have heard about it. Maybe this was a tactic to make me comfortable enough to let my guard down? I couldn't tell for sure.

"You're right. He's getting older now, but we have some good young players," I contended. "I think we'll be one of the best teams in a few years."

He cackled, leaning back in his chair a bit. "The Lakers will always be better. They are always the best team."

Typically, I would have doubled down on my disagreement, but I decided not to risk losing my freedom over an argument about NBA prowess.

"Yeah, they do always seem to exceed expectations."

"Have you been to Los Angeles before?"

"No. I'd like to go at some point, though," I replied, while thinking about how interesting (and amusing) it was that everyone I came across seemed obsessed with LA.

"My friend's nephew is studying chemistry at Cal Tech. Do you know that university?"

"Yes. That's a great school, he must be very smart."

"All Chinese students are very smart and work very hard. Do you have any Chinese friends back in America?"

"Some. I would like to make more, though."

"Well, now you have been to China, so you will have things to talk with them about!" He was too excited to just type this one into his phone. He almost screamed it in Mandarin as I was reading the text.

I was thoroughly conflicted. His shift to small talk was certainly a welcome change. But just moments ago, this man was trying to get me to incriminate myself. I'm also sure he would have been far less friendly if I weren't an American, let alone if I were Uyghur. Despite this, I couldn't help but view him in that moment as a truly pleasant and likable guy.

"You should tell them that you had an enjoyable time in Xinjiang. We want more people to visit," he added.

"I'll be sure to let them know all about how beautiful a place it is."

Our relaxed conversation went on for another thirty minutes or so, until the chief got a buzz on his phone. He promptly got up and left the room.

The foreign affairs police had arrived.

# Chapter 20
# Ürümqi, Day Two
## —More Questions

"If a superior man abandon virtue, how can he fulfill the requirements of that name? The superior man does not, even for the space of a single meal, act contrary to virtue . . ."
—Confucius

The chief returned minutes later, holding the door for a petite Uyghur woman with short black hair. She was wearing the standard (non-commando) Chinese police uniform: a light blue, short-sleeved collared shirt tucked into navy blue chino pants. She walked straight past me without a glance in my direction. A lanky Han Chinese man followed right behind her, sporting the long-sleeved version of the same standard police uniform, but with a crisp navy blue necktie. He approached me directly as he entered to shake my hand.

"Sorry to keep you waiting," he said, so dispassionately as to hardly be considered an apology. He was the first English-speaking officer I had met thus far, but given his hollow introduction, I wasn't entirely sure that this was a good thing.

Another deputy officer trailed behind them, holding two more metal folding chairs. He set them up next to the police chief's and exited as the two of them settled in.

"Why are you all the way out here by yourself?" the Han Chinese officer asked pointedly, in perfect English. When the other officers had questioned me through the WeChat app, I had several seconds to contemplate my response, and a few seconds more to make slight edits. That I now had to answer promptly, and verbally, only added to my fear of making a mistake.

"I wanted to come see this mosque. I saw it online and thought the architecture was beautiful."

"There are many beautiful mosques in the city. There is no reason for you to be at this one, especially as a foreigner," he corrected me. "Are you a Muslim?"

"No, I am not."

"How do you feel about Muslims?"

"I don't know that many. I know that some have committed terrorist attacks, but I don't think that all of them are like that." Obviously, my full honest answer to this question would be much different than the one I gave him. But I was trying my best to reinforce the politically disinterested student-traveler persona that I had constructed for myself.

"What do you know about China's security policies in Xinjiang?" he asked.

"Not much."

The tone of this questioning was dramatically different from any of my earlier encounters. The other officers I'd spoken with were direct, but they were also very polite. At times they even tried to be reassuring. The foreign affairs officer's approach and tone, in contrast, gave me the impression that they had already determined my guilt; as if all they were waiting on was for me to give some carelessly incriminating answer that would create a smooth segue into pronouncing their verdict.

"Xinjiang's security policies are the reason it is one of the safest regions in the world. The Western media lies about us," he stated, ignoring my response to his previous question.

"I'm sure. I haven't seen it, though. I don't check the news that much," I answered calmly.

He glanced over and commented something in Mandarin to his Uyghur comrade, who had been sitting beside him silently this entire time. She had a small notepad on her lap, and a pen in her right hand, observing our conversation intently. With my attention being on the Han Chinese officer who was grilling me, I hadn't been aware of her notetaking.

He began another round of the same recycled questions I had already heard a number of times that day. Having just answered them all repeatedly using the translation app, my answers were well rehearsed, and came out as cleanly as I could have hoped.

Eventually, after what must have been an hour of full-on, uninterrupted interrogation, he revisited the "why are you in Xinjiang?" question, but from a deeper, more specific angle that I hadn't been confronted with before:

"So you are visiting Xinjiang because of your interest in Silk Road history, yes?"

"Right."

"The Silk Road was very big. It covered many countries and regions. Why were you so interested in coming to the section in Xinjiang?"

I had no prepared response to fall back on this time, so I did the best I could on the fly.

"Xinjiang was the most important part of the Silk Road. The whole trade network wouldn't have been possible if not for the centers here. I have already been to Beijing, and I plan to go to Turkey at some time in the future."

Leaving aside the fact that it was mostly the oasis cities in the Tarim Basin to the south that were known for their central role in the Silk Road—the northern half of modern-day Xinjiang, where I was, much less so—I was totally satisfied with that answer at the time. The officer may well have been, too, if I had left it at that.

"Why should I have gone to visit other parts of the Silk Road instead?" I asked him. "Should I not have come to Xinjiang as a tourist?"

I felt a pang in my chest the moment this came out.

*Idiot. You answered his question perfectly, why the hell didn't you stop there? Why would you risk antagonizing a man who you know can do whatever he wants to you with impunity?*

As I berated myself in my own head, I looked up to see something unexpected and extraordinary. The Han officer, who just moments ago had been supremely confident, now seemed to be struggling to come up with an answer.

I could hardly believe it, but I might have just inadvertently trapped him in a catch-22.

On the one hand, he had to uphold the Party narrative—that there's nothing wrong with Xinjiang, it's the safest place on earth. Uyghurs and Han Chinese live together in perfect harmony under the CCP's benevolent rule, as is demonstrated by the ubiquitous, definitely-not-staged pictures of Uyghurs smiling alongside President Xi.

On the other hand, he needed to find out why this American student was really wandering around the outskirts of the city. He evidently suspected that I was hiding something—that I was more than just a simpleton Silk Road super-fan. But he couldn't seem to figure out how to continue without exposing the CCP's rosy characterization of life in Xinjiang as pure fiction.

His eyes darted to his Uyghur colleague and back to me again. She still hadn't spoken at all, in any language, but the Han foreign affairs officer now appeared quite mindful of her presence. Was he concerned that, if he said the wrong thing, she would jot it down on her notepad to be handed to his superiors?

Finally, after a long pause, he conjured up a response: "No, of course not. . . . Xinjiang is a great place for tourists, and we're happy that you have come. It is beautiful and has many entertaining things to do." His once-forceful voice was shaky and uncertain. "We just don't get many Americans visiting here, because Western media treats us so unfairly."

Now I too was unsure how to answer. No part of me had anticipated being in this advantageous position.

"Ah, okay, I understand," I managed to carefully reply.

The officer's eyes continued to swerve between me, the ground, and his Uyghur colleague's notepad. He seemed paralyzed by the thought of a potential mistake.

"Um, so, when will you be leaving Xinjiang?" He asked.

"The day after tomorrow. I have a flight booked to Astana."

"And then, after that, you will go back to America?"

"I plan to stay for a week in Kazakhstan, and then I will return home, yes."

He paused again, for a moment. He turned to the Uyghur officer and said something to her in Mandarin. She closed her notebook and they both got up.

"Thank you for your time, George," the Han officer said. "We are sorry to have inconvenienced you. Enjoy the rest of your travels."

He, his companion, and the station chief, who had been sitting there silently the entire time, all walked out the door, closing it behind them.

I couldn't believe how abruptly it had ended. One minute I think I'm going to be put in handcuffs; in the next, my interrogator and his colleague have bid me a nice farewell and are on their way. Even more astonishing was that my one question seemed to have had such a pivotal impact.

I fought off the temptation to feel as though my show-stopping query had been born of my own quick wit. I knew full well that what had happened had been pure luck. Ironically, this very slipping into my usual disputatious bent, which I had been mindful to try to keep at bay in Xinjiang, may have ended up securing my freedom.

As I was accustomed to by this point, I waited alone in the room for about forty minutes until the police chief returned, this time with my passport in hand. *Finally.* I took it from him as he began typing something into the translation app. I expected some sort of farewell message;

similar to the one I'd received from the foreign affairs officer, perhaps with some pro-Lakers sentiment added on.

"The police chief from the district where you are staying wishes to speak with you," it read. "We will drive you there and you will talk with him."

Just when I thought I was being let go, after enduring five hours of inquisition, I was facing yet another round of questioning, in a new setting with more new faces.

"Can't I just go now? I've answered all of your questions."

"You failed to register as a foreigner who would not be staying at a hotel. The police chief wishes to speak to you and your host about the procedure you must now take."

Needless to say, I was frustrated that this was the first I had heard of this additional registration requirement.

"My host knows about this?" I asked sheepishly.

"Yes. We have instructed her to meet you at the station."

Considering how intensely shy Nancy was, I worried that she would be ill-equipped (to put it mildly) for confrontation with the police.

"Let's go," the chief said (in English) with characteristic zeal.

I followed him out of the interrogation room and outside the building to the gravel front parking lot. It wasn't as nice out now. The scattered clouds from before had amassed into a solid layer of grey covering the sky. Still, I couldn't think of a time in my life that I had been so happy to be outdoors.

One of the deputies came around with a police pickup truck. The chief offered me shotgun, and I hopped in, as he got into the back seat. Despite my general disaffection with not yet being released, I felt thankful for not having to ride, this time, with the barrel of a carbine digging into my ribs.

As we merged onto the highway, the deputy's eyes were glued to his phone, which he had plugged into the truck's console. Seconds later, electronic dance music began blaring.

This, oddly enough, put me at ease. The familiar music genre, along with the gorgeous mountain scenery, reminded me of road trips I'd taken in Colorado.

"Hey!" I exclaimed, louder than I'd intended, in the direction of the deputy.

He looked at me, wide-eyed. I pointed to the speaker and gave a thumbs up paired with a grin.

He and the chief both laughed. The deputy then unplugged his phone from the auxiliary cord, handing the end of the cord to me.

Is this really happening? Just an hour ago I thought my next ride might be a one-way trip to Chinese prison. Now we're sharing music playlists.

I enthusiastically accepted, and took my phone out of my bag to plug in. I decided it would be best to stick with the same genre, so I put on a classic EDM album in my music library. The officers seemed to like it. The chief began a smooth, *Night at the Roxbury* style head-nod from the moment the first song came on. When the beat dropped, the deputy took one of his hands off the steering wheel and started pumping his fist in the air.

"Very good!" the chief praised.

*Unreal.*

But then I realized: I was using my *American iPhone* to play this music. When I was asked earlier, by a different officer, to give him my phone, I handed over my Guangphone, clearly implying that *that* was my phone. The chief and his comrade must not have been aware of my having two different phones—or maybe they were just taken by the music—because they didn't seem to notice. Unplugging at this point would only have drawn attention, so I continued jamming along like there was no problem.

Meanwhile, it also occurred to me that these two officers, with whom I had developed a short-lived but congenial relationship, were surely complicit—at the very least—in horrible human rights abuses. It was probable that they had personally detained Uyghurs for morally indefensible reasons. They might have previously been assigned to guard a cotton field full of Uyghur slave workers, or even a re-education camp. I was taken by the morbid juxtaposition of these realities: the bonhomie treatment I was receiving from them in that moment, and the unconscionable abuses that they were likely party to.

We had gotten through almost the entire album when the deputy turned off the speakers as we exited the highway. I recognized my surroundings as we got off the exit ramp; I had come this way in the taxi from the train station on my first day. We were not far from Nancy's place.

It wasn't long before we turned off the main road onto a long, newly-paved driveway, with concrete walls on either side topped with razor wire. At the end of it was a thick black iron gate, with a small guard tower peeking over it on the left side. It didn't look so different from the front of the mosque.

The chief barked something into his phone in Mandarin. Moments later, the gate slowly opened, and we drove in.

Four tan concrete buildings, each of them larger than the police station we'd just come from, were positioned on either side of the driveway, with police vehicles of different sizes parked outside. At the far end, maybe a football field away from the gate, was the main building. It was multiple stories, and had the dark blue shield insignia of the Chinese police hung over its entrance.

On the front steps of the main building, I could see Nancy standing next to a man towering over her. Presumably this was the next, and hopefully the last, Chinese official who would be questioning me this afternoon.

When we pulled up, I discreetly slid my iPhone back into my daypack and stepped out of the truck. I expected the chief and his deputy to come with me, to make a brief introduction, at least. Instead, all I got was a "goodbye Gerg!" from the chief, and a wave from them both, before they turned and drove off. Perhaps some new and urgent police matter needed their immediate attention.

I peered up the short flight of stairs to see Nancy staring down at her feet. She was wearing black and pink sweatpants with an extra-large T-shirt, and her hair looked slightly unkempt. It appeared that she had been enjoying a relaxing day inside, until she got called down to the police station to collect her miscreant houseguest. To say that I was embarrassed would be a monumental understatement.

The man standing next to her—who I took to be the local police chief who wanted to speak with me—couldn't have been a more perfect contrast to the last one. He was wearing a navy blue police polo shirt that was several sizes too small. The sleeves, in particular, were bearing a seemingly unmanageable load, the fabric struggling to hold the line against his notably large biceps. Also unlike the last chief, this one chose to wear his sunglasses, rather than prop them on his head as an accessory. It being too late in the now-cloudy day for this to be a practical eye-protection decision, I interpreted it as a sign of the commando-esque persona he sought to convey. I'd be lying if I said it wasn't effective.

When I arrived at the top of the stairs, he acknowledged my presence with a nod, then swung around toward the front door without saying a word. I turned to Nancy to see if she had anything to fill me in on, but she just followed right behind him, still staring down at the ground.

We walked inside and up two flights of stairs, down a dimly lit hallway, and into the chief's office. To my surprise, it was quite welcoming. There was a sizable window that took up most of the back wall, allowing a generous amount of natural light to cover the room. A few strategically placed plants added refreshing color. His desk was decorated with a bobble-head figure of a Chinese basketball player, next to an ancient-looking desktop computer. I couldn't help but note the irony in there being thousands of high-tech surveillance cameras to monitor every inch of the city's streets, while the police chief was typing on a clunker made more than a decade ago.

What most caught my attention was a picture, hanging on the wall right next to his chair, of the chief on a tropical vacation with his family. Two kids, who looked no older than six, stood in the center. One of them had hair caked in sand, while the other appeared to be teasing him about it. The chief, in an uncharacteristically well-fitted Hawaiian shirt, was crouched next to his wife, behind their children, each of them with an arm around the closest child. It looked like a portrayal of a loving family, showing a human side of the chief that he suppressed in his official demeanor.

Yet his need to suppress it made perfect sense. I can't imagine it being possible to excel as a police chief in contemporary China—a job that requires one to oversee and directly participate in, and even to initiate, crimes against humanity—without walling off one's personal life. I wondered whether his wife came to mind when he considered the frequency with which Uyghur women are raped by guards at the camps, or even in their own homes by their male Han "relatives." Did he think about his own kids while he and his comrades rounded up the children of interned Uyghurs to lock them away in "boarding schools?" Could he easily tell distraught Uyghur husbands and fathers, who came to him seeking answers, that everything that happens to their family is "for their own benefit," or "to improve China's ethnic unity"? Would he be satisfied with that answer about the fate of his own family members?

I would expect any person in his position, had they a shred of compassion, to be haunted by these questions.

The police chief gestured for us to take a seat in the two chairs against the side wall, as he poured tea for us from an electric kettle on his desk. He handed each of us a cup, and took one of the guest seats directly across from us, placing himself much closer than he would have been in his desk chair. He took off his sunglasses and hung them on the collar of his shirt, revealing a pair of fierce brown eyes.

I was taken aback when Nancy spoke up first. Her voice was feeble, like a nervous whisper, as she continued to look straight down for most of her delivery. I assumed that the two of them had already exchanged some words prior to my arrival, as I couldn't imagine her speaking to anyone unprompted—especially to her local police chief.

Once she had finished her cautious explanation, the police chief leaned forward in his seat, his hands together and fingers intertwined on his lap, and responded in a deep-throated, booming voice—a voice that would surprise absolutely no one after seeing him. It seemed excessive, considering that Nancy exhibited a clear regret for her transgression. That he was scolding her about something having to do with me made it deeply uncomfortable to hear.

Without warning, his already-harsh tone abruptly elevated to a shout—so immediate and intense that it almost shook me out of my seat.

He slapped his hand on the small wooden table beside him, almost knocking over his tea, as he went on at a fever pitch, gesticulating aggressively with every few words. I turned, mortified, in the direction of Nancy. She had her head down, with tears streaming down her face. I felt terrible, both for what she was going through, and because I knew there was no way for me to placate him. All I could do was to sit there, entirely ignorant of what was being said, hoping that his excoriation wouldn't end with one or the both of us being arrested.

This went on for about fifteen minutes. Nancy interjected small responses every so often through her sobs, but she could never get more than a couple of timid sentences in before being interrupted. Eventually, the police chief lowered his voice, and after getting in a few more words, he concluded his tirade. Nancy sprang out of her chair and signaled to me with her hand that it was time to leave.

The police chief gave me another robotic nod on my way out, but stayed seated, as I followed Nancy out of his office and out of the building, walking in the direction of the now-opened entrance gate.

Of course, I wanted to ask Nancy what had just happened, but we walked side-by-side silently until we got to what seemed like a safe distance from the compound. Then I tapped her and pointed to her phone, indicating my desire for an explanation.

Her condition had improved, but she still had a few fresh tears trickling down her dispirited face. I took the phone from her after she had finished typing.

"We have to go back to the apartment and move you out. I will help you to get a hotel, but then I have to go back to the police station."

This change of residence was surely going to make a significant dent in my funds. I knew that only the most luxurious hotels in Xinjiang accept foreigners, and I was already running somewhat short of funds in my budget.

In that moment, though, I was thinking more about her.

"Okay, if he said that I need to move then I will do that. No problem. Will you be alright?"

We had just made it to a busy crosswalk at the main road where Nancy's apartment was. She typed out her response carefully, and handed her phone back to me just as the light came on for us to cross.

"Yes, I'll be fine. The police chief had a really good attitude."

I had no idea how to respond to that.

I handed back the phone, and gave her a nod and the most genuine-looking smile I could muster, though she didn't look at me for either of them. There wasn't anything I could say or do that wouldn't jeopardize us further. I knew that she was probably terrified, with good reason, that our conversation was now being monitored by the police.

We walked, silently, back to her apartment. I packed my things as quickly as I could while she booked a hotel for my last two nights. When I came out of my room with my bags, I saw her sitting on the couch in front of the fish tank, with her forehead resting defeatedly on her palm. As she stood up to inform me of my new living situation, I gave her a hug. I doubt she would have been comfortable with this under any other circumstance, and I wouldn't have attempted it otherwise either. But I ignored my reservations. It was the only thing I could think of doing to show my earnest sympathy for the horrible situation she was in.

The subtle smile I saw on her face when I let go suggested it was well-taken.

Nancy took me back outside to the main road to hail a taxi. She flagged one down, told the driver the location of my new hotel, and paid the fare for me in advance. Before I was able to protest her typically kind gesture, the driver sped off. We waved goodbye to each other through the rear window.

---

In September, 2020, the Australian Strategic Policy Institute launched the "Xinjiang Data Project," an incredibly useful resource that features an interactive map of the region,[108] where they have marked all of the detention facilities, cultural sites, and mosques (as well as more detailed information on many of them) that they have been able to identify through analysis of satellite imagery.

According to their map, when I was picked up on the side of that road by the police, I was just half a mile from a detention facility.

Chapter 21

# Ürümqi Day Three
## —Heavenly Lake

"He who offends the Gods has no one to pray to."

*—Confucius*

I couldn't find any surveillance cameras in my hotel room. I gave the entire place a thorough sweep—from the ceiling lights, to the bedposts, to the mini-fridge—with no results. But I was convinced that they were there—somewhere. After what had happened just hours earlier, how could they not be watching me?

Spending the night in this room, sensing the presence of cameras that I couldn't see, wasn't conducive to a peaceful night's sleep. Nor was the recurring image of that apoplectic police chief berating a tearful Nancy. Nor the thought of what might have happened to her when she returned to the police station to face him again.

In the early hours of the morning, I sat on the edge of my bed, wide awake, pondering what I should do for my final day. The first idea that popped into my head was to get my flight changed—to just go to Astana a day early, where I could finally return to being an ordinary traveler again, and leave the anxieties of Xinjiang behind me. But it would be difficult to do this without accessing the internet. And subjecting my American iPhone to infiltration by going online was out of the question.

But I also couldn't wait out the whole day sitting in my hotel room. Beyond the fact that this would drive me insane, it could also attract further suspicion. No ordinary tourist spends their last day holed up in a hotel room, watching Chinese soap operas and gorging themselves on room service. I needed to come up with an innocuous activity that would take up the bulk of my day. *But what?*

Then I remembered—I already had several options to pick from, in the list Nancy had texted to me when I first met her. Even in her absence, she was a lifesaver.

I retrieved my Guangphone from the bedside table and pulled up her text. The first item on the list seemed like a perfect fit:

> Tianchi or "Heavenly Lake." Say "Tian shur" and people will know it. Beautiful lake outside of Ürümqi, where you can hike and take a boat tour around the lake. Ticket cost is ninetyfive Yuan without transportation or tour fees. You can get there by taking a bus from Ürümqi bus station that takes a little bit more than one hour.

A beautiful lake with a fifteen-dollar admission would be a very unlikely place to accidentally get myself into further trouble. Maybe not less likely than the Ürümqi museum the TV host had recommended during my interview at the park two days ago; but it would do. And I knew I'd enjoy a full day at a lake far more than the inside of a sterile building, looking at the CCP's curated collection of miscontextualized artifacts and demonstrations of gratuitous praise for its pacification of Xinjiang. "Tian shur" it was.

I got dressed in my last remaining clean outfit, grabbed my daypack and a bottled water from the mini fridge, and headed downstairs. I chose to keep my iPhone in the secret pocket of my daypack, reasoning that the chance it would be searched was higher if I left it unattended in my new government-sanctioned hotel room.

In the lobby, I asked the receptionist—in English, since this hotel catered to international guests—how to get to Ürümqi bus station. In lieu of an answer, she offered to have one of the bellboys hail a taxi to get me there, saying I should wait for him at the front sidewalk.

The hotel was on an even busier road than Nancy's place, beneath the same elevated highway. The dreary weather of the previous afternoon had cleared up. And, for the first time since I arrived in Ürümqi, the air pollution outside was negligible. The few visible clouds were dispersed, revealing the strikingly bright blue sky surrounding them. I could only imagine the rest of the sky, because most of my view was obstructed by the vast concrete underside of the highway.

I understood the rationale for building this highway. It was an infrastructure decision surely conceived in commercial practicality, meant to support increased development around the greater city—but with scant concern for the people who lived in the dwellings, and who occupied the offices, underneath the highway. I couldn't imagine that the bit of time shaved from their commutes made up for never getting a good look at the sun when they stepped outside.

The bellboy waved me over to where he'd successfully stopped a taxi driver who had agreed to take me.

I tipped him as I climbed into the back seat.

\* \* \* \* \* \* \*

The security line at Ürümqi bus station was by far the quickest, and the least invasive, of any I'd encountered in Xinjiang. I still had to put my bag through the X-ray, and I was asked the same basic questions, but the whole process took less than fifteen minutes.

I approached the single open window at the bus ticketing area, ready to give the ticket-seller my best attempt at clearly pronouncing "Tian shur." He preempted me with a single-word question—"English?"

"Yes!" I declared with relief. "I'd like to go to Heavenly Lake please."

"There is a tour bus leaving in five minutes, just out the glass doors over there," he said, pointing over his right shoulder down a hallway. "Would you like to take that one?"

"Definitely."

The ticket-seller handed me two small tickets; one for the ride there, the other to get back.

Outside was a large parking lot, with a dozen coach buses lined up, their drivers standing at their bus's entrance. There weren't any indicators as to which bus was mine. So I figured that the way to find out was to approach each of the drivers and announce "Tian shur," starting with the bus closest to me.

Tian shur?" I asked as I approached the driver, who was just lighting up a cigarette.

He glanced up at me and thrust his thumb over his shoulder.

"Tian shur?" I repeated to the next driver behind him.

His smile told me he was more receptive to actually helping.

"Tian shur!" he shouted behind him, saving me the trouble of having to inquire a dozen more times.

A hand shot out from the lineup of buses, nearly all the way at the end. When I made it down there, I saw in the bottom corner of the windshield a picture of a bright blue lake, surrounded by mountains.

"Tian shur?" I asked the driver, already fairly confident I knew the answer.

He nodded his head, and outstretched his hand to verify my outbound ticket.

When he handed it back to me, he pointed to a small number 48 at the top of the ticket. I assumed that was my seat number.

The bus was virtually full with tourists, all of them Han. My walk down the aisle to my seat was a gauntlet of shameless stares and unsubtle snapping of pictures; another part of Xinjiang that I was eager to be done with.

As I crammed myself into what was, at most, half of my seat—the other half occupied by a middle-aged man in tourist garb—a young woman at the front of the bus began speaking into a microphone, giving what I could tell was her introductory tour-guide speech. When we pulled out of the parking lot, I retrieved my iPhone from my bag and inserted my earphones.

Just as Nancy had said, it took a little over an hour to reach the park entrance. We were on a highway for a brief period initially, but the bulk of the trip was spent along a narrow, winding road, leading into the heart of the mountains that, until then, I had only been able to admire from inside the city.

The bus eventually stopped in the middle of a parking lot filled with dozens more identical tour buses, in front of a large, modern-looking building. The building was separated from the parking lot by—you guessed it—a security checkpoint line.

*The lake must be just on the other side,* I thought to myself.

I got off the bus with the rest of my group, following them to the security check-in line. I hadn't even made it halfway before I was stopped by a Han man in a blue polo shirt with the park logo.

"Hello, you need to go to the desk over there first," he said curtly, pointing to an opaque black booth immediately to my left.

He escorted me to the front of the booth, then went back to monitoring the incoming crowds.

"Passport, please," a woman said through the microphone. Her face was barely visible from behind the indigo tint of the windows.

"Sure." I retrieved it from my bag and handed it to her through the window slot.

"Where are you from?" she asked, as she opened the blue booklet.

"United States."

"Why are you visiting Tian shur?"

"Because I have heard about how beautiful it is, and I wanted to see it before I leave tomorrow," I replied.

She looked down at my passport again.

"You made the right decision. I hope you enjoy it," she said, handing it back to me. "Can we search your bag, please?"

I didn't know who she meant by "we," since she appeared to be alone in the booth.

"Just leave it on the counter, please."

She pressed a button on her desk. Moments later, the Han security guard returned to grab my bag from the counter, entering the booth without even glancing at me.

He emptied the contents onto the table. I couldn't see clearly through the dark window, but it looked like he was going through every pocket of my bag—even the interior one that held my American iPhone.

He quickly examined the items, not seeming to pay any special mind to the phone, before dumping them haphazardly back into my bag.

"You can come with me," he said after he exited the booth.

He moved the steel barrier next to the booth aside, and gestured at me to follow him through the opening. We walked toward the ticket building entrance, avoiding the burgeoning security line beside us, where the rest of my tour group was still waiting.

*Am I being taken somewhere else for further questions?*

He brought me into the building's crowded atrium, and, with a quick "goodbye, thank you," handed back my daypack. His thorough search of my bag had excused me from the main security line.

I almost laughed at my incredible good fortune: Of all the times when having my iPhone found could have been catastrophic, the previous day's prolonged interrogation prominent among them, it finally gets discovered not by a police officer, but by an ordinary security guard at perhaps the most visited tourist attraction in Ürümqi. And not only did I not incur any adverse consequences; I actually saved time because of his search.

I now had to wait for about thirty minutes in another line to purchase my park ticket, no longer having a park security guard to help me circumvent the usual process. After handing me my ticket, the ticket seller pointed toward a set of glass doors I had seen other visitors exiting from. I assumed I would see the legendary Heavenly Lake on the other side.

But I saw no lake. Instead, there was yet another long line—more than twice as long as the line outside that I had skipped—that zig-zagged up to a shuttle bus stop about fifty feet ahead. The outgoing buses cycled through every fifteen minutes or so, but only carried about fifteen passengers each. I prepared for another long wait.

After about an hour, I made it to the front, getting on a bus with a tour group completely different from the one I'd arrived with.

As our new guide began her speech, in Mandarin, from the front of the bus, we started down the road. Next stop, scenic lakeside views.

The drive, as I had expected, was gorgeous. We were now in the depths of the valley I had first entered on the bus from Ürümqi, with mountains lining both sides, stretching back behind us as far as I could see. The upper reaches of the mountains were brown, jagged, and barren. But farther down their slopes, I could see evergreen trees; scattered sparsely at first, then gradually converging to cover the entire base as they neared the valley floor. The road we were on bisected a verdant field that ran a hundred feet or so on either side before it met the edge of the evergreen forest. To our right, a shallow, rocky creek glinted up from the thick grass.

It took about thirty minutes before we pulled into a small turnout in a moderately forested area. Two other shuttle buses were already parked, and some tourists were milling about near them. Just ahead of the buses was a narrow dirt trail, with food and gift stands, and teeming with Han tourists. This certainly wasn't how I had pictured the entrance to Heavenly Lake.

Our tour guide made a brief announcement in Mandarin, and everyone began to exit the bus.

After getting a lukewarm egg-and-scallion pancake from the first food stand I came to, I ventured down the trail. The farther I went, the more convinced I became that we had not yet made it to the lake. To the contrary, it was as if they had taken a cutout of the least-interesting section of Erdaoqiao Bazaar and relocated it to the woods next to this roadside turnoff. Incredibly, the others in my group seemed to find this setup exhilarating; like they couldn't bear to be away from the kitsch souvenir shops of Ürümqi city's tourist hubs for even a single day's excursion.

I continued until I rounded the second bend in the trail, where the path revealed itself to be a large semi-circle, leading from one end of the parking lot around to the other. There was no attraction here—only shopping.

I hoped it wouldn't be long until we moved on, but I decided to get my fill of food while I was here, seeing that so much of it was available.

The now-unmistakable scent of cumin on grilled lamb led me straight to a kabob stand. I ordered four—thinking to save a couple to snack on later—and moved to the side while the grill man worked his magic.

While I was waiting, I noticed a heavy-set Han man in a light blue shirt standing just a bit farther down the trail, peering over at me with a theatrically bright smile. Seconds after I saw him, he excitedly began to walk over, grinning like he was recognizing an old friend. I assumed he had probably mistaken me for some American celebrity, and I prepared to temporarily pretend to be whichever movie star he thought I was.

"Hey, dude!" he shouted as he approached. I couldn't remember the last time I'd been called "dude," so right away I was intrigued.

"Hey, what's up?" I replied.

"What's your name?"

"Grayson. What's yours?"

"Jin," he said, stretching his hand out for a handshake. "Which country are you visiting from?"

"America," I told him, as the grill man handed me my kabobs and a plastic bag.

"I figured. You look like an American."

I would have been wary now of any Han stranger striking up a conversation with me in English, given what had happened to me the previous day. I didn't think it was out of the question that my long engagement with the police had earned me a personal government tail.

"Where'd you learn to speak English so well?" I asked.

"I learned it in school. I am studying to be a diplomat," Jin declared proudly.

"That's awesome. I'm sure you'll do very well."

"Thank you. This is good practice for me."

Piercing honks from the buses interrupted us, and the other tourists began heading in that direction.

"I guess that means we're leaving now," I posited. "Do you think we'll actually be going to the lake this time?"

"I'm not sure, I haven't been to this place before." A couple of older men who had come from farther down the trail walked up to Jin from behind, one of them saying something to him in Mandarin.

"These are my uncles," he said as he turned back in my direction. "They want to know if you like it in Xinjiang."

"Yes. Very much. It's beautiful here." Each of them gave approving smiles after Jin had translated. We all began walking to the parking lot.

"You should come with us on our bus." Jin suggested.

It didn't seem important that I stick to the same bus I'd started on, as I was already with a completely new tour group from the one I'd started with.

"Yeah, why not," I said.

We got on, followed by Jin's two uncles, and took a pair of seats in the front.

"How long are you staying in China?" Jin asked.

"I'm actually leaving tomorrow."

"Why would you leave, dude? You should come and visit Gansu Province!"

(Gansu is the Chinese province that borders Xinjiang to its northeast, just below Mongolia.)

"I wish I could," I lamented, despite not knowing what Gansu Province was at the time. "Is that where you're from?"

"Yes, we're all from there," he replied. The bus turned out of the parking lot and started back along the road.

*All?*

When I saw that most of the passengers on the bus were looking at me, I realized that he was referring to more than just himself and his two uncles.

"Oh, did you come here with your whole family?" I inquired.

"Yes, man, of course!" he said, as if it was strange to be even asking this question. "You can meet them."

He then proceeded to introduce me to his relatives—all twelve of them—adding biographical details about each. For a few, he even took the time to digress into full-length stories. Some of these stories, such as the time his brother-in-law got attacked by a wild boar while walking home from the supermarket, were actually quite funny and interesting (he escaped without serious injury). But many were much less so, frankly, and consisted of equal amounts of Jin rambling through mostly incoherent storylines in English and asking his family members to remind him of the relevant details in Mandarin. They all seemed like the friendliest of people, so I did my best to stay engaged. But I'll admit to zoning out a bit by the end of it.

"That's so cool that you all came here together," I noted once he'd finished. "This really must be a popular destination."

"It is, dude!" Jin confirmed, giving me a playful shove to my shoulder.

Shortly thereafter, the bus turned off the road again and into what seemed to be the same parking lot we'd just come from.

"I wonder what this one has," he pondered excitedly.

"Weren't we just here?" I asked, as the tour guide at the front of the bus made a brief announcement and everyone began getting off.

"No. This is the second market village."

*You don't say.*

"What do you think you will buy this time?" Jin asked, while his family members split off in different directions.

"Probably nothing," I replied. "I thought that the last one was the only stop we were going to make before the lake, so I bought everything that I needed there."

"There will be more things you will want to buy here. Just come with me."

Jin's confidence seemed unwarranted.

As we began down the trail, I made a game of trying to find something that I didn't recall seeing on our previous stop. I couldn't. Except for, maybe, the precise order of the line-up of specific shops, it was identical. It was—again—one big loop of redundant, frivolous trinkets.

Jin was nonetheless determined to examine nearly every shop we passed. He persistently asked for my advice on his purchasing ideas, and not in the casual way you might expect. He seemed entirely serious, consulting me on which Xinjiang-themed T-shirt he should get with the earnestness and deference that one might use with a tax lawyer, or a stock advisor.

My desire to hang out with Jin had run its course, and I began to look for a polite way to peel off.

"Jin, it was so nice to meet you," I began, interrupting his deep concentration on the latest product he was thinking of buying. "I should go back with my old shuttle bus now, since they're probably wondering where I am."

"Oh, you don't have to do that," Jin replied obliviously.

"Yeah, I know I don't have to. But I don't want them to worry that I've gotten lost."

The buses honked their horns, signaling that it was time to go.

"No, it's okay, they won't worry," Jin assured me as we began walking back to the parking lot.

We arrived at the bus, where we met up with his family members. I might have continued to insist on leaving, but I felt it would be too uncomfortable to do so in front of his family, having just been introduced to all of them. I followed Jin back onto the bus, hoping for a better opportunity later, when we got to the lake—or, God forbid, at the next in the series of souvenir villages.

"I'm happy that we got to stop there!" Jin declared.

"Yeah . . ." I could feel myself rapidly losing the energy to keep up with his enthusiasm.

After another twenty minutes or so, the road changed from straight and flat to a series of sharp switchbacks that ran up the side of a mountain. As we climbed progressively higher, I watched as the evergreen trees that had towered over us just minutes earlier became mere points on a vast canvas, stretching interminably to the distant horizon. The creek that had accompanied us through the valley had turned off to the right, emptying out into a turquoise pond surrounded by—

"Are you always this quiet, man?"

I had to gather myself before turning around to be greeted by Jin's face, bearing an incandescent grin.

"No, I was just looking at the view," I replied coolly.

"Oh yeah, it is quite nice!" he exclaimed, glancing out the window for a second. "So what do you want to do once we arrive at the lake?"

"I'm not sure," I said. I didn't want to close off any escape routes.

"You should come with us on the boat tour!" he enthused. "It doesn't cost much extra, I don't think, and we can go out on the lake together that way."

*That sounds absolutely unbearable, Jin.*

"Yeah, that sounds fun. I'll think about it."

There was one thing that I strangely liked about Jin: He was the only person I'd met in Xinjiang who I would bet my life had absolutely no connection to the CCP. It was hard to imagine that Sue and Nancy were anything other than incredibly generous hosts; but there was at least a *chance* they were just putting on a convincing front. Even my fermented-egg-loving drinking buddy from the beer festival might conceivably have had a hidden agenda. I couldn't really know whether anyone I met in Xinjiang was who they claimed to be.

But nobody could pretend to be Jin.

We cleared the final switchback, and turned up onto a straight road on a slight incline. We came to a large parking lot minutes later, filled with dozens of other tour buses, and countless tourists walking a gravel pathway that led up and over the grassy ridge about two hundred yards ahead.

It appeared that we had finally made it to the lake.

The bus parked, and after the tour guide gave a brief speech in Mandarin, we were allowed to get off.

"The lake is up that way," Jin informed no one as we stepped off the bus. The majority of his family members were already walking toward the gravel pathway.

Posted at the start of the pathway was a large map, denoting the various trails around the lake as well as key destination points. It showed that the nexus of all the trails was just up ahead.

"I need to figure out which trail I want to take," I stated, recognizing an opportunity. "You should go catch up with the rest of your family. It was nice meeting you, Jin."

I stretched my hand out for a handshake as I finished my sentence, with the hope that this would make it clear to him that it was time to go our separate ways.

"That's okay," Jin said. "They will wait for us."

"I think I'm going to do a hike instead of the boat tour, Jin. Thanks for your offer, though."

"Well, actually the boat tour will take you to all the main hikes, so you can ride with us until you have to get off."

I knew that our breakup was not going to be easy, but I'll admit, I did not anticipate this level of persistence. I looked back to the map for a moment, hoping to conjure some perfect excuse out of thin air—and there I found it, staring me in the face.

"Uhh, I'm actually going to do the whole perimeter trail," I explained, pointing to the thick black outline of the lake. "So I can't take the boat at all."

"The whole thing?!" Jin gasped. "You won't have time to do that."

"No, I will. I'm a fast walker."

"It will take hours. You won't be able to make it in time for the final bus back to the city."

"I think I might run for parts of it, too." I was all in at that point. Nothing was going to stop me from shedding Jin and having a relaxing lake day.

I noticed a perceptible shift in Jin's countenance, a wrinkle in his face. He had just come to a realization.

"It doesn't seem like a good idea . . . but it's your choice."

*Bingo!*

"Thanks Jin, it really was great meeting you," I insisted, doing my best to contain the relief dripping from every word. "I hope you have a nice time on the boat, and say goodbye to your family for me as well."

"Okay, be careful, Grayson. It was nice to meet you too," Jin said, finally accepting my outstretched hand and shaking it in farewell. With that, he turned around and slogged up the hill.

I was happy to be on my own again. Although I did feel a touch of remorse at having to end the partnership so insistently. I had no doubt that beneath the quirks that had been distracting me from enjoying the trip, Jin was a friendly guy who sincerely meant well.

I thought it would be best to stick around the map a while longer, just to make sure there was a safe distance between me and Jin. This also allowed me time to decide on what I actually did want to do with my day.

It was almost one o'clock, meaning that a hike around the entire perimeter trail was completely out of the question, as Jin had correctly pointed out. Luckily, there were a number of destinations on the map that still looked realistic to visit in the amount of time I had. "Queen Mother Temple," on the eastern side of the lake, looked interesting, and there were a couple of other spots that I kept in mind as backups. I took a photograph of the map with my iPhone, for later reference, and started up the hill.

The sun emerged from behind a mass of fluffy clouds as I made my way up the trail, its rays washing over the lush grass on either side. I could feel the freshness of the mountain air rush over me in punctuated gusts of cool, light wind.

As I neared the top of the hill, the distant snow-capped peaks beyond the lake came into view, then the smaller and snowless rocky peaks in front of them. Gradually these gave way to the evergreen of the forested smaller slopes forming the lake's perimeter, and ultimately, once I had reached the crest of the ridge, to the deep turquoise of the lake itself, dotted at two separate points by large yellow-and-white tour boats creeping along the water.

It was the most beautiful place I'd seen in China—and one of the most beautiful places I'd been to in my life. The mountains from that angle joined in immaculate symmetry, from the smaller evergreen slopes to the left and right of the lake, then inward to the larger, rocky peaks, and finally culminating at the two tallest, snow-capped peaks at the very center of my line of sight, directly across the lake and off in the distance. Those twin snowy peaks appeared to be more illuminated than everything else, as if the radiant sun were actively leading my gaze in their direction. It seemed a fitting placement for the Gates of Heaven.

Ensconced on one of the grassy slopes to my left, overlooking the lake, I could see the vague outline of Queen Mother Temple. I consulted the picture of the map on my phone to see how to get to it. The trail began to the side of the viewing area, just below me at the bottom of the ridge.

It was surprisingly crowded at first, and even featured a few more souvenir stands, just in case anyone hadn't purchased enough at the two souvenir villages on the way here. Once I'd made it past the turnoff leading to the boat launch, the trail cleared out significantly.

I encountered only a handful of people for the rest of the hike to the temple. Most of the trail wasn't a trail at all, but a sturdy wooden walkway built into the side of the cliffs around the lake, low enough to the water for me to see fish schooling in the various coves below it.

When I arrived at the "entrance," I realized that my hike to the temple was just beginning. The trail had taken me to the bottom of a staggeringly long flight of stone stairs, running several hundred feet up. They were so steep that I couldn't actually see the temple. I had to rely on what I had seen earlier from the other side of the lake.

It looked like a daunting climb, but I had already steeled myself for a rigorous hike, and my eagerness to see the view from the top served as the needed motivation. I began my ascent just as one of the tour boats was pulling into the dock, and I worked to put some space between myself and the swarms of tourists about to spill out from it.

At the top was a ticket booth, and then another, equally long flight of stairs. At the top of that flight, I could make out a small section of the temple's green-tiled roof. By now, I wasn't concerned with the price of an entry ticket. I would pay it, no matter how unreasonable it might be. But the commercialization of seemingly everything, everywhere, was off-putting.

I handed over the additional fee of thirty yuan and plodded up.

The stairs led onto a spacious white stone courtyard with a large bronze sculpture in the very center. It was maybe twenty feet tall, and resembled a seven-story pagoda, with small silver bells that adorned each of its seven pagoda "roofs" running up to the top. In front of this was a large trough of ash, holding several metal jars containing sticks of burning incense. An elderly couple were facing it, prostrating themselves.

The climb to get there must have been especially arduous for them at their age, and I admired their determination. I tried not to disturb the silence, but I could hear the faint voices of the mass of tourists from behind me, slowly growing louder, and I worried that the couple's prayers would soon be disturbed no matter how quiet I was.

The temple itself, painted a relatively plain green and yellow, loomed over the courtyard from the opposite side. It was accessible by another thirty-foot climb, up grey stone stairs carved into a jagged stone wall. In the middle of the wall, directly in line with the bronze sculpture and the ritual space in the courtyard, a circle of the stone had been smoothed over for a Taoist yin-yang symbol painted in the essential black and white. I paused briefly in front of it before heading up the stairs.

At the top was the entrance to the temple. Its exterior was bright yellow, aside from the Chinese characters above the entrance that were colored dark green, and two white surveillance cameras on its outside corners.

Inside, I found glistening golden statues depicting various deities lined against the back wall, with symmetrical paintings of dragons behind them. Leather cushions were laid out in front of the statues, where people could quietly pay their respects and burn incense offerings, which wafted throughout the room. Bright red and gold banners with Chinese characters hung from the ceiling around the room's interior perimeter. The ceiling was decorated with intricate murals of people and animals; each of them I imagined might represent some profound allegorical truth.

---

I couldn't help but reflect on how this temple spoke to the immeasurable number of positive contributions that have come from Chinese civilization. The Chinese were the first to invent paper, porcelain, silk, cast iron, gunpowder, the magnetic compass, and many other world-changing innovations.[109] But their contributions to philosophy and religion are also foundational—with Taoism and Confucianism dating back two and a half millennia, and other traditions reaching back even further in time. The Chinese, specifically the Qin Dynasty (221–206 B.C.), can even be credited as the first to develop the "modern state"—defined, according to political scientist Francis Fukuyama, as a "centralized, bureaucratic" state that "operates according to rules rather than being governed by the mere whim of the ruler."[110] It really is tragic for the Chinese people, and for the world, that these rich sources of wisdom have been supplanted by the spiritually stultifying doctrines of Socialism with Chinese Characteristics, Han-centrism, and Xi Jinping Thought.

---

I stayed for several minutes before leaving by a different exit, taking me out the left side of the temple. Outside, there was to my left a stone path that would take me back to the front steps. But to my right, I noticed another, inconspicuous set of steps, leading farther up the slope through fields of overgrown grass, ending at another, smaller temple.

I saw nobody else around me, or anywhere on or near those steps, so I doubted that this was part of the tourist attraction. But I saw no sign telling me I wasn't allowed up there.

Like the two long flights of steps I had taken to get to the main temple, these steps were made of a grey stone. But they were much less sturdy. Many of them wobbled as I put my weight on them, and a couple even broke off and rolled down the hill behind me. Still, I continued upward, taking special care with each step.

Thankfully, I reached the top without incident. To my surprise, this secondary temple's exterior was far more involved than the main temple's. The walls were dark blue on the top half, and maroon with diagonal white hash-marks below. Multicolored geometric paintings were etched into a line dividing the two. Almost immediately, I noticed how silent it was up there. The chattering of tourists had vanished, replaced by the buzzing of insects and the faint sough of the light breeze breaking through the tall grass.

I entered the temple somewhat carelessly, not paying any mind to silence my steps, assuming that I would be the only one up there. But when I entered the meditation room, I found a young Han man kneeling in front of a row of three deities, with a lit jar of incense in front of him. When he turned around to look at me, I was prepared for him to scold me for having thoughtlessly interrupted his prayer. Instead, he just smiled at me, and said "Hello!"

"Hello!" I echoed, happy to have not upset him. Still, I thought it best to leave him alone, so he could finish his ritual undisturbed.

I retreated outside to search for a comfortable spot to rest—preferably one with a good view. There didn't appear to be any place to sit at the front of the temple, so I went around the side to try my luck there.

Rounding the corner, I spotted a large boulder not far away. It looked smooth enough for me to sit on comfortably. But as I began to wade through the tall grass, I stepped into a clearing about five feet wide. It was *another* path—this one leading yet farther up the slope. I couldn't see any more structures anywhere higher up, so it was unclear where exactly this path would take me. But given how I had just happened upon it, I felt obliged to see what might await me up there.

The path snaked along the side of the slope in a switchback, neutralizing the steep incline. Old wooden boards were placed over the dirt trail, with tall grass overgrowth spilling over from its edges that I would need to brush aside or step through, but not so much as to make the path unwalkable. While the earlier path seemed as though it hadn't been worked on in a while, this one looked like it had been completely forgotten about.

After about ten minutes of walking, I got to a point where the tall grass had overtaken the entire pathway, rendering invisible the wooden boards I'd been relying on to guide me. It would be too unsafe to continue farther.

I was disappointed that I wouldn't be seeing the view from the very top of the hill, which was maybe another hundred feet or so higher up the slope. But when I turned around, my disappointment vanished.

I had climbed high enough to now have an aerial, panoramic view of the entire lake, from the far end and the twin snow-capped peaks beyond, all the way back to the lower ridge I had summited when I first arrived. I could see over some of the smaller mountains around the lake's perimeter, to where the deeper layers of the range continued endlessly into the horizon. The clouds overhead cast navy blue patches on the bright turquoise lake, and the tour boats slowly carved through them, creating tiny white wakes that rippled from their sterns.

As I stood at that last clean step, fully immersed in the breathtaking beauty that surrounded me, and the tranquility of the private perch I had discovered, I forgot where I was.

But after a few peaceful minutes, reality reasserted itself. I remembered where I was, and the unspeakable things that were happening there. It was impossible to separate this moment of serenity from the context in which it was taking place. Nothing in today's Xinjiang can be disconnected from genocide. Every item I'd held, every experience I'd had, and even every person I'd met was inextricably tied in some way to the atrocities being committed by the CCP.

The tour boats on the lake below, and the two buses I had taken to get to the lake; the train that I took from Kashgar to Ürümqi; the many taxis I had ridden in to get around each of those cities—they were all probably built or maintained, at least in part, by Uyghur slave labor. The trinkets and clothing items I'd seen in the New Old City of Kashgar, in Erdaoqiao Bazaar, and in the souvenir villages earlier that day, these too were most likely produced by Uyghurs in re-education camps, or under threat of being sent, or sent back, to one. The profits accrued from the multiple entrance fees to tourist sites I'd paid during that week, including the fee I'd paid just minutes earlier to gain access to this temple, would help subsidize the construction of a new guard tower, or the latest model of surveillance camera. At best, that money would be circulated back into the Xinjiang economy—an economy that functions in lockstep with the malevolent ambitions of the Chinese Communist Party.

*Everything*, even this pristine moment of solitude, was sullied by the darkness of the ongoing subjugation, enslavement, and ethnic cleansing of the Turkic peoples of East Turkistan.

\* \* \* \* \* \* \*

When I did come down from there, the rest of my day was uneventful.

I hiked back to the bus lot, and the shuttle bus took me to the main park entrance. I took a coach bus back to Ürümqi bus station, and a taxi back to my hotel, where I stayed until leaving for the airport the next morning.

Despite my fears that I might encounter issues leaving the country the following day, I got through the security checks one last time, and onto my flight to Kazakhstan, with no trouble.

# Epilogue

About six months after I had left China, I sat down in a quiet corner of the University of Colorado Law Library in Boulder, for a phone interview I had arranged with a man named Teng Biao.

Mr. Biao is a soft-spoken man, in the literal sense, but a more accurate way to describe him would be "carefully spoken." The best lawyers—as Mr. Biao had been in Beijing more than a decade ago—have a deliberate style of communicating, taking long pauses between trains of thought, and seeming sometimes to talk in slow motion when they come to a topic that they feel is especially important. They value clarity above all else. I've encountered a few people in my life who I recognized in this way, but Mr. Biao may be the foremost example.

To call him soft-spoken also does not do justice to the man's bravery. As a prominent lawyer and professor at the University of Beijing, Mr. Biao founded several human rights organizations in the early 2000s, including the since-banned Open Constitution Initiative, which focused on promoting the rule of law and expanding constitutional protections for Chinese citizens. Mr. Biao was later imprisoned on two separate occasions by the Chinese police, after the relatively liberal policies that had allowed him to be so publicly outspoken on sensitive issues were tightened by the Party. The second time, in 2011, he was imprisoned for more than two months, and tortured. He was released due to intense pressure from the international community and human rights organizations like Amnesty International. He now lives in the United States, and continues to be an unwavering critic of the Chinese Communist Party.

During the interview, I asked him about a variety of topics. His answers were as enlightening as one would expect from a man with his background. But there was one answer that has had a particularly significant influence on my thinking:

> **GS:** "In your view, what is the difference between the mass internment going on in Xinjiang and other types of extra-judicial internment elsewhere in China?"
>
> **Mr. Biao:** "Yes, there are different types of extra-judicial internment. Some have been abolished, like 'Re-Education Through Labor,' and the 'Custody and Repatriation System.'

"But there are still some other types of extrajudicial detentions. What's happening in Xinjiang is very different. It's not only extrajudicial facilities, it's extra-legal detentions. There is no legal basis for the internment camps. More than one million Uyghur and Kazakh people were detained there arbitrarily. They were tortured and they were forced to study Chinese. They brainwashed them. They were forced to sing the patriotic songs. That's totally illegal.

"And the scale, the number of the detainees, is shocking. In other Chinese cities there are legal education centers which are extrajudicial detention that target the Falun Gong practitioners. And some other black [secret] jails detaining petitioners. But the concentration camps are very different. The targeting of the whole ethnic group and without any process and without any legal procedure, that's quite similar to the concentration camps in Nazi Germany."

The point Mr. Biao makes here is among the most important for understanding the situation in East Turkistan. The Chinese Communist Party has long been known to violate the human rights of its citizens. Even during periods in which many influential people thought (quixotically, it turns out) that China was slowly moving toward some semblance of liberal governance, no serious observer would have disputed that the CCP's human rights record had serious flaws. But what they're doing today in East Turkistan is very different.

As Mr. Biao notes, none of China's other, long-running extrajudicial detention facilities are meant to brainwash entire ethnic groups. None of them, horrible as they are, are designed as mechanisms to erase entire cultures. The surveillance state that the CCP has constructed elsewhere in China comes nowhere close in its invasiveness to the ever-present, ethnically-targeted panopticon in East Turkistan. The re-education camps constitute an unprecedented escalation in China's human rights abuses, compounding the manifold other abhorrent anti-Turkic policies that have been implemented there.

This isn't to say that these policies will remain confined to East Turkistan, or to ethnic Turks. There is some evidence to suggest that the "success" of these "totally correct" policies—as President Xi described them during a Party meeting in September 2020[111]—has convinced the CCP to expand them to deal with non-Han ethnic groups in other Chinese provinces. In Tibet, the CCP has put half a million ethnic Tibetans through a "vocational training program" since the beginning of 2020, a program that Adrian Zenz has said "shows a disturbing number of close similarities" to the policies in East Turkistan.[112] There have been similarly troubling recent developments in Gansu, Inner Mongolia, and Guangxi provinces as well.[113]

Nor is it inevitable that these policies will stay confined to China. For all the condemnation that can and should be leveled at the CCP's policies in East Turkistan, it would be difficult to argue that they haven't been effective at reinforcing the CCP's control in the region. And there is no shortage of authoritarian leaders in the world who are perfectly comfortable violating the human rights of their citizens in order to stay in power. These leaders have taken note of the recent developments in East Turkistan.

And an unsettling number of countries publicly approve of the steps China has taken. In July 2019, fifty countries signed on to a letter sent to the United Nations Human Rights Council that praised China for its "counter-terrorism and de-radicalization measures in Xinjiang," characterizing them as "remarkable achievements in the field of human rights."[114] Although it's unclear how many of these countries would adopt a version of China's policies themselves, their painting the genocide in East Turkistan in such rosy terms implies that they might hold the same favorable view of other countries should they take similar "counter-terrorism and de-radicalization measures" against their own populations.

Tragically, human rights are too often reduced to a mere cudgel, used by nations to cynically attack their geopolitical rivals—attacks intended to advance their own strategic interests rather than to protect vulnerable people. This self-serving dynamic has had a profoundly corrosive effect, creating an environment in which nations are reflexively skeptical of calls to defend human rights, and nations that systematically violate human rights are placed on equal footing to those who (imperfectly) seek to protect them.

This is what is happening now with the genocide being committed in East Turkistan. It is at risk of being normalized, of becoming just another human rights issue on which nations take sides based on geopolitical self-interest instead of the credibility and severity of the claims. This is the worst possible outcome; and it's precisely the outcome that the CCP wants.

But there are ways that we can push back against this normalization. The most effective way is to make sure that we carefully draw the necessary moral distinctions between human rights violations, like Mr. Biao did in his response to me. This can un-muddy the waters of the human rights discourse, and ensure that we recognize the very worst violations where there is the greatest need to find common ground. We can separate the injustices that regularly occur throughout the world from those that are so comprehensively evil that to disregard them means to reject the very concept of human rights.

We must consistently reiterate the truth: that there is no equivalent, anywhere in the world, to what the Chinese Communist Party is doing to the Turkic peoples in East Turkistan. We must underscore the need to prioritize attention to this humanitarian crisis, so as to live up to the solemn promise of "Never Again." And we must accept that all of us—every international organization, every nation, every corporation, and every individual—has a moral duty to do whatever we can to help put a stop to it.

# What We Can Do

Regardless of what we might seek to do as individuals, what's happening in East Turkistan right now is a problem that can only be solved definitively at the level of geopolitics. China is, unquestionably, the second most powerful country in the world today, according it significant sway over many other countries, as well as over international institutions such as the United Nations—which shamefully elected China to the UN Human Rights Council in October 2020.

For China to reconsider its policies, it will not be enough for citizens of the free world to make pleas based on human rights and morality. The CCP's leaders must be convinced that abandoning these policies is the best way to serve China's own geopolitical interests. And this shift will only occur once the CCP feels the plausible threat of severe consequences for the Uyghur genocide; consequences so severe that they would outweigh the callously calculated benefits of continuing it.

We are already seeing significant multilateral actions from Western democracies. Most recently as of this writing, the United States, Canada, the United Kingdom, and the European Union placed sanctions in March 2021 on several Chinese officials and entities in regard to their connection to the Uyghur genocide.[115] This is a hopeful sign that the world is now waking up to China's malevolence. But these measures will need to be sustained, and augmented, to secure human rights protections for the people of East Turkistan. The West, and like-minded nations throughout the world, must send a clear, strong message (in whatever form that might take in practice) to the CCP that their genocidal policies are an affront to the most fundamental of human rights, and that, should they continue, China will pay a high price.

Despite the primacy of geopolitics, there are things that individuals can do to help make a difference:

***Contact your Congressional Representative and your Senators, and ask them to give this issue the attention it deserves.***

The geopolitical struggle to compel China to forgo its policies in East Turkistan will be difficult. It is not unwinnable; but it can only be effectively waged by those who possess the requisite political power. By contacting your elected representatives in Congress, you can influence them to put this issue on their agenda, and to prioritize the development of strategies to counter China's genocidal campaign. We have already seen hopeful beginnings of bipartisan support for this effort—even in America's present hyper-polarized political environment.

### Abstain from purchasing goods made in China.

The federal government has taken some significant steps to curtail Xinjiang-made products from entering the U.S.[116] However, as I noted in chapter 12, Uyghur slave-labor is so deeply interwoven and widely dispersed throughout Chinese manufacturing that we cannot reliably disconnect any Chinese-made product from the CCP's human rights abuses in East Turkistan. Thus, the only way to ensure that we are not subsidizing these abuses is to refuse altogether, to the fullest extent that we can, to buy anything that has been made in China. If enough consumers boycott enough Chinese-made products, and make clear that they are doing so in solidarity with the Uyghurs, it could be a strong enough supplement to requisite national- and international-level actions to convince the CCP that continuing its genocidal policies in East Turkistan is not worth the cost.

### Support the Uyghur diaspora in your community.

One of the modes of control over the Uyghurs that I wasn't able to discuss in detail in this book is how the CCP seeks to intimidate and silence Uyghurs throughout the world—not just within China's borders. This can manifest itself in a variety of ways, but the most common is the general, implicit threat to all Uyghurs living outside China: if they speak ill of the CCP in any public way, then their loved ones back in Xinjiang will suffer for it. During my research for this book, I spoke with several members of the American Uyghur community who have lost contact with their family members in China. These stories are each heartbreaking in their own unique ways; but the basic components of them are all-too common in the Uyghur diaspora.

This makes it especially important for us to help make sure that Uyghurs feel welcome in our own communities. We can shop at Uyghur-owned stores and dine at Uyghur restaurants. Or if you know Uyghurs in your community on a personal level, you can invite them to community events. We can't hope to truly replace the communities that the CCP has disenfranchised the Uyghurs from, but we can do our best to support them here.

**Donate to organizations that fight for human rights in East Turkistan.**

By purchasing *Middle Country*, you have already done this. One hundred percent of my royalties from this book are going toward pro-Uyghur causes. But if you would also like to donate directly to organizations that are championing the cause of human rights in East Turkistan, here are a few to consider:

East Turkistan National Awakening Movement, https://nationalawakening.org/

Uyghur Human Rights Project, https://uhrp.org/support

Campaign for Uyghurs, https://campaignforuyghurs.org/

Xinjiang Victims Database, https://www.shahit.biz/eng/

Uyghur Tribunal, https://uyghurtribunal.com/

**Use your own voice to spread awareness.**

The easiest thing that you can do is inform the people around you about the situation in East Turkistan. Most people have little, if any, awareness of what is happening there. This lack of awareness can partially be attributed to the unfortunate silence of many of our most important American cultural institutions that have a presence in China, such as Hollywood and the NBA. These institutions have been at the forefront of efforts to promote social justice at home, but at the same time have calculated that protecting their access to the lucrative Chinese market is a higher priority than speaking out against the egregious injustices committed by the CCP. We can only hope that they eventually muster the courage to use their platforms to promote human rights for all people, everywhere, even if it means missing out on Chinese money.

Nevertheless, each of us still has the ability to help move attention to this crisis on our own. We can utilize social media platforms, we can attend and help organize peaceful protests, and we can simply inform people we know. If enough of us speak out, the plight of the Uyghurs will be impossible to ignore any longer.

# Notes

1. Kwok, Caroline. China promotes tourism in Xinjiang region where detentions of Muslims continue. South China Morning Post, July 17, 2019, https://www.scmp.com/video/china/3018776/china-promotes-tourism-xinjiang-region-where-detentions-muslims-continue.
2. Allison, Graham. Is war between China and the US inevitable? TED Talk, Nov. 20, 2018, https://www.youtube.com/watch?v=XewnyUJgyA4.
3. Anderson, Ross. The Panopticon Is Already Here. The Atlantic, Sept. 2020, https://www.theatlantic.com/magazine/archive/2020/09/china-ai-surveillance/614197/?utm_source=twitter&utm_medium=social&utm_campaign=share. Hannon, Paul and Eun-Young Jeong. China Overtakes U.S. as World's Leading Destination for Foreign Direct Investment. Wall Street Journal, Jan. 24, 2021. https://www.wsj.com/articles/china-overtakes-u-s-as-worlds-leading-destination-for-foreign-direct-investment-11611511200.
4. Schuman, Michael. *Superpower Interrupted: The Chinese History of the World*. New York, Public Affairs, 2020, p. 145.
5. Weatherford, Jack. *Genghis Khan And the Quest for God: How the world's greatest conqueror gave us religious freedom*. New York, Viking Penguin, 2016.
6. Bonavia, Judd, et al. *The Silk Road*. Chicago, Passport Books, 1993, pp. 63–64.
7. Osborne, Hilary and Sam Cutler. Chinese border guards put secret surveillance app on tourists' phones. The Guardian, July 2, 2019, https://www.theguardian.com/world/2019/jul/02/chinese-border-guards-surveillance-app-tourists-phones.
8. Standish, Reid. Our Government Doesn't Want to Spoil Relations With China. The Atlantic, Sept. 3, 2019, https://www.theatlantic.com/international/archive/2019/09/china-xinjiang-uighur-kazakhstan/597106/.
9. National Minorities Policy and Its Practice in China. Information Office, State Council of the Peoples Republic of China, Sept. 1999, Permanent Mission of the People's Republic of China to the United Nations Office at Geneva and Other International Organizations in Switzerland, http://www.china-un.ch/eng/bjzl/t176942.htm.
10. Chinese ship, Vietnamese fishing boat collide in South China Sea. South China Morning Post, April 3, 2020, https://www.scmp.com/news/asia/southeast-asia/article/3078286/chinese-ship-hits-and-sinks-vietnamese-fishing-boat-south.
11. Oscars: Hong Kong selects "Operation Red Sea" for foreign language category. The Hollywood Reporter, Sept. 24, 2018, https://www.hollywoodreporter.com/news/hong-kong-picks-operation-red-sea-foreign-language-oscar-1146410.
12. Friend, John M. and Bradley A Thayer. *How China Sees the World*. Lincoln, University of Nebraska Press, 2018, p. 33.
13. Ibid, p. 64.
14. The Soviet-Sponsored Uprising in Kuldja/ The Establishment of the East Turkestan People's Republic. Central Intelligence Agency (April 13, 1953;

Sanitized Copy Approved for Release July 21, 2011), https://www.cia.gov/library/readingroom/docs/CIA-RDP80-00809A000600040004-3.pdf.
15. Millward, James A. *Eurasian Crossroads*. New York, Columbia University Press, 2007, p. 234.
16. Qin, Amy. "In China's crackdown on Muslims, children have not been spared." New York Times, Dec. 28, 2019, https://www.nytimes.com/2019/12/28/world/asia/china-xinjiang-children-boarding-schools.html.
17. Zenz, Adrian. Parent-child separation in Yarkand County, Kashgar. Medium, Oct. 15, 2020, https://adrianzenz.medium.com/story-45d07b25bcad.
18. Qin, note 16.
19. Beach, Sophie. Leaked speech shows Xi Jinping's opposition to reform. China Digital News, Jan. 27, 2013, https://chinadigitaltimes.net/2013/01/leaked-speech-shows-xi-jinpings-opposition-to-reform/.
20. Document 9: How much is a hardline party directive shaping China's current political climate? ChinaFile, Nov. 8, 2013, https://www.chinafile.com/document-9-chinafile-translation.
21. McDonell, Stephen. China's Xi allowed to remain "president for life" as term limits removed. BBC News, March 11, 2018, https://www.bbc.com/news/world-asia-china-43361276.
22. Millward, note 15, pp. 83–88.
23. Wines, Michael. To protect an ancient city, China moves to raze it. New York Times, May 27, 2009, https://www.nytimes.com/2009/05/28/world/asia/28kashgar.html.
24. Weatherford, note 5.
25. Millward, note 15, p. 84.
26. Jacobs, Andrew. In China, myths of social cohesion. New York Times, Aug. 18, 2014, https://www.nytimes.com/2014/08/19/world/asia/in-china-myths-of-social-cohesion.html.
27. Rivers, Matt. More than 100 Uyghur graveyards demolished by Chinese authorities, satellite images show. CNN, Jan. 2, 2020, https://www.cnn.com/2020/01/02/asia/xinjiang-uyghur-graveyards-china-intl-hnk/?utm_medium=social&utm_source=twCNN&utm_content=2020-01-02T12:03:55.
28. Ruser, Nathan, et al. Cultural erasure: Tracing the destruction of Uyghur and Islamic spaces in Xinjiang. Australian Strategic Policy Inst., Sept, 24, 2020, https://www.aspi.org.au/report/cultural-erasure#:~:text=We%20found%20that%20across%20the,destroyed%20and%20undamaged%20mosque%20numbers.
29. Hoshur, Shohret and Joshua Lipes. Chinese authorities jail four wealthiest Uyghurs in Xinjiang's Kashgar in new purge. Radio Free Asia, Jan. 5, 2018, https://www.rfa.org/english/news/uyghur/wealthiest-01052018144327.html.
30. Mao Statue, iStock by Getty Images, accessed Jan. 7, 2021, https://www.istockphoto.com/photo/giant-statue-of-mao-tse-tung-in-kashgar-xinjiang-china-gm820873118-132758401.
31. Somin, Ilya. Remembering the biggest mass murder in the history of the world. Washington Post, Aug. 3, 2016, https://www.washingtonpost.com/news/volokh-conspiracy/wp/2016/08/03/giving-historys-greatest-mass-murderer-his-due/. (Citing Dikötter, Frank. Looking back on the Great Leap Forward. History Today, Aug, 8, 2016, https://www.historytoday.com/archive/looking-back-great-leap-forward.)
32. Dikötter, Frank. *The Cultural Revolution: A People's History, 1962–1976*. New York, Bloomsbury Publishing, 2016, p. xviii.

33. Holdstock, Nick. *China's Forgotten People: Xinjiang, Terror and the Chinese State*. London, I.B. Tauris, 2015, pp. 38–39.
34. Millward, note 15, pp. 254–257.
35. Friend and Thayer, note 12, p. 52.
36. Holdstock, note 33, pp. 19–21.
37. Drexel, William. Kashgar Coerced: Forced Reconstruction, Exploitation, and Surveillance in the Cradle of Uyghur Culture. Uyghur Human Rights Project, June 2020, p. 16, https://uhrp.org/sites/default/files/UHRP-Kashgar-Coerced-Report-06_03_20%20Final.pdf.
38. Zenz, Adrian. Beyond the Camps: Beijing's Long-Term Scheme of Coercive Labor, Poverty Alleviation and Social Control in Xinjiang. Journal of Political Risk, 7:12, Dec. 2019, https://www.jpolrisk.com/beyond-the-camps-beijings-long-term-scheme-of-coercive-labor-poverty-alleviation-and-social-control-in-xinjiang/.
39. Drexel, note 37, p. 16.
40. Ibid, p. 55.
41. Perper, Rosie. "'This Is Mass Rape': Uighur Activist Condemns Program Said to Pay Chinese Men to Sleep with Uighur Women to Promote 'Ethnic Unity'." Insider, Insider, 24 Dec. 2019, www.insider.com/uighur-activists-mass-rape-chinese-men-xinjiang-2019-12.
42. Drexel, note 37, p. 16 .
43. 'Many Uygurs like to drink': Chinese academic defends beer festival in Muslim region. South China Morning Post, June 24, 2015, https://www.scmp.com/news/china/society/article/1825456/many-uygurs-drink-chinese-academic-defends-beer-festival-muslim.
44. Adrian Zenz, Twitter post, May 20, 2020, 10:14 PM, https://twitter.com/adrianzenz/status/1263291925991510016.
45. Bonavia et al, note 6, p. 262.
46. Holdstock, note 33, , p. 12.
47. Millward, James A. *Violent Separatism in Xinjiang: A Critical Assessment*. Washington, DC, East-West Center in Washington, 2004, p 31.
48. Shih, Gerry. Uighurs fighting in Syria take aim at China. Associated Press, Dec. 22, 2017, https://apnews.com/article/79d6a427b26f4eeab226571956dd256e.
49. Roberts, Sean. Imaginary Terrorism? The Global War on Terror and the Narrative of the Uyghur Terrorist Threat. Elliott School of International Affairs, George Washington University, March 2012, https://www.ponarseurasia.org/sites/default/files/Roberts_WorkingPaper_March2012.pdf.
50. In the Matter of the Designation of the Eastern Turkistan Islamic Movement Also Known as ETIM as a "Terrorist Organization" Pursuant to Section 212(a)(3)(B)(vi)(II) of the Immigration and Nationality Act, as Amended. U.S. Dept. of State Pub. Notice 11252, Oct. 20, 2020, 85 F. Reg. 70703, Nov. 5, 2020, https://www.federalregister.gov/documents/2020/11/05/2020-24620/in-the-matter-of-the-designation-of-the-eastern-turkistan-islamic-movement-also-known-as-etim-as-a.
51. Millward, note 15, p. 24.
52. Ibid.
53. Schuman, note 4, p. 309.
54. Holdstock, note 33, p. 208.
55. Madani, Doha. Disney faces more "Mulan" backlash after film thanks Xinjiang government agencies in credits. NBC News, Sept. 9, 2020, https://www.nbcnews.com/news/asian-america/disney-faces-more-mulan-backlash-after-film-thanks-xinjiang-government-n1239679.

56. Yilei, Feng. Wusu: Xinjiang beer, a new option for Chinese consumers. CGTN News, Oct. 8, 2020, https://news.cgtn.com/news/2020-10-08/Wusu-Xinjiang-beer-a-new-option-for-Chinese-consumers-UqlyBECc8M/index.html.
57. Olesen, Alexa. Tea Leaf Nation: China's Vast, Strange, and Powerful Farming Militia Turns 60. Foreign Policy, Oct. 8, 2014, https://foreignpolicy.com/2014/10/08/chinas-vast-strange-and-powerful-farming-militia-turns-60/.
58. Ibid.
59. Holdstock, note 33, p. 90.
60. Bao, Yajun. The Xinjiang Production and Construction Corps: An Insider's Perspective. Blavatnik School of Government, University of Oxford, Jan. 2018, p. 4, https://www.bsg.ox.ac.uk/research/publications/xinjiang-production-and-construction-corps.
61. Holdstock, note 33, p. 61.
62. Ma, Alexandra. China is reportedly tracking ethnic minorities by sticking QR codes with their personal information on their front doors. Business Insider, Sept. 13, 2018, https://www.businessinsider.com/china-tracks-uighur-minority-qr-code-kitchen-knives-doors-human-rights-watch-report-2018-9.
63. China: "Changing the soup but not the medicine?": Abolishing re-education through labour in China. Amnesty International, Dec. 17, 2013, p. 9, https://www.amnesty.org/en/documents/asa17/042/2013/en/.
64. Xu, Vicky Xiuzhong et al. Uyghurs for sale: 'Re-education', forced labour and surveillance beyond Xinjiang. Australian Strategic Policy Institute, March 1, 2020, https://www.aspi.org.au/report/uyghurs-sale.
65. Zenz, Adrian. Coercive Labor in Xinjiang: Labor Transfer and the Mobilization of Ethnic Minorities to Pick Cotton. Center for Global Policy, Dec. 14, 2020, https://cgpolicy.org/briefs/coercive-labor-in-xinjiang-labor-transfer-and-the-mobilization-of-ethnic-minorities-to-pick-cotton/.
66. Ibid.
67. Millward, note 15, p. 287.
68. Horwitz, Jeremy. Apple, Foxconn, and 81 others are accused of using Uighur forced labor. Venture Beat, March 2, 2020, https://venturebeat.com/2020/03/02/apple-foxconn-and-81-others-are-accused-of-using-uighur-forced-labor/.
69. Rajagopalan, Megha and Alison Killing. US Solar Companies Rely on Materials From Xinjiang, Where Forced Labor is Rampant. Buzzfeed News, Jan.14 2021, https://www.buzzfeednews.com/article/meghara/forced-labor-xinjiang-solar.
70. Xu, note 64.
71. Albergotti, Reed. Apple's longtime supplier accused of using forced labor in China. Washington Post, Dec, 29, 2020, https://www.washingtonpost.com/technology/2020/12/29/lens-technology-apple-uighur/.
72. Albergotti, Reed. Apple is lobbying against a bill aimed at stopping forced labor in China. Washington Post, Nov. 20, 2020, https://www.washingtonpost.com/technology/2020/11/20/apple-uighur/.
73. Xu, note 64.
74. Millward, note 15, p. 8.
75. Martina, Michael. China says Xinjiang has 'boarding schools', not 'concentration camps'. Reuters, Mar. 12, 2019, https://www.reuters.com/article/us-china-parliament-xinjiang/china-says-xinjiang-has-boarding-schools-not-concentration-camps-idUSKBN1QT1E4.
76. Rivers, Matt and Lily Lee. Former Xinjiang teacher claims brainwashing and abuse inside mass detention centers. CNN, May 9, 2019, https://www.cnn.

com/2019/05/09/asia/xinjiang-china-kazakhstan-detention-intl/index.html.
77. "Eradicating Ideological Viruses": China's Campaign of Repression Against Xinjiang's Muslims. Human Rights Watch, Sept. 9, 2018, https://www.hrw.org/report/2018/09/09/eradicating-ideological-viruses/chinas-campaign-repression-against-xinjiangs.
78. Rivers and Lee, note 76.
79. Moore, Mark. China reportedly secretly built hundreds of prison camps to hold minority Muslims. New York Post, Aug. 27, 2020, https://nypost.com/2020/08/27/china-secretly-built-hundreds-of-prison-camps-to-hold-minority-muslims/.
80. Schmitz, Rob. Ex-Detainee Describes Torture in China's Xinjiang Re-Education Camp. NPR, Nov. 13, 2018, https://www.npr.org/2018/11/13/666287509/ex-detainee-describes-torture-in-chinas-xinjiang-re-education-camp.
81. Hill, Matthew et al. 'Their goal is to destroy everyone': Uighur camp detainees allege systematic rape. BBC News, Feb 2, 2021, https://www.bbc.com/news/world-asia-china-55794071.
82. Mauk, Ben. Weather Reports: Voices from Xinjiang. Believer, Oct. 1, 2019.
83. Graham-Harrison, Emma and Lily Kuo. Uighur Muslim teacher tells of forced sterilisation in Xinjiang. The Guardian, Sept. 4, 2020, https://www.theguardian.com/world/2020/sep/04/muslim-minority-teacher-50-tells-of-forced-sterilisation-in-xinjiang-china.
84. Smith, Saphora. China forcefully harvests organs from detainees, tribunal concludes. NBC News, June 18, 2019, https://www.nbcnews.com/news/world/china-forcefully-harvests-organs-detainees-tribunal-concludes-n1018646.
85. Hoshur, Shohret. At Least 150 Detainees Have Died in One Xinjiang Internment Camp: Police Officer. Radio Free Asia, Oct. 29, 2019, https://www.rfa.org/english/news/uyghur/deaths-10292019181322.html.
86. Zenz, Adrian. "Wash Brains, Cleanse Hearts": Evidence from Chinese Government Documents about the Nature and Extent of Xinjiang's Extrajudicial Internment Campaign. Journal of Political Risk, Vol. 7, No. 11, Nov. 2019.
87. Ibid.
88. Feng, Emily. "Illegal Superstition": China Jails Muslims For Practicing Islam, Relatives Say. National Public Radio, Oct. 8, 2019, https://www.npr.org/2019/10/08/764153179/china-has-begun-moving-xinjiang-muslim-detainees-to-formal-prisons-relatives-say.
89. Holdstock, note 33, p.166.
90. Millward, James and Dahlia Peterson. China's System of Oppression in Xinjiang: How It Developed and How to Curb It. Brookings Inst., Sept. 2020, https://www.brookings.edu/wp-content/uploads/2020/09/FP_20200914_china_oppression_xinjiang_millward_peterson.pdf [figure as later corrected].
91. https://www.behindthename.com/name/aynur.
92. Ingram, Ruth. Sexual Abuse of Uyghur Women by CCP Cadres in Xinjiang: A Victim Speaks Out. Bitter Winter, Sept. 19, 2020, https://bitterwinter.org/sexual-abuse-of-uyghur-women-by-ccp-cadres-in-xinjiang/.
93. Zenz, Adrian. China's Own Documents Show Potentially Genocidal Sterilization Plans in Xinjiang. Foreign Policy, July 1, 2020, https://foreignpolicy.com/2020/07/01/china-documents-uighur-genocidal-sterilization-xinjiang/.
94. Kashgarian, Asim. China Video Ad Calls for 100 Uighur Women to 'Urgently' Marry Han Men. VOA News, Aug. 21, 2020, https://www.voanews.com/east-asia-pacific/voa-news-china/china-video-ad-calls-100-uighur-women-urgently-marry-han-men.

95. Millward, note 15, p. 88.
96. Ibid, p. 93.
97. Ramzy, Austin and Chris Buckley. 'Absolutely No Mercy': Leaked Files Expose How China Organized Mass Detentions of Muslims. New York Times, Nov. 16, 2019, https://www.nytimes.com/interactive/2019/11/16/world/asia/china-xinjiang-documents.html.
98. Ibid.
99. Sulaiman, Eset and Paul Eckert. China Runs Region-wide Re-education Camps in Xinjiang for Uyghurs And Other Muslims. Radio Free Asia, Sept. 11, 2017, https://www.rfa.org/english/news/uyghur/training-camps-09112017154343.html/.
100. List of United States cities by population, Wikipedia, https://en.wikipedia.org/wiki/List_of_United_States_cities_by_population (accessed Jan. 8, 2021).
101. Miller, Tom. *China's Asian Dream.* London, Zed Books, 2019, p. xii.
102. Green Belt and Road Initiative Center (official website), https://green-bri.org/countries-of-the-belt-and-road-initiative-bri#:~:text=As%20of%20March%202020%2C%20the.
103. Osnos, Evan. Born Red: How Xi Jinping, an unremarkable provincial administrator, became China's most authoritarian leader since Mao. The New Yorker, March 30, 2015, https://www.newyorker.com/magazine/2015/04/06/born-red.
104. Holdstock, note 33, pp. 183–194.
105. Urumqi riot commencement 2009 07 05. Youtube, 25-minute video, posted May 26, 2013, accessed Jan. 9, 2021, https://www.youtube.com/watch?v=5A5o4nThUmg.
106. Yip, Hilton. Beijing Blames Foreigners When Hong Kongers March: Belief in foreign spies is projection about the Party's own overseas activities. Foreign Policy, June 19, 2019, https://foreignpolicy.com/2019/06/19/beijing-blames-foreigners-when-hong-kongers-march/.
107. Kharpal, Arjun. LeBron James says Houston Rockets' GM was not 'educated' on Hong Kong situation when he tweeted. CNBC, Oct. 15, 2019, https://www.cnbc.com/2019/10/15/lebron-james-daryl-morey-not-educated-with-hong-kong-protest-tweet.html.
108. Map of Xinjiang Uyghur Autonomous Region Detention Facilities and Destruction of Cultural Sites and Mosques. The Xinjiang Data Project, Australian Strategic Policy Institute's International Cyber Policy Centre, accessed Jan. 11, 2021, https://xjdp.aspi.org.au/map/.
109. Schuman, note 4, pp. 143–173.
110. Fukuyama, Francis. What Kind of Regime Does China Have? The American Interest, May 18, 2020, https://www.the-american-interest.com/2020/05/18/what-kind-of-regime-does-china-have/.
111. Buckley, Chris. Brushing Off Criticism, China's Xi Calls Policies in Xinjiang 'Totally Correct.' New York Times, Sept. 26, 2020, https://www.nytimes.com/2020/09/26/world/asia/xi-jinping-china-xinjiang.html.
112. Xiao, Eva et al. Beijing Accelerates Campaign of Ethnic Assimilation. Wall St. J., Dec. 31, 2020, https://www.wsj.com/articles/beijing-accelerates-campaign-of-ethnic-assimilation-11609431781.
113. Ibid.
114. Yellinek, Roie, and Elizabeth Chen. The "22 vs. 50" Diplomatic Split Between the West and China Over Xinjiang and Human Rights. China Brief, Jamestown

Foundation, Dec. 31, 2019, https://jamestown.org/program/the-22-vs-50-diplomatic-split-between-the-west-and-china-over-xinjiang-and-human-rights/.
115. Gauette, Nicole et al. US and allies announce sanctions against Chinese officials for 'serious human rights abuses' against Uyghurs, CNN, March 23, 2021, https://www.cnn.com/2021/03/22/politics/us-eu-china-uyghur-sanctions/index.html.
116. Ordonez, Victor. US bans all cotton and tomato products from Xinjiang over slave labor. ABC News, Jan. 13, 2020, https://abcnews.go.com/International/us-bans-cotton-tomato-products-xinjiang-slave-labor/story?id=75226217.

# Acknowledgements

I would first like to thank Eric Koester of the Creator's Institute, who gave me the inspiration to turn my story into this book. I would also like to thank my friends and colleagues who provided me feedback on the draft manuscripts. Thanks, too, to the several people who took time out of their busy schedules to allow me to interview them.

I would like to thank my family for their unwavering support of me throughout my life, and even more so during this past year, with all of the special difficulties of writing a book in the middle of a pandemic. And, most of all, I would like to thank my father, who contributed countless hours and many late nights to helping me make *Middle Country* the best possible version of itself.

www.ingramcontent.com/pod-product-compliance
Lightning Source LLC
Chambersburg PA
CBHW061303110426
42742CB00012BA/2037